THE RISE OF THE
DEVON SEASIDE RESORTS

1750–1900

EXETER MARITIME STUDIES

General Editor: Stephen Fisher

EXETER MARITIME STUDIES No. 8

THE RISE
OF THE DEVON
SEASIDE RESORTS
1750–1900

John F. Travis

UNIVERSITY
of
EXETER
PRESS

First published in 1993 by
University of Exeter Press
Reed Hall
Streatham Drive
Exeter, Devon EX4 4QR
UK

British Library Cataloguing in Publication Data
A catalogue record of this book is available
from the British Library

ISBN 0 85989 392 8

Typeset by Kestrel Data, Exeter

Printed and bound in Great Britain by
Short Run Press Ltd, Exeter

Contents

Tables

Maps

Plates

Illustration Acknowledgements

Special thanks are due to Sheila Stirling, Librarian at the Devon and Exeter Institution; Ann Inscker, Curator of the Torquay Museum; and Joy Slocombe, Curator of the Ilfracombe Museum, for allowing the copying of photographs and topographical prints from the extensive collections in their care.

The author and publishers would also like to thank the following institutions for granting permission to reproduce illustrations in this book:

Ilfracombe Museum for plates 4, 7, 8.
Torquay Museum for plates 2 and 6.
Devon and Exeter Institution for the jacket illustration and plates 1, 3, 5.

Acknowledgements

I should like to express my gratitude to all the librarians, archivists, correspondents and friends who have given me so much help in the preparation of this book.

Particular thanks must go to the staffs of the Devon and Exeter Institution, the Westcountry Studies Library, the University of Exeter Library, the Devon Record Office, the North Devon Athenaeum, the North Devon Local Studies Library, the Public Record Office, the House of Lords Record Office and the British Library. They bore patiently with my stream of requests for obscure documents, newspapers and books; they searched for little-known items hidden away on top shelves or stored in remote annexes; they called my attention to treasure troves of information in unlikely pamphlets and papers.

I should also like to thank Mathew Amner, who processed my photographs, and Rodney Fry, who drew the maps.

I owe a particular debt to Stephen Fisher and Edmund Newell, both of whom gave freely of their time to read the manuscript and made constructive suggestions for its improvement.

A list of all those to whom I am grateful for information would be unacceptably long, so I hope that I may be excused if I do not mention them individually by name. An exception must, however, be made in the case of Bernard Hallen, who put me on to Samuel Curwen's journal and provided answers to a whole string of queries about Exmouth.

Finally, I should like to thank my family. Justin, Emma, Sarah, Ruth and Simon were always understanding when their father closeted himself away to write. Peter and Carol, my brother and sister-in-law, provided warm hospitality whenever I needed a base while researching in London. Most of all, I am grateful to Gwyneth, my wife, for her support and practical assistance. This book is dedicated to her.

Introduction

This is a book which has evolved gradually over a long period of time. It is the product of years of research, with information being gleaned from a wide range of sources.[1] The text has frequently been revised as new evidence has come to hand. Yet it makes no claim to present a complete account of the rise of the Devon seaside resorts. The evidence is extremely fragmentary, so the picture pieced together can at best be only a partial one. Nor does it pretend to cover all the issues. It seeks only to analyse some of the main forces influencing the development of tourism on the Devon coast and to trace some of the main trends in the emergence of the watering places.

The rise of seaside resorts was for many years a neglected subject. Histories of the British Isles usually ignored the development of the tourist industry or dismissed it in a few lines. Histories of individual coastal counties frequently gave inadequate emphasis to this important subject and often failed to examine the causes and effects of the growth of holiday resorts. Devon was perhaps more fortunate than most counties, for when in 1954 W.G. Hoskins first published his comprehensive history and description of Devon, he devoted four pages to its seaside resorts and briefly discussed a few of the factors influencing their development.[2] Usually, though, it was labour rather than leisure which was the focus of attention for historians. There was a scholarly preoccupation with technological achievements and working conditions, but little interest was shown in the growing demands for relaxation and recreation.

In recent years, however, our nation has become increasingly pre-occupied with the fruitful use of free time. Reductions in the working week and lengthening holidays with pay have both helped to stimulate greater interest in leisure activities. It is in response to this growing interest that the history of leisure has at last begun to attract the serious attention of academics. The rise of the seaside holiday is one aspect of this fascinating subject which is currently being explored.

Several general histories of the English seaside holiday have been published since the Second World War. J.A.R. Pimlott's *The Englishman's*

Holiday: A Social History was the pioneer study. His book was a perceptive study of the evolution of the holiday as a social institution.[3] James Walvin's *Beside the Seaside: A Social History of the Popular Seaside Holiday, 1750–1914* appeared in 1978 and included sections on the origins of the seaside holiday and life at the resorts.[4] Then in 1983 John Walton's *The English Seaside Resort: A Social History, 1750–1914* was published. His book analysed the range of factors influencing the rise of seaside holidays and was a major contribution to the historiography of our country's holiday resorts.[5]

A number of histories of individual Devon seaside resorts have also been published. Among the best of these may be mentioned: Percy Russell's *History of Torquay*, J.A. Bulley's *Teignmouth in History*, Lois Lamplugh's *History of Ilfracombe* and Ronald Mayo's *Westward Ho!*.[6] F.B. May has published two papers on Ilfracombe, based on his valuable unpublished thesis entitled 'The Development of Ilfracombe in the Nineteenth Century',[7] but no other Devon resort has received such a detailed treatment.

This book attempts a much broader survey, for it examines the rise of all the Devon seaside resorts. It argues that, while each watering place was unique, certain underlying trends were common to them all. Yet it also stresses that their development differed in a number of important respects from that of many other British coastal watering places. It is these distinctive characteristics which make the Devon seaside resorts particularly interesting to study.

Here it is necessary to explain that, for the purposes of this book, a seaside resort will be defined as a place which owed a substantial part of its prosperity to the fact that people visited it for a holiday by the sea. All coastal settlements on the Devon coast that met this criterion will be studied whether they were large or small in size.

Plymouth does not qualify as a seaside resort when this test is applied, despite the fact that it was the principal urban centre on the Devon coast and had some of the facilities found at coastal watering places. Plymouth provided accommodation for many tourists, but this was because it was, like the inland city of Exeter, an important stopping point for travellers going on sightseeing tours of the West Country or wanting to break their journey to Cornwall. In the late eighteenth and early nineteenth centuries the nearby dockyard was an important attraction, but many inland towns likewise found that tourists enjoyed being shown round their factories. In that period Plymouth had assembly rooms, circulating libraries and a rich social life similar to that found at fashionable seaside resorts, but so too did Exeter and many other English provincial centres that were a long way from the sea. It is true that Plymouth had sea-water baths by 1767[8] and that a few people began to bathe in the sea nearby, but most of the bathers seem to have been local residents and there is no evidence to suggest that there was ever an influx of holiday-makers visiting Plymouth in order to bathe. It is also true that in 1884 a pier was opened at Plymouth,[9] but once again this seems to have been used principally by the local citizenry and it was not an important tourist attraction. While Plymouth did occasionally attempt to promote itself as a health resort,[10] it never succeeded in gaining general recognition as a coastal watering place. Catering for seaside holiday-makers was never one of Plymouth's principal functions. It owed its importance mainly to the nearby docks, to its varied industrial and commercial activities and to its role as a route centre.

The period covered by this book is from *circa* 1750 to *circa* 1900. The choice of 1750 is governed by the fact that the mid-eighteenth century saw the birth of the first seaside resorts in Devon; 1750 is in fact the year of the first extant reference to sea-bathing on the Devon coast. The choice of 1900 as a finishing point does however require more explanation. The end of the nineteenth century marked the end of an era for the Devon health resorts. Reputations founded on natural salubrity, and later bolstered by major sanitary improvements, were to count for far less in the early twentieth century, as pleasure rapidly supplanted health as the dominant reason for holidaying on the Devon coast. Social attitudes also changed at the turn of the century; improving recreations were no longer held in such high esteem, mixed bathing was allowed at many resorts, pierrots and the so-called 'nigger minstrels' began to strum on the beaches, music halls and cinemas were to become popular at the larger resorts in the years immediately before the First World War. The early twentieth century also saw the advent of motor cars and charabancs, bringing growing numbers of visitors into established resorts and opening up stretches of coast previously placed beyond common reach by their distance from the nearest railhead. The transition from health to pleasure, and from narrow exclusiveness to a more open society, was a gradual one, but the year 1900 does seem to stand out as a watershed. It has, therefore, been chosen as the termination of the period to be studied, although, whenever necessary, sallies will be made across the chronological divide.

It is hoped that this book will throw new light on some important aspects of the history of English seaside resorts. There have been a number of studies of large, popular resorts within easy reach of major centres of population.[11] Yet until now there has been far less interest in examining small but select seaside resorts located in more remote parts of the country. Devon was far removed from the major conurbations and, whilst one large watering place emerged at Torquay, many smaller watering places evolved which were quite different in size and character from most of the English seaside resorts that have previously been studied. This book also ventures down little-trodden paths by attempting a regional synthesis rather than making a case-study of a single watering place. It aims to avoid the parochial perspective and whenever possible tries to place developments at the Devon resorts in their national context. If it adds to the general understanding of the history of seaside tourism it will have served a valuable function. If at the same time it proves of interest to those who know and love Devon, the work of researching and writing it will be considered time well-spent.

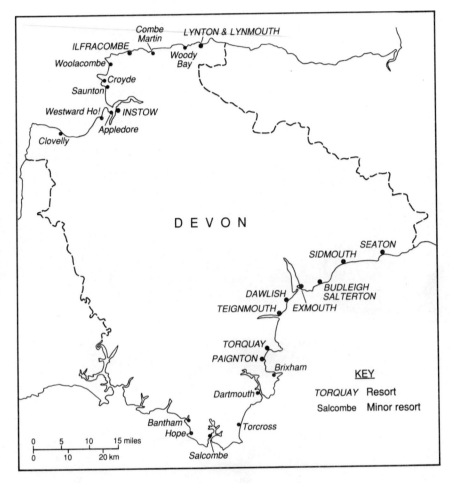

Map 1. The Seaside Resorts of Devon.

One

Early Beginnings: South Devon Resorts, 1750–1788

Seaside resorts began to develop at an early date on the south Devon coast. In 1750 Bishop Pococke visited the estuarine village of Exmouth and found that it was 'a place to which the people of Exeter much resort for diversion and bathing in the sea'.[1] Less than a decade had elapsed before there was a report of a second watering place emerging only a few miles along the coast. It was in 1759 that Andrew Brice, the Exeter publisher, stated that the little seaport of Teignmouth was developing a holiday trade and was being 'visited both for health and recreation'.[2] By the 1770s two more coastal settlements had begun to attract visitors. In 1776 Sidmouth was said to be playing host to 'company resorting hither for the benefit of bathing and drinking the waters'.[3] Two years later it was reported that Dawlish was entertaining sea-bathers, drawn there by its recently acquired reputation as a small health resort.[4]

These four seaside resorts were some of the first to develop on the British coast. Sea-bathing had been reported at Scarborough, Brighton and Margate in the 1730s, and also at Deal, Eastbourne and Portsmouth by 1750,[5] but it only gained general recognition as a fashionable pursuit in the following decades. It was in the second half of the eighteenth century that a number of villages and towns on the English and Welsh coast began to take on an important holiday function. The principal concentration of early seaside resorts was on the Kent and Sussex coast, where they benefited from their proximity to London, the principal centre of demand for seaside holidays. On coasts more distant from the influence of the metropolis, regional holiday demand was sufficient to encourage a scattered development of provincial seaside resorts at places as far apart as Southampton, Great Yarmouth and Blackpool.[6] The only other cluster of early coastal watering places was this group of resorts in south Devon, in what was then an extremely remote part of the country. It testified to the strength of the local demand for seaside holidays in a region far removed from the fashionable world of the capital.

The cult of sea-bathing had developed as a natural consequence of the popularity of the spas. For many years rich gentlefolk had frequented inland watering places, hoping to benefit from bathing in the spring waters and drinking the unpalatable liquid. Health had been the ostensible reason for visiting the spas, but, for the physically fit, the opportunities for amusement and social intercourse had often been more of an attraction than the spring waters. The popularity of spas like Bath, Tunbridge Wells and Epsom had encouraged a search for new mineral springs, so that by 1740 one observer had been able to count no less than 228 'spaws'.[7] Not all of these spas had developed into health resorts but, as each new spring had been discovered, so extravagant claims had been made for it by local members of the medical profession, who sought to increase their practices by attracting wealthy invalids to take the waters.

As physicians sought new sources of mineral water, it was at last realized that the sea offered a limitless supply of water containing all the necessary salts. In 1702 Sir John Floyer published the first edition of his *History of Cold Bathing*, and this book, advocating sea-bathing as a cure for many diseases, is thought to have persuaded a few members of the leisured class to seek renewed health at the seaside.[8] It was, though, Dr Richard Russell's *Dissertation on the Use of Sea Water in the Diseases of the Glands*, first published in 1750, which was principally responsible for the wakening of interest in the sea as a potential source of health. Dr Russell regarded the sea as a huge medicated bath and recommended that all health-seekers should be dipped in it. He went one step further, advising invalids that they should also drink sea water.[9] The thought of gulping down glasses of sea water may seem revolting to our generation, but it must be remembered that wealthy invalids were already accustomed to imbibing nauseous chalybeate and sulphurous waters at the spas. They certainly seem to have accepted this 'elixir of life' without question. The success of Russell's book encouraged many other doctors to publish treatises extolling the medical virtues of sea water taken both externally and internally.[10] Sea-water treatments became fashionable and wealthy people began to seek both health and pleasure at the seaside.

Many of the early visitors to the south Devon resorts were attracted there by the extravagant claims being made for the healing properties of sea water. In 1762 the *Royal Magazine* advised its readers that at Teignmouth:

For the sake of drinking that fashionable purging draught, sea water, and bathing, for which purpose two machines were lately constructed, numbers of people from all parts resort here in the summer season, and cripples frequently recover the use of their limbs, hysterical ladies their spirits and even the lepers are cleansed.[11]

Such stories of miracle cures seem hardly credible to our more sceptical generation, but the seaside resorts were anxious to attract invalids and sometimes exaggerated the effectiveness of their sea-water treatments. In 1789 the Teignmouth correspondent of the *Exeter Flying Post* claimed that over the years at his resort, 'bathing in the sea and drinking the salt water had been attended in many cases with great success'. He cited the case of an elderly clergyman who, after losing the use of both hands and legs, had visited Teignmouth in the hope of a cure:

> By bathing a few weeks, and drinking the sea water every other morning, he recovered the use of his limbs so far as to walk with crutches . . . and before he left Teignmouth was entirely restored.[12]

Faith must have been a great healer in such serious cases.

When the ailment was only a minor one, the disagreeable nature of the marine medicine perhaps spurred the patient into a rapid recovery. Yet it is clear that quaffing the ocean cordial did not always result in a miracle cure. In 1765 one Devon doctor prescribed a pint of sea water every morning for a girl with a swollen lip and was surprised to find that his patient was taken seriously ill after taking this unpleasant drink for ten days.[13]

Bathing machines made an early appearance on the south Devon coast. In this early period men nearly always bathed naked; women sometimes did the same or otherwise wore only flimsy dresses for their dip. Bathing machines were introduced to shield modest bathers from prying eyes while changing and then being transported down the beach and into the sea. In reality little more than sheds on wheels, these ugly but essential amenities were usually pulled along by bathing attendants or horses and were moved forward and back according to the dictates of the tide and the whim of their occupants. It seems likely that this new innovation was perfected in 1753 by Benjamin Beale of Margate.[14] Only six years later Exmouth was boasting of 'a conveniency made for safely and privately bathing in the sea water, of late much used and found beneficial'.[15] By 1762 Teignmouth had two machines in use.[16] At this early date they were still a novelty, but in later years they would become a familiar sight at all self-respecting English coastal resorts.

Sea-bathing was usually regarded as a necessary ordeal rather than as a pleasure. Bathers were forcibly dipped under the waves by the attendants accompanying the bathing machines; an unpleasant practice, particularly for those who were physically frail or of a nervous disposition. It was modelled on time-honoured custom at the spas, where 'dippers' were employed to submerge 'the quality' under the healing waters. At the south Devon seaside resorts the brawny women attendants were a formidable breed who struck fear into the hearts of many shivering customers. Fanny Burney, the young diarist, was terrified at Teignmouth in 1773 when she was dipped under the waves by the bathing women. She recorded in her journal:

> The women here are so poor and this place till lately was so obscure and retired that they wheeled the bathing machine into the sea themselves . . . I was terribly frightened and really thought I should never have recovered from the plunge.[17]

Sea-bathing usually took place at an extremely early hour. The medical faculty advised patients to dip before ten in the morning, to invigorate the constitution for the remainder of the day. So bathers were obliged to mortify the flesh by plunging into an icy-cold sea. In 1783 this daily ceremony was eulogized in an *Ode Addressed to the Bathing Machines at Exmouth*, which described the bathing machines as 'temples of health' from which 'priestesses each early morn salute the fragrant brine'.[18] Elegant words, but this ritual dip at the crack of dawn must have been a harsh penance for invalids who had made a pilgrimage to the seaside in the hope of renewed health.

While sea-water cures were very much in vogue, some early visitors also hoped to benefit from breathing pure sea air. As early as 1759 Andrew Brice reported that the gentry of Exeter were visiting Exmouth 'for the benefit of fine fresh air', as well as for the sea-bathing, and Teignmouth, 'the air being very wholesome here especially in summer'.[19] In 1771 Dr Downman, a celebrated Exeter physician, published a didactic poem declaring that cities like Exeter had an 'unwholesome atmosphere, gravid with seeds of latent sickness' and that smoke contaminated them with a 'darkening plume of poison and death prolific'. He advised the invalid to escape from the 'crowded town . . . that court of death where every gale is tainted with pollution' and to visit Dawlish, where, by turning his pallid face to 'the refreshing breeze' and 'inhaling . . . the briny spray', he might hope to obtain better health.[20] In 1795 John Swete, a local clergyman, stated that it was this doctor's recommendation that had led to the development of Dawlish as a seaside resort:

> Wonderful since the doctor's visit to it has been its transformation. What was then a fishing hamlet consisting of a few cots, one or two of which had been fitted up for the occasional reception of an invalid stranger, is now converted into a town.[21]

How could a considerable number of local people afford to spend long holidays at these emerging seaside resorts? The answer lies in the wealth being created in inland Devon. By the eighteenth century the woollen industry had brought prosperity to the county. Tiverton was the principal centre for both spinning and weaving, but many other towns had grown rich spinning yarn and manufacturing woollen fabrics. Exeter was the major centre for the finishing, dyeing and marketing of the cloth. Some of the city's merchants began importing linen, wines and spirits from the countries they exported woollen goods to, and they gradually diversified into general trade with Europe and the West Indies. Exeter's commercial prosperity was at its peak; it was one of the largest and richest of England's provincial cities. Exeter's professional class rapidly expanded, with many lawyers, doctors, teachers and clergymen taking up residence in the city. The business and professional classes were also expanding in the prospering market towns and other smaller centres of the woollen industry.[22] As the inland centres of population grew rich so they generated a demand for watering places on the nearby coast, where those with surplus wealth could seek new leisure-time opportunities.[23]

There was not a similar level of demand from the large coastal town of Plymouth. We have already seen that, while it was not itself a seaside resort, Plymouth did have some sea-bathing facilities of its own and it could offer a good range of entertainment facilities. So there was never much incentive for Plymouth people to visit the Devon seaside resorts.

While the burgeoning prosperity of inland Devon caused holiday resorts to germinate at an early date on the local coast, there was one adverse factor which seriously curtailed their ability to grow. The south Devon seaside resorts were badly handicapped by being virtually cut off from major centres of holiday demand in distant parts of the country. In 1752 the *Gentleman's Magazine* published an article calling attention to the atrocious state of the main highways leading into Devon. The author argued that the dreadful condition of the roads was a major deterrent to travellers and as a result the county was little-known:

> All beyond Sarum or Dorchester is to us *terra incognita* and the map-makers might, if they pleased, fill the vacuities of Devon and Cornwall with forests, sands, elephants or savages or what they please.[24]

Only the intrepid tourist ventured into Devon in the mid-eighteenth century. The roads leading into the county were probably in a worse condition than they had been in the Middle Ages. These highways had originally been designed for pack-horses and riding traffic, but by this time they were being deeply rutted by heavy coaches and wagons. The problem was that local parishes were still responsible for the upkeep of the major roads passing through their area, and they had neither the finance nor the expertise to do the job properly.[25]

A solution had been available from 1706 onwards, for Parliament had been authorising independent bodies of trustees to improve highways and then to charge road users a toll.[26] But in Devon not a single road was turnpiked before 1753, the year when the Exeter, Honiton and Exminster trusts were established. Several other turnpike trusts were set up in the county by the end of the decade.[27] Slowly then, more scientific and efficient methods of road construction were adopted. But it was many years before all the main highways into Devon were widened and their courses improved.

Most of the roads leading to the coast were little more than tracks and they were quite inadequate to cope with tourist traffic. Only in the late eighteenth century were the first steps taken to improve access to the nascent resorts. The road from Exeter to Exmouth was turnpiked as far as Lympstone. There was no coast road from Exeter to Dawlish and Teignmouth in this period, but a road linking the two resorts to the main Exeter to Newton Abbot road was improved. A new road was made from Sidmouth to join the main Exeter to Lyme Regis road. As the seaside resorts began to grow on both the east and west side of the Exe estuary, so the need increased for a new crossing over the Exe. In 1774 the Countess Wear Bridge was built. This enabled travellers from the direction of Sidmouth to make their way to resorts west of the Exe, without having to use the ferry from Exmouth to Starcross or having to pass through Exeter.[28]

The journey to the south Devon coast was long and tiring. In 1760 it still took coaches four days to travel the 170 miles from London to Exeter. Major road improvements then took place and by 1764 a coach was advertised to cover the distance in 48 hours.[29] Only those with strong constitutions could contemplate this bone-shaking ride, for it allowed very little time for stops. Tourists arriving at Exeter still had to make the journey on to the south Devon coast. The first coach services to the resorts began in the late 1760s. In 1768 the 'Exmouth Machine' was advertised to run from Exeter at 8.00 a.m. each day for Exmouth.[30] In the following year a coach began operating between Exeter and Teignmouth on three days a week during the summer season.[31] The south Devon resorts were gradually being made more accessible from the outside world, but the prospect of an arduous journey to Exeter, followed by a night in an inn, and then a further coach ride to a Devon resort, was still enough to discourage many potential visitors from distant parts of the country.

Resorts on the Kent and Sussex coast were certainly much easier to reach from London. Brighton, for example, was only some 57 miles by road from London and by 1762 a coach was being advertised to make the journey in a day.[32] Margate was also popular with Londoners, for it was only 72 miles away, and by 1771 the coach journey there could be completed in 13 or 14 hours, at a time when the journey to Exeter was still taking two days.[33]

It was not only the time and inconvenience of the long journey to south Devon which deterred potential visitors from the capital; the high cost of travel was another serious obstacle. In this period the coach fare from London to Exeter ranged between £1 16s. and £2 12s. 6d.[34] Then there was the expense of overnight accommodation at an inn. To this had to be added the cost of travel from Exeter to a resort: the coach fare from Exeter to either Exmouth or Teignmouth was 2s. 6d. in the late 1760s.[35] The cost of travel from London to resorts on the south-east coast was much less: the coach fare from London to Brighton in 1770 was only 14s.,[36] and from London to Margate in 1771 only 16s.[37] Sailing vessels provided an even cheaper way of travelling from London to Margate; between 1763 and 1780 the minimum fare for the sail down the Thames was 2s. 6d.[38]

Given the difficulties and high cost of travel from London to Devon, it is hardly surprising that some of the coastal watering places within easy reach of the capital expanded quicker than the remote south Devon resorts. Much of the early demand for seaside holidays stemmed from London. It was the social capital where aristocrats and gentry congregated and it was also the commercial metropolis with many prosperous middle-class citizens. The fashionable society and *nouveaux riches* of London generally preferred to holiday on the easily accessible coast of south-east England, rather than to make the long journey to Devon.

Another reason why the south Devon coastal resorts failed to become nationally important in the period prior to 1789 was that they had insufficient natural advantages as sea-bathing stations to attract visitors from London. While the beaches at Exmouth, Dawlish and Teignmouth were sandy and had relatively gentle gradients, they were no better than those at seaside resorts like Margate and Ramsgate, which were much easier to reach from the capital. Moreover the south Devon seaside resorts all had the disadvantage of being situated at river mouths. Medical experts were attaching great importance to the health-giving properties of sea water, so it was considered a significant disadvantage to be located where there was a flow of fresh water.[39] The sea-bathing facilities at the south Devon resorts were quite adequate to meet local needs, but they were not sufficiently exceptional to entice fashionable visitors from the metropolis to undertake the long journey into Devon.

Early visitors to the south Devon seaside resorts originated mainly from within the county. In 1759 Andrew Brice wrote of Exmouth that 'here many of the gentry of Exeter much resort in the summer'.[40] Exmouth was the easiest seaside resort to reach from Exeter, so it was not surprising that it attracted the lion's share of the holiday demand from that city. Indeed when Maurice Margarot visited Exmouth in 1780 he formed the impression that the resort was 'only frequented by the merchants of Exeter'.[41] Yet Exmouth, like its local rivals, also attracted rich families from many other towns of inland Devon. Landed gentry from the rural districts of Devon also began to congregate at the emerging seaside resorts for the summer season. The leading county families had long been accustomed to gather in Exeter, which was regarded as the social capital of south-west England.[42] Now the new coastal resorts became an alternative rendezvous for some members of this élite group.

The first 'strangers' to arrive only made the comparatively short journey from Somerset. It had taken the coach three days to cover the 75 miles from Bath to Exeter in 1727, but the journey time was reduced to 1½ days in 1768 and to only 15 hours in 1777.[43] These transport improvements persuaded a few wealthy inhabitants of the Somerset market towns to visit the south Devon coast for the sea-bathing season.[44] More importantly for the social tone of the developing resorts, they also encouraged a few members of the fashionable society frequenting Bath to spend the summer months at the south Devon seaside. Thus, when in 1773 Fanny Burney travelled from Bath to spend July, August and September at Teignmouth, she found that a few other visitors from the spa were among the company already assembled there.[45] It is interesting to note that at this time other members of the genteel society at Bath were beginning to make summer visits to the new seaside resorts on the adjacent Dorset coast.[46]

Evidence about the size and social composition of the visiting public is difficult to obtain. In the absence of precise statistics, the lists that local papers published of either visitors newly arrived at a resort or visitors present in a resort will sometimes be referred to in this book, so at this point it is necessary to call attention to some of the problems involved in analysing them. One problem with both arrival lists and visitor lists is that it is impossible to judge how carefully they were prepared. It is also difficult to be sure how representative they were. It is possible, or even probable, that some editors chose not to include the names of visitors at the lower end of the social scale. Yet another difficulty is caused by the fact that these lists often contain the words 'and family' or 'and party' without specifying the number included in these groups. The solution adopted when counting numbers from either arrival or visitor lists has been to add two to the total each time these words appear. There are, therefore, considerable problems in using these lists but, if their limitations are kept clearly in mind, they can provide useful information about the size and nature of demand at particular resorts.[47]

The first and only sequence of arrival lists available for this early period is that for Teignmouth published in the *Exeter Flying Post* in 1774. These lists run from June to August suggesting that this was the main season. They also indicate that the resort had only a small company of visitors. Only 147 people were listed as arriving at the resort in these three months. Among the names given were those of two knights and their ladies, together with a number of army officers and several clergymen. But not a single peer of the realm was recorded.[48]

The journal of Samuel Curwen also provides valuable information about the number and quality of the visitors to the south Devon resorts in the 1770s. Arriving at the new resort of Sidmouth in August 1776, this exiled American found it had only a small company of visitors. Fashionable tourists holidayed there only rarely and were greeted with surprise and admiration.[49] In July 1778 Curwen visited Teignmouth and noted that it was an established resort attracting visitors with a higher social standing:

> It is a bathing town and resorted to by men and company of a much higher rank than Sidmouth can boast ... the houses [being] of incomparably better appearance ... Here are some well-filled shops and a face of success.[50]

On the same tour he visited Dawlish and found 'a few persons only resorting there'.[51] This coastal village had but one bathing machine and had only recently begun to develop a tourist trade.

Finally in 1779 Curwen spent the whole summer at Exmouth and discovered that, while it was easily the busiest of the Devon resorts, it was riven with social tensions. At first he was pleased to find a substantial number of gentry among the company and was particularly impressed when told: '375 strangers have been numbered here at one time'.[52] He soon realized that at weekends the resort was invaded by fun-loving bourgeoisie from nearby Exeter. The people of Exmouth resented the fact that these weekenders had purchased some of the finest houses in Exmouth and spent little in the resort on either accommodation or meals. Curwen observed:

> Exeter people who come down in shoals on Saturday P.M. for purpose of pastime or festivity among themselves on Sunday ... not, as I am told, to the emolument or wish of the inhabitants, to whom they are of no advantage.[53]

It was the brash and vulgar manners of the Exeter citizenry which most offended the more 'respectable' visitors. There were frequent complaints that these weekenders spent the Sabbath in 'jollity and indolence' when many felt their time would have been better employed at worship.[54] Samuel Curwen was outraged when he encountered some of these pleasure-seekers while out on an evening promenade.

> Walked ... amidst shoals of Exeter damsels, whose insufferable undress and ill-breeding justly exposes them to the contempt and derision of strangers.[55]

He noted that the weekenders from Exeter and the more genteel long-stay visitors never mixed, and that they shared only a 'reciprocal dislike'.[56] Even at this early date there were signs of the social conflict which in later years was to bedevil life at so many English seaside resorts. It seems clear then that the visiting public was small in size and largely provincial in origin. Very few Londoners made the difficult journey to the Devon coast in this period. Nearly all the visitors came from the Westcountry and they included members of both the urban and country gentry together with some less polished merchants and manufacturers from local towns. The few fashionable arrivals from Bath had an importance far beyond their numbers, for they brought with them the manners and conventions of a more sophisticated society.

Tourism at first played only a small part in the economy of these coastal settlements. They were all old-established fishing communities. Teignmouth, Dawlish and Sidmouth all had substantial inshore catches of pilchards, while Exmouth had important oyster and mussel fisheries at the mouth of the Exe. All four of these seaside villages had for many years derived most of their income from the Newfoundland trade. As early as the sixteenth century they had sent small ships on hazardous voyages to catch cod in the teeming waters of the Grand Banks. Vessels were away for several months at a time, fishing and also trading with the coastal villages of Newfoundland. When the south Devon tourist industry began to develop in the second half of the eighteenth century, the Newfoundland trade was still the principal source of employment at all four of the infant resorts. Teignmouth sent no less than 43 vessels to the Grand Banks in 1770.[57] Yet by this time the trade was in decline. One visitor to Sidmouth in 1776 noted that the inhabitants were 'chiefly hired out to the Newfoundland traders and for the most part in low circumstances'.[58] At a time when the fishing industry was faced with recession, the development of the tourist industry provided new employment opportunities and regenerated the economies of these coastal communities.

In this early period most of the visitors had to stay in unsophisticated accommodation, usually renting accommodation in old houses which had been adapted to take holiday-makers. When Fanny Burney visited Teignmouth in 1773 she stayed in a 'small, neat, thatched and white-washed cottage'. It was owned by a sea captain and was quite simple, containing only a parlour, a kitchen and two bedrooms.[59] On arrival at Exmouth in 1779, Samuel Curwen was directed to a little cottage inhabited by a widow. He wrote: 'I quickly struck a bargain for lodgings and dressing my food that I was to buy exclusively for 6s. a week'.[60] In 1782

Exmouth was described as a pretty village, 'composed for the main part of cot-houses, neat and clean, consisting of four or five rooms, which are generally let at a guinea a week'.[61]

Investment in tourism was cautious and small in scale, but gradually a limited amount of purpose-built holiday accommodation was provided. In 1759 Andrew Brice reported that Teignmouth had 'of late begun to be beautified with diverse handsome and delightful buildings' for the use of visitors.[62] In 1776 newly-built dwellings, with coach houses and stables, were advertised for sale at Exmouth and were intended for the use of those seeking 'the benefit of the air and the conveniency of the sea-bathing'.[63] Three years later Samuel Curwen noted at Exmouth that while the houses were 'chiefly small and low, mud walls and thatched roofs', there were also 'a considerable number of brick, covered with slate, very reputable and handsome'.[64] Existing inns at the emerging resorts were improved to accommodate visitors and at Teignmouth two new ones were built, with the Globe opening in 1773 and the London Inn in 1780.[65]

While some of the early visitors to the south Devon resorts were seeking relief from a chronic complaint, others arrived hoping to be delivered from the malaise of boredom. Health for them was merely the pretext for a seaside holiday and pleasure was their real objective. We have seen how the coastal watering places modelled their sea-water treatments on the formal ritual of taking the waters at the spas. The emerging south Devon resorts also tried to emulate their inland precursors by providing a few of the fashionable amusements available at the spas.

At the south Devon resorts in the late 1770s Samuel Curwen observed a daily ritual which was very similar to that at the spa resorts. After an early start at the bathing place, where some bathed, others drank the waters and the majority looked on, the rest of the day was spent in social display and time-frittering amusements. The company first paraded up and down the sea-front, admiring the 'brilliant appearance of well-dressed ladies'. Long hours were then spent at commerce, quadrille and other card games, before the whole company met again in the late afternoon for a 'public tea'. Sometimes, to make a change, bowls would be played or an excursion made into the surrounding countryside.[66]

Visitor numbers were too small to justify investment in large purpose-built assembly rooms comparable to those found at the major spas, but once the south Devon resorts became established they felt it necessary to at least provide a public room where the company could meet. The first assemblies at the south Devon seaside resorts were run by innkeepers in large rooms attached to their premises. In 1770 the proprietor of the Globe Inn at Exmouth announced that he had 'made a new assembly room together with a new bowling green which will be opened by subscription, and there will be a public breakfast every Thursday and a card assembly every Monday'.[67] Similarly at Teignmouth in 1773 new rooms were built onto the recently completed Globe Inn and the landlord advertised 'a card assembly to be continued Mondays and Fridays during the summer season'.[68] By 1781 the Teignmouth gentry were meeting in the 'long room' at the London Inn, with balls being held once a week and card assemblies taking place every day during the season.[69]

This practice of holding assemblies in rooms forming part of an inn was not uncommon. The first assemblies in many provincial towns and coastal resorts were held in rooms attached to a local hostelry. At Brighton, for example, the company started to assemble at the Castle Inn in 1754, while at Margate fashionable society began to assemble at the New Inn in 1762.[70] However, at these two watering places and at other centres of fashion, the clientele was soon large enough to justify investment in large, new buildings specially designed for the holding of assemblies,[71] whereas at the Devon seaside resorts visitor numbers throughout this period remained too small to warrant the building of purpose-built assembly rooms.

The assemblies at the south Devon seaside resorts had very few potential patrons and could not afford to be selective. Assemblies at leading English spas often had elaborate rules designed to protect and enhance the social status of the company, but on the south Devon coast the public rooms were open to all who could afford to pay the expensive admission charges. The price of entry to the first meeting of the Teignmouth assembly in 1774 was the substantial sum of 2*s.* 6*d.*[72] By 1781 the gentlemen there were being charged 3*s.* 6*d.* for admission to a ball, or a guinea for a season, and the ladies enjoyed only slightly reduced rates.[73] While such charges effectively deterred labourers, servants and other members of the 'lower orders', they were no deterrent to prosperous Devon businessmen, who found that the assemblies provided them with unique opportunities to mingle with their social superiors.

Any spirited spark holidaying on the south Devon coast in the years prior to the French Revolution would have been sadly disappointed by the size and nature of the company at the assembly rooms. At a time when fashionable young rakes were following the Prince of Wales to

Brighton, and many prosperous Londoners were sailing down the Thames to Margate, the Devon coastal assemblies had to rely on a small provincial clientele. In 1782 one bored visitor wrote in disparaging terms of the limited entertainment available at the Exmouth assembly:

> Exmouth boasts no public rooms or assemblies, save one card assembly in an inconvenient apartment at one of the inns on Monday evenings. The company meet at half after five, and break up at ten—they play at shilling whist or two-penny quadrille. We have very few young people here, and no diversions.[74]

While indoor amusements were few in number, the south Devon coastal resorts could boast a few novel outdoor attractions. The diary Fanny Burney kept of her stay at Teignmouth in 1773 captured her surprise at the strangeness of life on the remote Devon coast. She was particularly fascinated by the 'barbarous' fisherwomen who tended the nets while their menfolk were away at the Newfoundland fishing grounds. This was an age when it was not considered ladylike for members of the fairer sex to unduly exert themselves, and Fanny stared in astonishment when some of the muscular fisherwomen hauled in the heavy seine.[75] She was even more surprised to find them competing in a rowing match: 'The women rowed with astonishing dexterity and quickness: there were five boats of them: the prizes which they won were shifts with pink ribands'.[76]

Fanny was less impressed with her visit to a wrestling match at Teignmouth. She considered Devon wrestling a 'barbarous diversion' for it involved kicking as a principal form of attack. Fanny saw 'a strong labouring man come off victorious in the first battles', but was shocked to learn that the wrestler had to 'conquer twice, one opponent immediately after another, to entitle himself to the prize', and that 'while his shins were yet bleeding, he was obliged to attack another'.[77] Yet for many wealthy incomers this traditional Devon sport was a welcome novelty and they put up substantial prizes to encourage famous wrestlers from inland Devon to compete at the seaside resorts.

Not all the outdoor recreations were alien to arrivals from inland towns. A day at the races had long been a popular diversion at the spas, and this exciting spectator sport was one of the first forms of organized entertainment to be provided at leading south Devon resorts. Fanny went to the races at Teignmouth and was pleased to obtain 'a very good place in the stand, where there was a great deal of company'.[78] By 1779 Sidmouth had also begun to stage horse races, which took place on Salcombe Down as part of a local festival known as the Annual Diversion.[79] Cricket also reached the south Devon coast. Fanny went to see her host play in a 'grand cricket match on the Den' at Teignmouth. Cricket had become popular in Georgian England as a skilful game for gentlemen which could be watched and enjoyed by their ladies. Cricket games, like race meetings, were social occasions and Fanny recorded: 'The cricket players dined on the green where they had a booth erected, and a dinner from the Globe, the best inn'.[80] But fashionable visitors were still too few in number to support a large calendar of social events, and life at the south Devon resorts must have seemed very sedate to those accustomed to the sophisticated diversions of the principal spas.

The tourist trade of the south Devon seaside resorts was still in its infancy. The holiday industry had been grafted onto the economies of a number of long-established coastal settlements and, although it was beginning to flourish, it was still far from maturity. At a time when some specialized resorts were emerging on the Kent and Sussex coast, providing a wide range of social amenities for fashionable London society, the south Devon seaside resorts were still relatively small and provided only limited facilities for a restricted provincial market.

Two

A Delayed Start: A North Devon Resort, 1770–1788

The holiday industry was slow to develop on the north Devon coast. The first south Devon resorts had grown up in a prosperous region enriched by the close proximity of Exeter, but it was not easy for resorts to take root on the coast of sparsely-populated north Devon. Ilfracombe was the only watering place to emerge in the period up to 1788 and even there early growth was hesitant and stunted.

Paucity of local demand was the principal impediment to the early development of tourism. There were no urban centres in north Devon comparable in size or wealth with Exeter or Tiverton. The only towns of any consequence were the coastal settlements of Barnstaple and Bideford. These relatively small seaports had had an illustrious history, playing an important part in the development of the Atlantic trade. At the beginning of the eighteenth century they had still been dispatching many merchant ships on long voyages to Newfoundland, Maryland and Virginia. Since then long wars with France had decimated this trade and in 1775 the outbreak of the American War of Independence delivered its death blow. Traditional Continental markets were also lost as hostilities with France continued. Even local coastal trade with Wales and Ireland was adversely affected by the wars. Time after time French and Spanish privateers lurking off Lundy Isle plundered vessels trading out of the two ports. By the second half of the eighteenth century Barnstaple and Bideford's merchant fleets were only a fraction of their former size and only the memories of mercantile renown lingered on.[1] Their woollen industries had also been crippled, for they had lost their European markets during the wars with France.[2] Barnstaple and Bideford were both gripped by recession; with their trade and industry collapsing, few of their inhabitants could afford to contemplate a holiday. The small minority who still had money to spend on leisure activities showed little desire to visit a local seaside resort. It has to be remembered that Barnstaple and Bideford both had estuarine locations, so their citizens were not particularly attracted by the prospect of spending a holiday only a few miles along the coast.

Nor was there sufficient surplus wealth in the inland districts of north Devon to fuel a demand for holidays. The little market town of South Molton had had a flourishing woollen industry since medieval times, spinning and weaving wool produced on Exmoor. It had produced coarse cloths for export to Europe, but in the eighteenth century the frequent wars with France cut off this market.[3] With its staple trade almost moribund, South Molton had only a handful of citizens with the time and means to take a holiday on the local coast. The rural community was also suffering; wool prices had slumped, agricultural techniques were backward, the tenant farmers poor and the landed gentry far fewer in number than in the south of the county.[4] The whole region was sparsely populated and few of those who did live there could afford to contemplate a holiday at a seaside resort.

Difficulties of access from distant parts of the country also helped to prevent the early development of a holiday industry on the north Devon coast. Given the meagre local demand for holidays, it was obvious that the tourist industry could not develop significantly while transport links with areas of greater urban prosperity were so poor. The problem was that north Devon was almost completely detached from the mainstream of progress. The county's main transport artery was the road from London which went through Exeter and Plymouth, and followed a route much closer to the English Channel than to the Bristol Channel. The other major highways likewise avoided the region, running on more southerly routes. Most roads converged on Exeter, which was conveniently placed in relation to the southern coast of Devon, but far-removed from the northern one.

Land approaches to north Devon were made more difficult by the hilly terrain. The extensive uplands and deeply incised valleys posed formidable problems for the road engineer. Many of the early routes to the north of the county had to cut across the grain of the country, climbing and falling as they crossed the undulating uplands. The valley floors would have provided easier gradients, but the roads avoided them because the land was wet and marshy.[5]

The atrocious condition of the roads to north Devon added to the difficulties for would-be travellers. An Act had been passed in 1763 creating the Barnstaple Turnpike Trust, which was given powers in most of north Devon. The Trust had soon started to charge tolls on the principal access routes to the region. But only minor improvements had been made to existing roads and no new turnpikes had been constructed.[6]

Wheeled vehicles were an unusual sight on north Devon roads as they could not operate satisfactorily over surfaces pitted with craters and strewn with rocks. Consequently, most early visitors to the region were obliged to travel there on horseback. Attempts were made to start a coach service between Exeter and Barnstaple in 1778, but in 1787 it still took the coach over 12 hours to cover a distance of just 39 miles.[7] More difficulties lay in store for those who wished to travel further. The roads leading from Barnstaple to the Bristol Channel coast were little more than track ways and the traveller had of necessity to complete his journey on horseback or on foot. The prospect of such a slow and trying journey served to deter many potential visitors. So too did the fare. In 1778 it cost 13*s.* to travel by coach the relatively short distance from Exeter to Barnstaple,[8] and further costs were incurred in hiring horses to journey on to the coast.

Ilfracombe was the only north Devon coastal settlement to develop any sort of holiday trade in the period up to 1788. A report from Ilfracombe in the *Exeter Flying Post* in August 1771 was the first indication that a new watering place was emerging in the northern extremities of the county. It announced that visitors were arriving at the little seaport 'for the benefit of the air, salt water and to spend part of the summer season'. It went on to claim: 'Of the very many persons who have frequented Ilfracombe for their health, during the summer season for years past, but one have died; so salubrious is its air and waters'.[9] Yet it listed the names of only some ten holiday-makers present at the resort that season, indicating that in fact the town's tourist trade was still in its infancy. Ilfracombe was making exaggerated claims in the hope that it would establish a reputation as a health resort.

In 1788 the same newspaper again stated that Ilfracombe was developing a tourist trade, catering for a Devon clientele rather than a national one:

> Ilfracombe we hear is this season remarkably full of genteel company, being resorted to by numbers of respectable families from most parts of the county. What pleases strangers most is the conveniency of the bathing machines.[10]

This news item originated from a local correspondent and was typical of the puffed-up claims being made by many small watering places in the hope of attracting rich visitors.

The sparsity of information about Ilfracombe in this early period indicates that this coastal settlement was little-known and little-visited. What contemporary evidence there is serves to confirm that even at the very end of the period Ilfracombe still had only a very small tourist industry. In 1789 the Revd John Swete made his way there on horseback from south Devon. In his journal he gave a comprehensive account of the town's economic activities, noting that its coastal vessels were kept busy transporting coal from South Wales to Cornwall and then returning to Neath and Swansea with copper and tin. He described the manufacture of rope and cord for the numerous ships frequenting the port and he referred to the revival of the herring fishing industry. Yet he made no mention of either visitors or tourist amenities.[11] Elsewhere on his travels Swete displayed a keen interest in the growth of seaside resorts. His silence on this subject while at Ilfracombe suggests that tourism there was only of minor importance. After leaving Ilfracombe he did make a passing reference to his disappointment at finding the little town had only one bathing machine.[12] This once again suggests that claims for the development of a thriving resort were exaggerated and in fact Ilfracombe still had only a few visitors.

In the following year John Savage, a mariner, was driven by a storm into Ilfracombe harbour and discovered a poverty-stricken community. In his memoirs he gave an account of farmers from the town labouring to cultivate the rocky slopes of the surrounding hills, while in the valleys millers struggled to make a living grinding grain in dilapidated water mills. He described how herring were caught, cured and exported to the Mediterranean countries. He also provided information about 'near 100 sail of freighting sloops and brigs at this place whose chief employ is fetching coal from Wales for this and many other ports, or carrying any other merchandise that suits them'. Yet Savage made no mention of a holiday industry other than to comment on the fact that there were no hotels suitable for the gentry, but instead just 'one public house, a very good one, which is a tavern, coffee house and inn, sign the Britannia, all in one'.[13] It seems clear that at this time the tourist trade at north Devon's first seaside resort was still in an embryonic state.

Three

'Overflowing with Fashionables': South Devon Resorts, 1789–1815

The outbreak of the French Revolution in 1789 sent ripples of fear eddying through the English upper classes, but few people in south Devon realized that the upheaval abroad would soon divert a steady stream of wealthy English tourists down to their remote seaside resorts. The prospect of political disruption on the Continent was greeted with alarm in Devon. Not without reason, for the wars which followed cut off European markets and brought ruin to many of the county's cloth manufacturers and merchants.[1] At first it was thought that it was only the local farmers who were benefiting from the wars, with wheat prices soaring when it became difficult to import from abroad.[2] Soon it was realized that the holiday industry was also prospering. Existing coastal resorts expanded and new ones began to develop. This chapter will examine the reasons why tourism rocketed to importance on the south Devon coast in the period between 1789 and 1815. It will also consider the changes that took place as a group of small provincial resorts suddenly gained national recognition and found themselves playing host to many fashionable visitors from distant parts of the country.

The storming of the Bastille on 14 July 1789 sparked off a period of terror in France, and this caused many members of the British leisured class to seek alternative holiday destinations in their own country. When the guillotine swung into action, decimating the flower of the French aristocracy, most of the British gentlefolk still in France beat a hasty retreat back across the Channel, while those planning a holiday felt it prudent to find safer places to visit in England.[3] Then in February 1793 France declared war on Britain. This war finally closed the greater part of the Continent to British tourists, for the British government made it illegal for its citizens to visit France and it was dangerous for them to visit many other European countries.[4] Most of Europe remained out of reach for the next 22 years. Only in two brief intervals of peace did a few brave tourists venture into France, and on both occasions the renewal of hostilities caused them to stampede home. Not until the final defeat of Napoleon at Waterloo in June 1815 did British tourists feel safe to venture abroad again.[5]

Many delicate people of rank and fortune had been in the habit of wintering in Mediterranean France. It was the climate which was the principal attraction; the winters there were warm and the air was thought to be extremely healthy. The English had long frequented Montpellier, for it was famed for its salubrious air and skilled doctors. Other English colonies had grown up at Avignon, Toulouse and Aix.[6] In the later eighteenth century the Riviera coast had also become fashionable. One visitor to Nice wrote in December 1786: 'The town is much enlivened and enriched by the concourse of strangers, who resort here for the sake of the climate in winter'.[7] So by the 1780s Mediterranean France was firmly established as a favourite winter retreat for wealthy Englishmen. But the French Revolution brought an abrupt end to winter sojourns in that sunny clime and obliged the English gentry to find a new refuge from the icy blasts of winter.

South Devon then began to receive considerable publicity as the nearest English equivalent to the south of France. In 1791 the celebrated Dr Jebb, physician to George III, announced that he would 'aver the pureness and salubrity of the air at Exmouth equal to the south of France'.[8] By 1793 Sidmouth was 'being very commonly recommended to invalids, particularly those affected by consumptions, as many of the faculty think this situation equal to the south of France'.[9] Soon all the south Devon resorts were being favourably compared with those of Mediterranean France. In 1803 one national guide stated: 'The mild and genial softness of the air on the south coast of Devon is generally esteemed equally salutary with that of Montpellier or Nice, and is frequently prescribed for pulmonic disorders and declines'.[10] Even the landscapes were compared with those of the south of France; by 1809 the coastline of Torbay was being likened to 'the scenery on that part of the coast of the Mediterranean on which Monaco and other picturesque places are situated'.[11]

Linked to the change in the political situation was a concurrent change in medical fashion. The south Devon resorts may have had few special advantages as sea-bathing stations, but they soon started to attract invalids from distant parts of England, once the medical profession began to consider the merits of different local climates in the treatment of disease. We have seen that the health-giving properties of pure sea air were appreciated in Devon as early as the 1750s. National interest in the medical properties of sea air was greatly stimulated by the work of Dr Ingenhousz, who in 1780 gave a paper to the Royal Society entitled 'On the Degree of Salubrity of the Common Air at Sea'. At a time when thinking people had begun to realize that the polluted environment of the overcrowded towns provided a fertile breeding ground for disease, this paper provided a valuable service by calling attention to the purity of the air at the seaside.[12] It had an important effect on medical thinking. Doctors had been stressing the benefits of sea-water treatments, but now the medical faculty began to develop an additional interest in the nature of climates at coastal locations and their influence on health.

The climate of the south Devon coast offered a healthy blend of pure sea air and exceptionally mild winters. This combination was thought to offer important benefits to all invalids, but was believed to have special value in the treatment of respiratory complaints. In an age when lives were constantly threatened by disease, it was tuberculosis that was feared most, for it was a merciless killer. In the absence of any effective medical preventative, many doctors began to send consumptives to the south Devon coast in the hope of a miracle cure. 'Medical men are now so much convinced of the advantages resulting from the climate of the south of Devon and Cornwall that they recommend it to their patients in preference to Lisbon', wrote one commentator in 1794.[13]

As the trickle of invalids increased into a steady flow, publicity began to be given to the therapeutic advantages of a stay in a particular resort. In 1803, for example, a national guidebook stated that at Exmouth the climate had a 'relaxing quality always befriending weak lungs' and that this was why many consumptives took up residence there.[14] In the same year a Sidmouth cleric claimed that at his resort the invalid could 'inhale those breezes which so frequently suspend the ravage of disease, pour fresh oil into the lap of life, and send him back a renovated being'.[15]

The temporary closure of the Continent also encouraged a new interest in the scenery on the Devon coast. Adventurous Englishmen had previously enjoyed discovering the scenic attractions of remote parts of Europe, but during the French Revolutionary and Napoleonic Wars they could no longer visit those regions. In the late eighteenth century William Gilpin, a Hampshire clergyman, published a series of books pointing out that in Britain there were landscapes which, while less spectacular than those of the Alps and Italy, would make attractive subjects for pictures and might therefore be described as having picturesque beauty.[16] His books were a great success and helped to found the cult of the picturesque. Many were inspired to explore Britain in search of scenes which could delight the eye and inspire the artist's brush. The Lake District, Wye Valley and Snowdonia all gained recognition as areas of picturesque scenery. Then it was realized that picturesque views could also be found in Devon, and that this county had the extra advantage of having some of its finest scenery by the sea.

A south Devon clergyman played an important role in publicizing the scenic attractions of the county. The Revd John Swete had inherited a fortune, and this gave him the time and income to develop his interest in the cult of the picturesque. Between 1789 and 1801 he toured the county and then wrote and illustrated a twenty-volume journal of all that he had seen. This great work was entitled 'Picturesque Sketches of Devon'.[17] It was never published, but was shown to the many writers and artists who visited him at Oxton House, his country seat near Dawlish. His journals strongly influenced many subsequent topographical descriptions of the county.[18]

Travel writers soon began to bring to public notice the scenic attractions of south Devon. In 1793 two articles appeared in the *Gentleman's Magazine* advising a discriminating readership that at Dawlish and Teignmouth could be found landscapes which were 'remarkably picturesque'.[19] In 1797 William Maton's *Observations Relative to . . . the Western Counties of England* was published and it drew attention to the 'most romantic scenery' of the little-known seaside village of Torquay.[20] Then in 1804 T.H. Williams' *Picturesque Excursions in Devonshire* went on sale. This attractive book was published in London and was a fine advertisement for the charms of the Devon landscapes.[21] In the next few years the south Devon coastal scenery was praised in a whole string of travel books.[22] This flood of publicity enticed some tourists to venture on long expeditions into Devon. They were hoping for opportunities to exercise and display their aesthetic judgement as they searched for an ideal landscape on the south Devon coast.

The French wars had another stimulating effect on the south Devon tourist trade, for the emerging seaside resorts received the patronage of many army and naval officers. The threat of a French invasion made necessary the garrisoning of large numbers of soldiers along the coast and their officers often sought recreation and good company at the seaside resorts.[23] The Channel Fleet was often stationed in Torbay, because it

provided a sheltered rendezvous for vessels returning from blockading
Brest or guarding the Western Approaches. Many of the principal naval
officers spent much of their free time ashore and they formed an important
part of the fashionable society frequenting the coastal watering places.
Some of their wives and families took up residence in Torquay and helped
the nascent resort to gain fashionable acceptance.[24]

There was yet another way in which the war boosted tourism on the
south Devon coast. Some members of the upper classes were driven to
small seaside resorts by the need to cut costs at a time of rising prices
and increased taxation.[25] It was certainly cheaper to live on the remote
Devon coast than in London or the fashionable seaside resorts within
easy reach of the capital. Many early visitors expressed astonishment at
the low cost of living in Devon. In 1800 Mr Dunsford, a Tiverton
merchant, suggested that many fashionable visitors were being attracted
to the Devon coast at least as much by the need for economy as by the
'claims of sickness and infirmity'.[26] The cost of provisions on the south
Devon coast rocketed during the French Wars,[27] but still seemed
attractively low to people from the capital and other centres of fashion.
When the artist Joseph Farington toured south Devon in 1809, he was
told that 'a person might . . . live in Devonshire as well for £400 a year
as he could do in London for £600', and that was a powerful inducement
to take up residence on the Devon coast.[28]

The cost of accommodation also rose sharply during the war years, but
still remained well below that at leading seaside resorts located closer to
London. In 1795 John Swete visited Dawlish and noted:

> About twenty years ago the price of the best lodging house per week
> was not more, if it was as much, as half a guinea, but so fashionable
> is Dawlish in the present day, that in the height of the season not a
> house of the least consequence is to be hired for less than two guineas
> a week and many of them rise as high as four or five.[29]

In 1809 Joseph Farington reported that properties in Sidmouth were being
let for five guineas a week, while at Exmouth houses with good views
could command seven guineas a week.[30] These were high prices by Devon
standards, but they were quite moderate when compared with those on
the Kent coast where comparable houses were being let for as much as
eight or ten guineas a week.[31] While charges for accommodation had
soared, many fashionable incomers still considered them to be attractively
low. The south Devon resorts were inviting havens for those in financial

difficulties who wished to avoid the extravagance of a stay in a major watering place, and especially for those obliged to distance themselves as far as possible from their creditors in London or Bath.

Royal visits to the South West also helped to publicize the attractions of the region and brought in more new visitors. In July 1789, the month in which the French Revolution began, George III made his first visit to Weymouth on the Dorset coast. He was recovering from an attack of insanity and his doctors prescribed the fashionable therapy of a visit to the seaside.[32] After taking the air and bathing in the sea he was restored to 'full health and joyous spirits'.[33] To the nation this seemed conclusive proof of the effectiveness of the seaside cure. No single event ever did more to publicize the advantages of a seaside holiday in south-west England.

George III's subsequent expeditions to Weymouth brought in their wake many followers of fashion, all eager to follow in the royal footsteps by making the long journey to the South West. These newcomers, having visited the Dorset coast, sometimes extended their tour to include the south Devon resorts.[34] The monarch was the supreme trend-setter and, once it was known that he had benefited from his seaside visits, a visit to the remote south-west coast became fashionable.

The principal south Devon seaside resorts were themselves given the ultimate accolade of royal patronage at the beginning of the nineteenth century. In the spring of 1806, Sidmouth, Exmouth, Dawlish, Teignmouth and Torquay were all favoured by visits from the Princess of Wales.[35] These resorts profited from the cachet of royal approval for, as Robert Southey pointed out in 1814 in his 'Letter on Watering Places': 'Wherever one of the queen bees of fashion alights, a whole swarm follows after'.[36] Long before the advent of public relations consultants, it was recognized that a resort could secure no better publicity than that bestowed by the favour of royal patronage, and consequently these visits by the Princess of Wales were frequently alluded to in subsequent tourist guides.[37]

There was still another important factor encouraging visits by tourists from distant parts of the country and that was the acceleration of coach travel to south Devon which had taken place in the 1780s. We have seen that the long, gruelling journey had been the major obstacle deterring early holiday-makers from choosing to travel to this remote region for their holiday. But the journey time from London to Exeter had been cut to 32 hours by 1783 and then, on the new mail coach, to only 24 hours in 1785.[38] Travel times on other coach services to south Devon were

similarly speeded up. These transport improvements at last placed the
south Devon seaside resorts within reach for those who could afford the
high coach fares.

So far we have seen that in the period after 1789 there were a number
of important reasons why the south Devon coastal watering places gained
national publicity and came to be regarded as extremely attractive holiday
destinations. But we need to know more about the people who began to
holiday on the south Devon coast in this period, so we shall now attempt
to assess the quality and size of the visiting public at these developing
resorts.

Contemporary reports indicate that the new arrivals included many
members of the nobility and gentry. The quiet south Devon resorts had
previously catered for a mainly provincial clientele only embellished by a
few fashionable arrivals from Bath, but suddenly they found themselves
playing host to the 'cream of society', with many of the new patrons
originating from distant parts of the country. In October 1789 the *Exeter
Flying Post* reported in awed tones that in the courtyard of the Globe Inn
at Teignmouth had been seen the unprecedented sight of 'seven carriages
with coronets'.[39] The arrival lists occasionally published in the local press
began to include the names of many aristocrats as well as high-ranking
officers and clergy. On 25 December 1794, for example, the *Exeter Flying
Post* published an exceptionally distinguished list for Teignmouth which
included the Duke and Duchess of Devonshire and 15 other nobles.[40] It
seems likely that these lists were usually published when a resort had
present a particularly impressive number of aristocrats. Local newspaper
reports, however, frequently referred to resorts having a 'numerous
assemblage of nobility and gentry' or 'overflowing with fashionables'.[41]
The journal of the Hon. Frances Mackenzie, kept during her visit to
Sidmouth in 1811, helps to confirm the general impression that the
company at the south Devon resorts included many distinguished visitors,
for she mentions several members of the nobility among her circle of
acquaintances.[42] The south Devon resorts were certainly being patronized
by a far more august clientele than had ever previously been the case.

Among the new visitors were many invalids, with some arriving in a
last desperate attempt to recover their health. Sadly, for many tuberculosis
victims neither the genial climate nor the skills of the resident doctors
could arrest an inevitable decline. One sad entry in a local diary for 1812
perhaps can speak for them all: 'Poor George Bright came down from

London in a deep consumption; he was at Exmouth for the change of air, but it was of no service to him. He died about three weeks ago'.[43] When Joseph Farington visited Sidmouth and Dawlish in 1809, he found many new gravestones in the churchyards, erected to the memory of young people who had come from distant parts of the country in search of a miracle cure, only to die there.[44]

It is clear that in this period there was a marked increase in the number of visitors arriving for the summer season. At Teignmouth, for example, it was reported in September 1792: 'The arrivals this season have greatly exceeded any other season; and at this time there is not a single lodging vacant. Indeed numbers of families . . . have been obliged to go to other watering places for want of room'.[45] The same resort claimed in August 1796: 'This fashionable place has more company now than were here at any time before'.[46] Other resorts were equally busy in the summer months: Sidmouth in June 1791 was reported to be hosting 'many fashionable families',[47] Dawlish in July 1795 was said to be 'full of lodgers',[48] and Exmouth in August of the same year was reported to be 'full of the most respectable and fashionable families'.[49] Some of these summer visitors were hoping to obtain renewed health, but others were more interested in finding select company and fashionable amusements. When John Swete visited Exmouth that summer he noted that it was not 'merely sought for by the invalid, but was considered during the summer months as an eligible retreat for the children of idleness and gaiety'.[50]

The south Devon seaside resorts also benefited by being the first in England to gain the coveted prize of a winter season. It was in the winter months that the majority of invalids arrived, hoping that the mild sea air would restore their health. It was also in the inclement months that the south Devon resorts enjoyed the patronage of many fashionable visitors who had formerly been accustomed to winter in the south of France. The influx of winter visitors steadily gathered momentum. As early as December 1790 Exmouth was claiming that 'through the means of the vast improvements made for the reception of quality, many very respectable families still remain'.[51] By December 1794 the *Exeter Flying Post* could report that Exmouth was enjoying 'all the gaiety of the summer season' being 'extremely full of company, notwithstanding which genteel families arrive continually'. To further emphasize how busy the winter season had become the newspaper added: 'Earl Abergavenny's band of music plays twice daily on New Square. Balls and assemblies rage as in the season'.[52] At Teignmouth in the same month there were so many visitors that the *Exeter Flying Post* described it as the 'Montpellier of

England' and predicted: 'In the course of a few years this delightful watering place will be frequented as much in winter as in summer'.[53] In the same year William Maton visited Sidmouth and professed his astonishment at the number of wealthy families taking up winter residence there.[54]

The south Devon seaside resorts were enjoying what was for them an unprecedented boom, yet visitor numbers were still relatively small. Visitor lists were occasionally published: one for Teignmouth in September 1791 included only 119 names[55] and one for Dawlish in September 1813 gave only 143 names.[56] These may not have been complete visitor counts, but they do indicate that, while the south Devon resorts rejoiced to find themselves playing host to far more tourists than ever before, the actual size of their visiting public was still comparatively small. This impression is confirmed by Richard Polwhele, a local clergyman, who was obviously impressed with the numbers patronizing Sidmouth when in 1793 he stated: 'It is much frequented by people of fashion—near 300 yearly: and there is a constant succession of company'.[57] Although the holiday-makers had increased, such numbers seem very small when compared with the 4,300 visitors recorded at Brighton in 1794, or the 9,000 holiday-makers travelling by sea to Margate in 1792.[58] The south Devon watering places, however, did have the important advantage of a second season in winter, with a free-spending clientele residing there throughout the inclement months. It was this influx of winter visitors which gave the biggest impetus to their development. Our next task is to see how the tourist industry responded to this increased demand for both summer and winter holidays.

Given the sudden surge in the numbers of visitors arriving on the south Devon coast, it is not surprising to find new resorts starting to develop. In 1793 John Swete found Seaton 'beginning to have its share of company',[59] while two years later at Budleigh Salterton he noticed 'improvements in equipping a few cottages for invalids'.[60] These two seaside villages had had little to recommend them in earlier days when the emphasis was placed on sea-bathing facilities, for they had steeply-shelving pebble beaches. Both, though, could claim the advantages of a south-facing situation and mild sea air, and these became important assets when a change of medical fashion focused public attention on climatic factors. That is not to say that sea-water treatments were ignored at these nascent resorts. In 1791 one early visitor to Seaton observed 'many decent looking men going down the beach three or four times in as many hours, and drinking a pint of water each time'.[61] In this period Seaton catered for only a handful of holiday-makers who were seeking 'cheapness and retirement'.[62] It was attractive to those who were seeking renewed health without the expense of a stay at a more fashionable resort. But Budleigh Salterton soon began to expand. By 1811 it was claimed that it was 'rising fast to eminence as a watering place' with a row of new lodging houses having been 'lately built' which were 'much occupied'.[63]

Torquay, though, was by far the most important Devon resort to begin life in this period. Swete visited the coastal village in 1792 and found only a small fishing port with a few new houses erected for the accommodation of visitors. Swete was shown plans to create a new resort drawn up under the auspices of the principal landowner, Sir Robert Palk, and he commented: 'If the plans which I have seen be carried into execution, Torquay will one day be raised into importance'.[64] These were prophetic words, for Torquay almost at once embarked on a period of rapid expansion. William Maton was an early visitor, writing in 1794: 'Torquay far exceeded our expectation in every respect. Instead of the poor uncomfortable village that we had imagined, how great was our surprise at seeing a pretty range of neat new buildings, fitted up for summer visitors'.[65]

At first Torquay entertained only a handful of tourists, lured there by the publicity given to its picturesque scenery. But it soon began to attract a few infirm visitors who were seeking to benefit from its genial climate. In 1803 a local guidebook advised that 'the invalid also may rest assured of finding the lodgings and accommodations good for a place yet in an infant state'.[66] When Joseph Farington went to Torquay in 1809 he was told that the infant resort was 'peculiarly favourable for nervous and consumptive complaints, the air being warm and dry'.[67] It was Torquay's sheltered position and south-facing location which made it so attractive to the invalid and led to its endorsement by the medical profession. In years to come it would build its reputation as the country's premier winter health resort.

The south Devon resorts were expanding and we must now try to measure both their rates of growth and their relative sizes. Population figures are a valuable source of information and will be frequently referred to in this book, but there are problems in interpreting the statistics published in the decennial census returns. The first difficulty is that there are no reliable figures available for earlier periods to compare with the first census return of 1801. The second problem is that the census returns are for parishes, and this means that it is impossible to separate out the urban population from the rural population of the outlying area. The third difficulty is that none of these coastal settlements began life as a seaside resort, so they all had other functions, mainly of a maritime nature. This makes it hard to evaluate resort development, because the effect of seaside holiday-making on population growth is partly obscured by the decline or expansion of other activities.[68] So the population tables in this book are not intended as a precise measure of the progress of different resorts, but they are helpful in providing indications of general trends and they can be used for making crude comparisons of relative size.

It is clear that in 1801 the south Devon resorts still had relatively small populations. At a time when Margate's population was approaching 5,000 and Brighton had over 7,000 inhabitants, the population of Devon's two oldest resorts was much smaller. Table 1 shows that in 1801 Exmouth, Devon's largest resort, had a population of only 2,601, while Teignmouth had only 2,012 inhabitants. The newer watering places of Dawlish and Sidmouth both had populations of less than 1,500. The infant resort of Torquay had only 838 inhabitants.[69] These were small figures, particularly when it is realized that the census figures for these parishes included fishermen, farmers and many other people not directly connected with the holiday industry.

The south Devon resorts grew substantially in the first two decades of the nineteenth century. Table 1 shows that the increase in total population was especially marked at Teignmouth, which by 1821 had 3,980 inhabitants and had overtaken Exmouth to become the largest Devon resort. Table 2 considers growth-rates at the resorts. It shows that in percentage terms Torquay increased most, growing by almost 130 per cent between 1801 and 1821. Torquay, from a very small beginning, was setting out on a rapid rise to national prominence. In the same period Sidmouth achieved an impressive growth-rate of over 119 per cent. Like Torquay it was expanding rapidly from a small coastal village into an important watering place. All the other leading south Devon resorts experienced high growth-rates. This expansion was part of a broader pattern. Most of the resorts on the fashionable south coast of England achieved their highest rates of growth in the first two decades of the nineteenth century.[70]

In the period from 1789 to 1815 there was a rush of building activity at these coastal settlements, to provide accommodation for the growing resident population and also for the influx of visitors. Before the tourist trade developed, the only dwellings close to the sea had been those clustered round the centre of the fishing activities, and the majority of

Table 1 Population of the Principal
South Devon Resorts, 1801–1821

Resort	*1801*	*1811*	*1821*	*Increase 1801–1821*
Exmouth	2601	3160	3895	1294
Teignmouth	2012	2893	3980	1968
Dawlish	1424	1882	2700	1276
Sidmouth	1252	1688	2747	1495
Budleigh Salterton	1014	1190	1706	692
Torquay	838	1350	1925	1087

Table 2 Percentage Growth-Rates of the Population of the
Principal South Devon Resorts, 1801–1821

Resort	*1801–1811*	*1811–1821*	*1801–1821*
Exmouth	21.5	23.3	49.8
Teignmouth	43.8	37.6	97.8
Dawlish	32.2	43.5	89.6
Sidmouth	34.8	62.7	119.4
Budleigh Salterton	17.4	43.4	68.2
Torquay	61.1	42.6	129.7

Source for Tables 1 and 2: Decennial Census.
Exmouth figures are for Littleham and Withycombe Raleigh parishes. Teignmouth figures are for East and West Teignmouth parishes. Budleigh Salterton figures are for East Budleigh parish. Torquay figures are for Tormohun parish.

houses had been well away from the shore in sheltered positions protected from the winter gales. The new developments were usually as close as possible to the sea, reflecting the importance now attached to the therapeutic influences of the sea air and water, and also the new interest in coastal scenery. In 1790 the *Exeter Flying Post* reported from Teignmouth: 'A regular and genteel row of houses has been started . . . especially for the invalid, being within a few yards of the beach'.[71] Building operations steadily increased to meet the growing demand. In October 1799 a local banker wrote: 'Teignmouth is still full of company and enquiries are daily made for purchasing building plots . . . people are absolutely building mad'.[72] Development also went on apace at the other resorts. At Exmouth work started in 1791 on Beacon Terrace, a prestigious row of houses commanding fine views of the estuary. From Sidmouth a local clergyman reported in 1805: 'A great number of new houses have been erected . . . ranged upon the beach . . . numerous as the lodgings now are, there are frequently not enough to accommodate the company in the height of the season'.[73]

Local landowners were involved in most of the schemes to provide more tourist accommodation. In some cases they made a few building plots available for others to lease and develop, but usually they were themselves responsible for the whole project. At Exmouth Mr Rolle, the principal landowner, commenced building prestigious houses on Beacon Terrace in 1791.[74] At Teignmouth building ventures were controlled by Lord Courtenay, the local land magnate, who angered the inhabitants by encroaching onto common land.[75] At Sidmouth the development by the sea was 'a speculation of the lord of the manor, Mr Jenkins'.[76] At Torquay Mr Cary and Sir Lawrence Palk, the principal landowners, were separately engaged in constructing rows of houses close to the beach.[77] The situation was rather different at Dawlish where by 1809 an outsider, a Mr Manning of Exeter, had purchased most of the valley, drained the wet meadows and was building houses for the accommodation of visitors.[78]

Many of the fashionable new arrivals were accustomed to the social institutions and stylized pleasures of the spas and other fashionable provincial towns, so they expected to find a similar range of sophisticated amenities and entertainments on the south Devon coast. The increased demand justified investment, so the principal seaside resorts set out to meet this need, carefully modelling their new recreational facilities on those long in vogue at the inland watering places.

Baths were an important amenity sought by fashionable visitors familiar with the ritual of 'taking the waters' at the spas. Sea-water bathing establishments were soon opened at the principal seaside resorts on the south Devon coast to provide bathers with all the benefits of immersion in the healing brine without the need to be buffeted by strong waves. Hot baths were available if required, and these proved especially attractive to invalids whose parlous state of health did not permit a dip in the cold waters of the English Channel. Sidmouth was the first Devon seaside resort to obtain its own sea-water baths. The resort's steep shingle beach made bathing in the open sea extremely difficult and thus created a particular need for an indoor bathing establishment. So it was that in June 1791 the *Exeter Flying Post* reported that Mr Taylor, a Sidmouth surgeon, had 'erected conveniences for warm sea-bathing and the cold shower bath'.[79] Later in this period hot and cold sea-water baths were also opened at Exmouth, Teignmouth, Dawlish and Seaton.[80] These bath houses were usually to be found in prestigious positions on the sea front or principal thoroughfare, reflecting their importance in the social life of the resorts.

As these sea-water baths were a facility provided primarily for health purposes they were quite often owned by a local medical practitioner. At Exmouth, for example, Dr Black advertised in 1800 that he had erected a 'large and commodious bath' for 'warm sea-bathing',[81] while in the following year his fellow surgeon, Dr Land, set up a rival establishment and advertised his 'warm and cold marble sea-water baths on the approved plan'.[82] Soon afterwards Dr Land published a pamphlet entitled *A Treatise on the Hot, Cold, Tepid, Shower, and Vapour Baths* setting out the advantages of sea-water baths. The extravagant claims that he made echoed those frequently made by the medical faculty for the mineral baths at the spas:

> There is scarcely a disease in which the hot sea-water bath may not be used, not only to palliate but to relieve; as fever, rheumatism, nephritic complaints, spasm, stricture, suppressed evacuations of every kind, gout, scrofula, scurvy, diseased joints, epilepsy, convulsions, diseases of the uterus.[83]

This desire of the medical faculty to exercise control over sea-water treatments stemmed partly from their concern to promote good health. It also reflected what was to be a recurring theme: the desire of the medical profession to create profitable practices at the coastal watering places by maximizing their income from the wealthy visitors attracted there for health reasons.

The south Devon resorts also emulated the spas by providing elegant assembly rooms. It has already been shown that as early as the 1770s at Exmouth and Teignmouth, small assemblies had been organized by innkeepers in rooms attached to their own premises. In the period after the French Revolution the increase in visitor numbers justified the construction of purpose-built assembly rooms at several of the principal resorts. At Teignmouth, for example, the public rooms at the Globe Inn proved quite inadequate once fashionable visitors began to flood in. In October 1789 the *Exeter Flying Post* announced: 'A subscription is to be opened for erecting a large, handsome and commodious assembly room'.[84] The new public rooms on the sea front were opened in 1796.[85] Facilities included a billiard room, a reading room and an assembly room which was spacious enough for 'one hundred couples to dance with ease'.[86] These rooms at once enjoyed the patronage of 'those of the first fashion', with a splendid ball being held once a week and a card assembly taking place every night.[87] In July 1801 purpose-built assembly rooms were opened at Exmouth, on fashionable Beacon Hill.[88] By 1811 Dawlish had its own specialist building with a ballroom, billiard room and reading room, located in an imposing position on the sea front and run by William Gore, a local librarian.[89] At Sidmouth the company still met at the London Inn, but the facilities were improved and it was claimed that the assembly room was 'larger and better fitted up' than that at any other local resort.[90]

Complementing and sometimes competing for patronage with the assembly rooms were the circulating libraries, which again were modelled on a social amenity found at the principal spas. These libraries had become popular in eighteenth-century England, being stimulated by the spread of literacy, a widening interest in science, archaeology and topography, a love of poetry and, above all, by the rise of the novel. Circulating libraries appeared at many provincial towns, but multiplied most prolifically at the spas and later at the seaside resorts, for the gentlefolk who congregated there had left behind their own books in their town and country houses, but had the time, education and money to take full advantage of a library.[91] On the south Devon coast a circulating library was opened at Sidmouth by 1795,[92] at Dawlish by 1802,[93] at Exmouth by 1803[94] and at Teignmouth by 1815.[95] Like the assembly rooms, the circulating libraries were elegant, well-appointed buildings designed to attract the patronage of rich visitors. Like the assembly rooms, they were usually located in a prestigious position on the sea front or fashionable promenade.

These circulating libraries had many functions: part lending library where both academic tomes and sentimental novels could be borrowed, part reading room where newspapers and current periodicals could be scanned, part souvenir shop where gifts could be purchased, part social rendezvous where wealthy subscribers might debate national issues or exchange local gossip. The choice of books was sometimes limited, despite the substantial subscription fees. Jane Austen described the Dawlish library of 1802 as 'pitiful and wretched . . . and not likely to have anyone's publication'.[96] Yet for many genteel patrons the range of reading material available was of less consequence than the opportunities for relaxing and enjoying polite conversation. At Sidmouth, for example, the library opened by John Wallis in 1809 prided itself on being 'a lounging-place in a conspicuous and pleasant situation . . . where the news of the day may be collected and discussed, and an opportunity given to the saunterers at a watering place to chat and gossip together'.[97]

There was a wide range of goods on sale at the libraries, to tempt a leisured class with ample funds into indulging every scholarly interest or fashionable eccentricity. Each library had a shop and, in addition to retailing books, topographical prints, maps and music, they often sold a wide variety of frivolous souvenirs. John Wallis's library at Sidmouth, for example, had for sale not only a local guidebook and a large number of topographical prints published by the proprietor, but also 'a variety of elegant toys and trinkets and some articles of greater utility'.[98] The owners of these establishments could hardly be blamed for trying to maximize their profits. They had spent large sums in constructing and stocking their libraries, and, as the south Devon resorts had only a relatively small clientele, they had to diversify in the hope of obtaining a return on their substantial investment.

The theatre was another popular institution at fashionable spas and at other leading centres of fashion, so several of the south Devon resorts tried to provide this amenity for their visitors. A small theatre was erected at Sidmouth in 1791, which it was hoped would 'form an agreeable addition to the pleasures of the assembly',[99] but the venture soon failed. In 1805 a local clergyman wrote: 'An itinerant company were the performers, but the building, now converted into habitations for poor people, is a proof of the success they met with'.[100] A further attempt to operate a theatre at Sidmouth in 1813 was just as short-lived.[101] By 1795 Exmouth had its own theatre with performances being staged three times a week.[102] A playhouse was opened at Teignmouth in 1791, but was soon closed due to lack of support. In 1802 another attempt was made to provide theatrical entertainment at this resort, and this time it proved more successful. A playhouse was erected on a site given for the purpose by Lord Courtenay, the major landowner, and a regular theatrical season was presented there for many years.[103]

Theatres in south Devon were usually operated on the circuit system with a touring company performing in a different town every night. When Sidmouth's first theatre opened in 1791, the performances there were by a group of touring actors managed by the proprietor of the playhouse at Salisbury.[104] By the beginning of the nineteenth century Samuel Fisher had established a circuit on the south Devon coast. In 1802 Mr Fisher leased the new theatre at Teignmouth, 'engaged a company of approved abilities' and opened with a play entitled *The Heir at Law* and the farce *Of Age Tomorrow*, charging 3*s.* for a place in a box, 2*s.* for a place in the pit and 1*s.* for a seat in the gallery.[105] Mr Fisher's company performed regularly at Teignmouth, but also appeared at Sidmouth, Exmouth, Dawlish and many other local towns. His players were flatteringly described as 'a good company of provincial comedians and frequently aided by the attractions of the London actors'.[106] Yet he must have encountered both practical and financial problems when moving his company from one resort to another. On Mr Fisher's death in 1816 it was reported that local theatricals were in 'a depressed state' and that his concerns had 'not proved prosperous'.[107]

Theatre management on the south Devon coast must have been a hazardous occupation. While a mediocre performance by a group of touring actors might be well received in an inland Devon town, it was likely to face a searching examination before the discriminating audiences at the south Devon resorts; for many of the visitors were accustomed to high-quality performances in London, the spas and leading provincial cities. It is perhaps hardly surprising there was a high failure rate at theatres in the south Devon resorts, for while the audiences were sophisticated and critical, they were usually too small to make the productions economically viable.

Promenades were constructed at most of the principal resorts in the period after 1789, for this was another amenity that fashionable visitors from the spas and leading provincial towns were accustomed to.[108] In 1789 Sidmouth opened 'a pretty new gravel walk by the seaside for the company to walk on'.[109] In September 1792 the *Exeter Flying Post* announced that at Teignmouth: 'The new walk is nearly finished, and every fine evening is lined with a grand assemblage of genteel and fashionable company'.[110] By 1803 Dawlish likewise had a fine gravel walk fronting the sea, 'kept in excellent repair and affording a most agreeable promenade'.[111] The principal public walk did not always border the sea; at Exmouth a promenade was laid out on Beacon Hill in 1790 and it was there that the fashionable company paraded each day.[112]

The promenades attracted many visitors. Invalids congregated there, for they were ideal situations in which to inhale the therapeutic sea air. These public walks were flat and well-drained, usually having a gravel surface which was regularly rolled. These were important advantages for those who found walking difficult, and for those who had to push bath chairs containing the aged and infirm. Promenades also attracted those who sought vantage points from which to admire the coastal scenery and the varied maritime activity. Furthermore they provided splendid opportunities for visitors wishing to parade and impress, and equally to survey and evaluate the quality of the company frequenting the resort. These 'grand public malls' on the Devon coast saw the fashionable company promenading each day to ogle at the beautiful, stare at the strange and cast covetous eyes at the rich. This was, as one local guide pointed out, a rewarding diversion for 'such as are most happy in a crowd, whose grand enjoyment it is to see and be seen'.[113]

Two merchants visiting the south Devon coast formed very different opinions as to the quality of the company parading on the promenades. In 1800 Mr Dunsford came from the woollen town of Tiverton in mid-Devon to holiday at Teignmouth and strolled each evening on the esplanade, where he was delighted to meet visitors from more fashionable centres:

> I was much entertained with the acquaintance and informations of new society; the great variety of company which assembled every fine evening, walking on the promenade.[114]

In 1810 Mr Hayman, a businessman from sophisticated Bath, visited Exmouth and, perhaps not surprisingly, was less impressed with the class of people he saw thronging the public walk on Beacon Hill:

> Here the company which frequent Exmouth are accustomed to promenade in the summer evenings. Here we accordingly walked till dusk, desiring to see and, if possible, form an estimate of the rank and fashion of the visitants. We did not, however, see anything very remarkable for either elegance or beauty.[115]

The promenade was a free but universally popular amenity. Healthy, wealthy, sick or poor; everyone found something to look at and something to look forward to; whether it be the prospect of the sea, the prospect of renewed health or the prospect of a socially-advantageous encounter; the promenade was an attraction to all.

Jaunts into the country to view stately homes were popular at the spas and they soon became a favourite pastime at the south Devon resorts. Tourists were delighted to find so many fine country houses within easy reach of the coast.[116] Excursions to some of these splendid mansions were considered almost obligatory for those holidaying on the south Devon coast. 'These are spots which every tourist into the West of England will necessarily see and admire', declared one visitor in 1793.[117] Tourists dutifully traversed the region, intent on seeing as many of the showpieces as possible. The Revd and Mrs Rackett, for example, visited Lord Clifford's Ugbrooke, Lord Lisburne's Mamhead and Lord Courtenay's Powderham Castle in the course of a six-day tour of the south Devon coast in 1802.[118] Even this was a modest programme compared with the itinerary of Robert Clutterbuck, a dynamic tourist from Watford, who managed to see these three stately homes while on a twenty-four hour visit to Teignmouth in 1796.[119]

Some visitors gained entry to these stately homes, but others were obliged to view from afar. Those granted admission subsequently basked in reflected glory as they boasted of their visit and delivered judgements on the architecture and internal décor. Those refused entrance suffered a serious loss of face. The lower orders never had the temerity to present themselves at the main entrance, but the middle class often arrived there, only to find themselves being vetted by the housekeeper, who operated a screening process.

The difficulties experienced by some prospective sightseers were exemplified by the case of Mrs Price, a tourist from Bath, who, whilst holidaying at Exmouth in 1805, set off with a companion to visit some of the local country houses. Travelling first to Mamhead they saw members of the noble family 'very plainly through the windows . . . but were not permitted to enter'. They drove on to Oxton House, seat of the Revd John Swete, where, armed with a letter of introduction, they met with better fortune. Mrs Price recorded in her diary: 'We delivered Mrs Lee's note, on which Mr Swete invited us in to see the house and take some refreshment'. They left charmed by the 'very elegant manner and taste' of the proprietor, only to be humiliated on reaching

Powderham Castle. The housekeeper, acting on the instructions of Lord Courtenay, refused them entry:

> I then begged to be allowed to drive to the front of the house and through the grounds but that also was refused . . . we came away without seeing one thing but the back of the house . . . we also saw his Lordship cross the yard, he came past the carriage, but he never turned his head to look at us, feeling conscious I suppose how illiberally he had treated us . . . I really felt very much hurt and mortified at my disappointment.[120]

While most recreations at the south Devon resorts were modelled on those long popular at the spas, the annual boat race was a notable exception, for some of England's first regattas were staged on the south Devon coast. As early as 1772 a group of local gentlemen had founded a sailing club at Starcross, opposite Exmouth on the Exe estuary,[121] and in August 1775 they had organized their first regatta.[122] It was, though, in the period between 1789 and 1815 that the south Devon annual regattas became really popular events at the leading seaside resorts. Teignmouth, Sidmouth and Torquay all began to stage their own regattas,[123] while visitors holidaying at Exmouth and Dawlish could watch the races organized by the Starcross club.

The regatta was the crowning point of the summer season. The big day began early, with invited guests meeting at the assembly rooms for breakfast. Crowds gathered along the promenades and numerous craft from neighbouring resorts arrived offshore bringing competitors and spectators. Racing commenced about midday with the boats competing for silver cups and cash prizes, paid for by voluntary contributions. The major event was restricted to yachts which were 'the real property of reputed gentlemen',[124] but local boatmen were encouraged to compete in races for fishing vessels and rowing boats. The day invariably ended with a glittering ball at the assembly rooms which usually lasted until a late hour. In September 1812, for example, the *Exeter Flying Post* reported that the regatta ball at Torquay was 'kept up until four next morning, attended by all the beauty and fashion in that delightful watering place and the neighbourhood around'.[125]

The seaside was a stimulating new dimension and a welcome source of innocent amusement for visitors arriving with minds jaded by a surfeit of artificial pleasures at spas and other centres of fashion. The beach afforded an unfailing supply of natural curiosities to delight the stranger from an inland location. There were shells to be collected and displayed, seaweed to be dried and pressed, cliff-side fossils to be tapped out and identified.[126] The sea offered the landsman a whole range of new experiences: there were water excursions to places of interest, opportunities for sea fishing, and boat trips to remote cliffs where sportsmen could shoot countless sea birds without requiring permission from a landowner.[127] The swelling waves, toiling fishermen and bustling harbours all provided lively scenes to captivate the eye of the idle gazer or to inspire the brush of the enthusiastic painter.

The local countryside also held many attractions for visitors from an urban environment. Guidebooks were bursting with advice on places of interest. They directed visitors to a series of approved view- points such as Chudleigh Rock and Haldon Hill and helped them to formulate opinions on the quality of the scenes lying before them.[128] Tourists imbued with an interest in natural phenomena were encouraged to visit Kent's Cavern near Torquay where they could examine stalactites and savour the gothic gloom.[129] Antiquarianism was also fashionable and those wishing to delve into the past could visit prehistoric sites such as the barrow on Haldon Hill or the cromlech at Drewsteignton.[130]

The varied diversions available at the leading south Devon coastal resorts captivated those accustomed to the unsophisticated attractions of rural Devon. John Swete, for example, in 1795 was astonished at the multitude of pleasures on offer at Sidmouth: 'Sidmouth is the gayest place of resort on the Devon coast and every elegancy, every luxury, every amusement is here to be met with: iced creams, milliners' shops, cards, billiards, plays, circulation libraries, attract notice in every part'.[131] Yet the range and quality of entertainment found at the leading south Devon seaside resorts sometimes disappointed fashionable visitors from London and Bath, who saw only a pale reflection of the sparkling life they had left behind.[132]

Tiny watering places like Seaton and Budleigh Salterton had too small a clientele to sustain a full range of organized amusements, and instead advertised their cheapness and their advantages as 'retiring' resorts for those anxious to avoid the social demands and costs of more fashionable watering places. As small seaside resorts grew they changed their image. At first emerging Torquay tried to attract 'the lover of simple nature who can dispense with crowded assemblies, gaming tables and a train of luxurious refinements'.[133] Once it started to expand, it too began to boast that it provided some of the attractions expected at a fashionable watering place.

The period between 1789 and 1815 was then a time when the tourist trade rapidly expanded on the south Devon coast. These were the years when the region's earliest seaside resorts came of age and attracted fashionable visitors from distant parts of the country. This was the period which saw the birth and rapid growth of Torquay as a watering place. It was the time when the leading south Devon watering places became specialized health resorts. It was also the era which saw them become the first seaside resorts in England to reap the benefits of a second season in winter.

Four

Remote and Little-known: North Devon Resorts, 1789–1815

'It should seem that the Northern Devonians were not very anxious after the company of strangers,' wrote Richard Warner in 1800, 'for they certainly take the best possible means of preventing them from visiting this part of England by the execrable state in which they keep their turnpike roads.'[1] In one sense he was absolutely correct. At a time when tourists from distant parts of the country were travelling to south Devon in increasing numbers, the appalling state of the roads leading to the north Devon coast still deterred them from visiting that remote district. Yet Warner completely misjudged the local inhabitants' attitude towards visitors. In fact they longed to see holiday-makers arriving at their coastal towns and villages; not least because they desperately needed the financial rewards that would result from entertaining wealthy visitors. Their fear was that tourists would avoid the region because of the bad publicity their roads were receiving.

Our initial task in this chapter will be to consider these problems of access. Dreadful roads, however, were not the only impediment hindering the development of a successful holiday industry. We will also examine several other adverse factors which combined to prevent a tourist boom comparable to that experienced on the south Devon coast. The obstacles facing the tourist were quite exceptional, but so too were north Devon's attractions, for those with the time, means and fortitude to make the difficult journey. We will consider the nature and impact of these attractions, before moving on to see the part they played in the development of a few small resorts on this remote coast.

Everyone was agreed about the atrocious condition of the main highways leading into north Devon. In 1801 Charles Dibdin, the travel writer, commented: 'The roads are so dreadful that the difficulty of getting there is scarcely repaid by a view of so charming a county and thus the inhabitants seem as if they were in voluntary exile'.[2] Three years later T.H. Williams acknowledged the scenery on the north Devon coast to be 'by far the most magnificent and picturesque of which Devon can boast', but warned would-be visitors that it was 'only accessible by the worst roads in the Kingdom'.[3]

It was not only the clinging mud, deep ruts and scattered 'masses of stone larger than a man's head'[4] which made road travel difficult; steep gradients were an equally serious obstacle. One of the principal access routes to north Devon was from Taunton via Tiverton and South Molton to Barnstaple, but travellers following this route had to face steep hills, and a rough, stony road that was little more than a track, as they crossed the bleak expanses of Rackenford Moor. The other major road to north Devon had to climb over equally formidable hills. It ran from Exeter to Barnstaple, but avoided the marshy lowland by making a whole series of steep ascents as it crossed the valley spurs. In 1808 Charles Vancouver complained: 'The road . . . instead of being conducted through the valley of the Taw, is carried along the highest brows of the river hills, where the traveller is unceasingly compelled to ascend and descend the sharpest hills in the county'.[5]

Travel to north Devon was painfully slow along these appalling roads. Coaches still took the best part of a day to complete the 39-mile journey to Barnstaple from Exeter. By 1796 a coach service had been established on a more direct approach route to Barnstaple, from Taunton via Tiverton, but coaches on this road only averaged just over two miles an hour, taking 24 hours to cover a distance of under 50 miles.[6] By 1805 timings were somewhat improved, with coaches completing the journey from Taunton to Barnstaple in 14 hours. In that year the coach ride from London to Barnstaple via Taunton took 59 hours, with passengers being obliged to stop overnight in Taunton.[7] Yet by this time the mail coach from London to Exeter was completing its journey in less than half the time. Small wonder then that tourists from distant parts of the country usually chose to visit south Devon instead of opting to make the arduous journey to the north of the county.

The tourist's problems were far from over on reaching Barnstaple, for it was very difficult to travel from there to the emerging resorts. By 1803 a coach was running 'two or three times a week' to Ilfracombe,[8] but on days when there was no coach it was necessary to hire a post chaise. The ride from Barnstaple to Ilfracombe was extremely slow and uncomfortable, being over an ill-made road that was really little more than a cart track. There were no roads of any sort leading to the other emerging seaside resorts so, as wheeled vehicles could not reach them, the would-be visitor was obliged to travel there on horseback or on foot.

Those intending to visit Lynton and Lynmouth faced the prospect of a particularly difficult journey, for these adjoining coastal villages lay some ten miles from the nearest road. Some of the first visitors to Lynton and Lynmouth described in their journals the appalling condition of the ancient track-ways they had followed across the moor. John Swete approached Lynmouth in 1796 and was horrified at 'the ruggedness of the road which resembled more the bed of a torrent rather than a travelled way'.[9] His fellow cleric, John Skinner, arrived on a visit from Somerset in 1801 and commented: 'To travellers not accustomed to a mountainous country the approach to this place would have been deemed impassable'.[10]

The only other possible way of travelling to north Devon was by sea. For many years small trading vessels had linked Ilfracombe, and Lynton and Lynmouth with Bristol and South Wales. By 1800 a sailing packet 'with every accommodation for passengers, carriages and horses', was advertised to sail twice a week between Ilfracombe and Swansea, from where there were packet services to Bristol.[11] Sail, though, was a slow and unreliable form of transport, and there is no evidence to suggest that in this period any more than a trickle of visitors arrived at the north Devon resorts by sea.

The difficulties of travel to north Devon were experienced by Mrs Jackson, a wealthy resident of Bath, when in 1810 she decided to spend part of the summer season at Ilfracombe. After breaking her journey with a stay in Wells, she travelled on in her carriage, but averaged only four miles an hour on the road between Wells and Ilfracombe and took 'two long days' to complete a journey of less than a hundred miles. Even then her problems were not over. The carriage of bulky goods by land was so difficult that all the household baggage was sent by sea from Bristol in the care of the cook. Unfortunately the vessel sailed straight past the harbour at Ilfracombe while Mrs Jackson watched helplessly from her lodgings. She wrote: 'We were tantalized by seeing it pass our windows —for the captain could not or would not land—and we had to wait for both cook and her saucepans'. The vessel finally docked at Barnstaple, and a way then had to be found of bringing the cook and all the luggage to Ilfracombe by land.[12]

Another serious obstacle to the development of a holiday industry on the north Devon coast was its climate. In an age when temperatures and aspect became important criteria in selecting a holiday resort, this region was thought to have serious disadvantages. The emerging north Devon watering places claimed that their sea-bathing facilities and pure sea air equipped them to be health resorts. Yet by this time many doctors were placing more emphasis on the advantages of warm winters and shelter from cold winds, and in both of these respects the north Devon resorts were thought to compare unfavourably with their south Devon rivals.

The north Devon seaside resorts were also at a disadvantage because they lacked the publicity boost of an early royal visit. It has been shown that the south Devon resorts benefited from George III's visits to the adjacent Dorset coast, and particularly from the publicity they received in 1806 when they were honoured to entertain the Princess of Wales. The north Devon resorts, in contrast, were not favoured with any royal patronage in their formative years.[13] Royal visits were longed for, and sometimes confidently predicted, but never actually occurred, to the intense chagrin of all concerned with tourism. The north Devon coast was at that time a little-known holiday destination, so the publicity surrounding a royal visit would have been extremely valuable.

Yet, though there were formidable obstacles hampering the development of tourism, the north Devon coast did have a priceless asset in its superb scenery. In earlier times Exmoor had been avoided by travellers like Defoe as 'filthy barren land',[14] but at the end of the eighteenth century the vogue for the picturesque stimulated a new interest in the fine coastal landscapes of this remote region. William Maton was one of the first travel writers to publicize its scenery. His book *Observations Relative Chiefly to . . . the Western Counties,* published in 1797, enthused over Ilfracombe's 'truly romantic' scenery, but reserved its highest praise for the 'exceptionally picturesque' landscapes at Lynton and Lynmouth.[15] Extensive extracts from Maton's vivid descriptions were plundered by other topographical writers.[16] This sudden acclaim persuaded some tourists to make the difficult journey to north Devon to see for themselves the splendid scenery.

Reports of stone circles and other vestiges of Celtic religion also lured the curious. In 1789 John Swete visited the Valley of Rocks at Lynton and recorded in his journal that he had seen 'several circles, large masses of stone, in diameter above 40 feet . . . which seem to have been appropriated to the uses of the Druids'.[17] Travel writers were soon suggesting that prehistoric men probably practised their unhallowed rites in this rock-strewn valley. Some fancied they could identify altars used in ancient sacrifices and gazed in wonder at what they considered to be stone circles erected by the Celts.[18] Others were full of admiration for what they saw as the work of Nature.[19] Opinions differed, but the debate stimulated public interest. Tourists began to travel to Lynton to see these remarkable rock formations which were shrouded in mystery and defied logical explanation.

Some adventurous spirits were attracted to the north Devon coast by the challenge of exploring a little-known region, and for them the hardships encountered along the way were an attraction rather than a drawback. This group of tourists stemmed from that doughty breed that had been accustomed to roam the Alps, relishing the prospect of encountering hazards and danger. With the Continent in turmoil following the start of the French Revolution, they were obliged to seek out remote upland regions in their own country. They frequently cast themselves in the role of explorers rather than tourists. Their tours, planned as expeditions to investigate unfamiliar territory, often turned out to be adventures in self-discovery. They travelled on horseback or on foot, usually alone but occasionally accompanied by a single servant. Trials and tribulations were certainly experienced along the way, but these were often exaggerated in subsequent narratives, so their exploits would seem that much more impressive.[20] John Skinner, for example, enjoyed exploring the little-known Exmoor coast in 1801 and allowed the suggestion of peril to creep into his journal when describing his descent down the narrow track leading to Lynmouth:

> I found it absolutely necessary to dismount, the passage being cut on the side of a cliff, not above four feet wide, with a very steep descent towards the sea ... my faithful quadruped, who was following me with the bridle over his neck, being startled by something took a sudden spring to the brink of the precipice ... every second I expected to see him flung into the gulf below.[21]

Such accounts owed more to the influence of the Gothic novel then in vogue than to the analytical approach normally adopted by students of the picturesque when on flatter ground.

The prospect of joining the chase after wild red deer enticed others to the north Devon coast. Red deer had formerly ranged over most of Devon, but by the end of the eighteenth century relentless hunting had reduced them to a small remnant lurking in the north Devon woodlands and especially on the lower slopes of Exmoor.[22] Lynton and Lynmouth benefited from being at the heart of the only region in England where wild red deer were still found in sufficient numbers to warrant a staghound pack. In the early nineteenth century the emerging resort began to advertise itself in county newspapers as a hunting centre[23] and some leading members of the Devon gentry began to congregate there for the stag-hunting season.[24] Visitors from distant urban environments were also eager to participate in the pageant and excitement of an ancient custom far removed from their usual experience. This was a sport which gave them unique opportunities to mix with the local 'quality' and to share in the mystique of an old country ritual.

The low cost of living on the north Devon coast was another attraction, especially for holiday-makers who wished to avoid the expense of a stay at a major resort. Prices on this coast were extremely low.[25] While staying at Ilfracombe in 1810 Mrs Jackson wrote: 'Provisions . . . at their dearest are scarcely more than half the Bath prices'.[26] When Fanny Burney visited Ilfracombe in 1817 she was told that during the Napoleonic Wars a large family had been able to live at Ilfracombe for less than a single man could live in London or Bath. She suggested that this was one of the principal reasons why Ilfracombe had begun to attract a few more visitors, for, as she pointed out, once its 'secret of cheapness was . . . buzzed in society and heard by the common swarm', those with limited incomes 'hived themselves' there for 'economy'.[27]

The small north Devon watering places to some extent acted as overspill resorts for holiday-makers unwilling or unable to pay south Devon prices. We have already seen that the low cost of living at the south Devon watering places was an attraction for some early visitors, but that prices there increased when those resorts found favour with the rich. Some tourists with only limited means then began to seek out smaller, less-fashionable watering places where prices were still exceptionally low, and where the lack of assembly rooms, circulating libraries and other social diversions meant that they could avoid the extravagant lifestyle of an established resort. In 1811 one young gentleman arrived at Ilfracombe after first visiting the fashionable resorts of Sidmouth, Teignmouth and Dawlish. He wrote:

> We found it well filled with company of the middling ranks. Since washing in the sea has been thought necessary for all descriptions of people, new haunts are constantly sought by such as wish to combine health with economy. In a short time these too become fashionable

and poor dippers are obliged to shift their quarters and seek some unfrequented station.[28]

The tiny resort of Lynton and Lynmouth was another inexpensive haven for those forced out of the fashionable south Devon resorts by rising prices.

The decline of traditional maritime activities on the north Devon coast provided a spur for diversification into the holiday industry. For many years herring fishing had been the mainstay of the economy at both Ilfracombe and Lynmouth, but at the end of the eighteenth century the shoals disappeared, leaving the fishing communities in an impoverished condition.[29] Likewise on the south Devon coast there had been a recession in some branches of the fishing industry which had helped to prompt a move into tourism. On the north Devon seaboard the need to develop a holiday industry was rendered even more urgent by the 'wretched' state of farming in the immediate interior.[30]

North Devon had long been the poor relation casting an envious eye at the prosperity of the south of the county. In the 1790s there seemed every prospect of history repeating itself. The impoverished north Devon communities were obliged to look on from afar while the wind of change swept along the south Devon coast, bringing strangers in its train and scattering riches through the seaside towns. This time, though, there was reason for hope, for the isolated north Devon coast did have some important attractions for those tourists not scared away by reports of the atrocious roads. Now we will examine the development of four small seaside resorts which would cater for the few holiday-makers who were prepared to travel there.

Ilfracombe was first to benefit from an influx of tourists. Since the 1770s a handful of Devon families had been arriving there for the sea-bathing season. At the very end of the century this little group of visitors from inland Devon were joined by a small but growing number of arrivals from more distant parts of the country. Ilfracombe then began to acquire some of the trappings of a small coastal watering place. In 1800 one tourist commented favourably on its superior bathing machines and on the provision of a 'number of good houses, chiefly for the accommodation of strangers in the summer season'.[31] In 1803 Ilfracombe's status as a coastal resort was confirmed by its inclusion in the national *Guide to All the Watering and Sea-Bathing Places*, which noted the arrival of 'several genteel families in the town and neighbourhood; so that of late years it has become a fashionable place of resort in the summer months'.[32] Yet this publication devoted much more attention to the 'mild and genial softness of the air on the south coast of Devon', which had enabled the south Devon resorts to develop a second season in winter.[33] Ilfracombe was not considered to have any merit as a winter retreat, but was recognized solely as a summer watering place, being described in an 1805 guide as 'a pleasant and convenient place for bathing and much resorted to by the gentry for that purpose'.[34]

At the end of the eighteenth century the estuarine village of Instow became the second coastal community in north Devon to provide accommodation for sea bathers. In 1803 a national guidebook announced: 'Instow on the river Torridge possesses several advantages for bathing and has some good lodging houses erected by the late Dr Sibthorpe, lord of the manor'.[35] But the lack of road access was a barrier to any substantial development and in this period Instow was only an extremely small and little-known resort, with its handful of visitors coming chiefly from the nearby towns of Barnstaple and Bideford.

On the opposite shore of the Torridge estuary the fishing village of Appledore for a time acquired local recognition as a small coastal watering place. In 1815 one guidebook claimed that 'the salubrity of the air' there was 'celebrated for restoring health to the valetudinarian'. It also stated that Appledore was well-supplied with lodging houses and bathing machines, and that it was 'the resort of the neighbouring gentry when they wished to inhale the breezes and bathe in the waters of the Atlantic'.[36] This was exaggerated publicity. Appledore was never more than a small sea-bathing station with little accommodation and very few facilities for holiday-makers. It never had more than a few visitors, originating mainly from that neighbourhood and especially from the nearby town of Bideford. Appledore's natural advantages were insufficient to attract a national clientele, and it soon lost almost all of its local patrons to nearby Instow.

Ilfracombe, Instow and Appledore owed much of their early trade to the fashionable preoccupation with seaside health cures, but in the remote north-east corner of the county lay Lynton and Lynmouth; twin villages on the Exmoor coast with relatively few attractions for those seeking good sea-bathing or mild sea air, yet with a very special asset in their spectacular scenery. These two villages jointly developed into the only important Devon coastal resort originating principally in response to the allure of romantic scenery, rather than to the more tangible appeal of physical benefits derived from a stay by the sea. Their development as a seaside resort differed in several important respects from that of the health resorts emerging elsewhere on the Devon coast, so they will be given special attention here.

Romantic poets were among the first to make the arduous journey over the moor to Lynton and Lynmouth. The new Romantic Movement drew its inspiration from the world of nature rather than classical legend, so its leading spirits felt trapped in the blighted urban environs of the Industrial Revolution and longed to roam free in unspoilt countryside. Samuel Taylor Coleridge and William Wordsworth were staying in Somerset in November 1797 when Wordsworth recorded: 'Coleridge, my sister and myself started from Alfoxden with a view to visit Lynton and the Valley of Stones . . . in the course of this walk was planned the poem of the *Ancient Mariner*'.[37] Captivated by Lynton and Lynmouth's pristine scenery, they repeated the 30-mile walk several times in the following year. Robert Southey followed in their footsteps in 1799 and was profoundly impressed. He wrote: 'Lynmouth, a little village on the coast, is the most interesting place I have yet seen in this country. The roads to it on all sides are impassable by a coach and it is, of course, little known'.[38]

In 1812 Percy Bysshe Shelley took his child-bride, Harriet, to spend the summer at Lynmouth. 'This place is beautiful,' wrote Shelley soon after his arrival. 'All shows of sky and earth, of sea and valley are here.'[39] Shelley was inspired to pen his celebrated *Queen Mab*; but soon he busied himself in writing revolutionary tracts which his Irish servant, Daniel Hill, distributed in neighbouring towns. When Shelley heard that his servant had been arrested and imprisoned in Barnstaple, he found it prudent to flee by sea to Wales, leaving behind a string of debts.[40] Before they left Harriet wrote of Lynmouth: 'It seems more like a fairy scene than anything in reality'.[41] It certainly had magical qualities for the early Romantics, liberating minds formerly imprisoned in classical scholarship.

The main attraction for the majority of early visitors was the Valley of Rocks. Once Maton's graphic description was published in 1797, public curiosity was aroused and tourists made long journeys to marvel at this gigantic cleft overhanging the Bristol Channel. Southey described it as 'a spot which, as one of the greatest wonders in the west of England, would attract many more visitors if the roads were passable by carriages'.[42]

Travel difficulties were not the only problem. Having reached Lynton and Lynmouth, it was very difficult to find lodgings. When John Swete arrived there in 1789, he discovered only one 'little public house at Lynton called The Crown where, though the accommodations are indifferent, the people are civil and attentive'.[43] Swete realized that Lynton and Lynmouth had considerable potential for development as a resort. He recorded in his journal:

> It cannot but be an object of request that a better inn and even lodging houses were built on the plain at Lynmouth, for . . . if the roads for a few miles were made more passable . . . I know no place more likely to be resorted to in the summer months.[44]

William Litson, a Lynton wool merchant, was the first to provide tourist accommodation. Lynton had long had a wool-spinning industry supplying yarn to the weavers of Barnstaple. But the main foreign markets for cloth were lost following the outbreak of war with France in 1793 and Litson found that he could no longer sell Lynton yarn in Barnstaple. Faced with the collapse of his woollen business, Litson was obliged to find some other employment. An early guidebook explained how he established a holiday business in Lynton:

> Finding from time to time strangers wending their way to the spot on account of the unique and picturesque scenery, he opened in 1800 what is now the Globe Inn and furnished the adjoining cottages for the accommodation of visitors . . . The scenery becoming known, the visitors soon increased; this induced Mr Litson to build his Valley of Rocks Hotel which he opened in 1807.[45]

In the following year this new hotel was advertised in the *Exeter Flying Post*:

> William Litson returns his grateful thanks to the nobility, gentry and public in general for the great support he has received the past seven years, and respectfully informs them, for their better accommodation, he has, at considerable expense, erected a large and convenient house in a desirable situation commanding most delightful sea and land prospects, which he has furnished with good beds and every other requisite and has lain in a stock of choice wines and liquors.[46]

Other local people soon opened another inn and several more lodging houses. By 1815 Lynton and Lynmouth was established as a small watering place, catering for a discriminating clientele who made the arduous journey there in search of picturesque scenery rather than renewed health.

**Table 3   Population of the Principal
North Devon Resorts, 1801–1821**

Resort	*1801*	*1811*	*1821*	*Increase 1801–1821*
Ilfracombe	1838	1934	2622	784
Lynton and Lynmouth	481	571	632	151

**Table 4   Percentage Growth-Rates of the Population of the
Principal North Devon Resorts, 1801–1821**

Resort	*1801–1811*	*1811–1821*	*1801–1821*
Ilfracombe	5.2	35.6	42.7
Lynton and Lynmouth	18.7	10.7	31.4

Source for Tables 3 and 4: Decennial Census.

Tables 3 and 4 show the growth of population at Ilfracombe and at Lynton and Lynmouth between 1801 and 1821. The figures for 1801 show the position before these coastal settlements derived a substantial part of their income from tourism. Ilfracombe was still an important port and had a population of 1,838. Lynton and Lynmouth together had only 481 inhabitants, principally engaged in fishing and farming. The tables show that the population of both Ilfracombe and Lynton and Lynmouth grew significantly in the next 20 years, when they were establishing themselves as resorts. But their rate of growth was less than at most of the south Devon resorts, which were attracting more visitors. By 1821 Ilfracombe had 2,622 inhabitants, but a substantial proportion were engaged in economic activities other than tourism. Lynton and Lynmouth was still a very small resort with only 632 inhabitants.

The first edition of the Ordnance Survey for north Devon, published in 1809, serves to confirm the limited size of Ilfracombe and Lynton and Lynmouth. It shows that in both cases there was a group of houses clustered around the harbour, indicating the importance attached to maritime activities, and also a second nucleus on higher ground, reflecting their role as farming communities. Hotels and lodging houses were few in number. The tourist industry on the north Devon coast was still in its infancy and visitors were too few to warrant substantial investment in specialized holiday accommodation, or for that matter in grandiose public buildings providing sophisticated entertainment.

Lacking assembly rooms, circulating libraries,[47] theatres and promenades, the small north Devon resorts had little to attract those who visited the seaside in search of artificial pleasures and fashionable company. But for those who sought seclusion and natural beauty they held a strong appeal. When John Swete first visited Lynton and Lynmouth in 1789 he exclaimed: 'With such a scene before me how poor in comparison seemed the gaieties of the town'.[48]

At a time when watering places on the south Devon coast were attracting growing numbers of fashionable visitors, the resorts on the north Devon coast were in comparison of only minor importance and had a much smaller clientele. At a time when the principal south Devon resorts were becoming specialized watering places attracting holiday-makers from a wide catchment area, tourism at the north Devon resorts was still overshadowed by fishing and agriculture, and their small visiting public was made up in large part of people from the immediate hinterland. Yet it is clear that a few strangers from distant parts of the country were sufficiently impressed by the reports of the region's natural attractions to make the difficult journey there. The arrival of these tourists gave grounds for hope that, once the difficulties of access had been removed, the region might yet become a popular holiday destination.

Five

Trade Declines: South Devon Resorts, 1816–1843

On the morning of 24 July 1815 sensational news spread along the south Devon coast. Napoleon Bonaparte had arrived in Torbay, a prisoner on board the British warship *Bellerophon*.[1] A few weeks earlier the French had been defeated at Waterloo and now their Emperor was about to be sent into exile on the remote island of St Helena. A flotilla of small craft put out from Torquay and Teignmouth, for everyone wanted to catch a glimpse of the deposed tyrant.[2] The inhabitants of the coastal resorts rejoiced, for the fear of invasion had been finally removed and they looked forward to a period of great prosperity.

Sadly these hopes were never realized, for the years of peace saw a downturn in the fortunes of most of the local seaside resorts. While Napoleon had been pillaging Europe, the south Devon tourist trade had flourished, but in the period between 1816 and 1843 the pace of development slackened. Torquay was the great exception, the resort continuing its rapid rise to national importance at a time when its older rivals were experiencing a relative decline in trade. This chapter will examine the factors which adversely affected the tourist industry at most of the south Devon resorts, but it will also try to explain why Torquay managed to capture an increasing share of a contracting demand for holidays on the south Devon coast.

After the Napoleonic Wars ended, great changes took place in the pattern of English upper-class tourism. For many years English tourists had been cooped up on their own island, but once peace was restored many of the wealthier members of society felt the urge to visit the Continent. Older gentlefolk revisited the haunts of their youth, while their offspring sampled for the first time the delights of foreign travel.[3] The exodus gathered momentum: by 1830 it was estimated that there were

150,000 Englishmen visiting France.[4] The tourists who had been making the long and expensive journey to south Devon since 1789 were just the type of people likely to have the time and money needed to undertake a foreign tour. Once the Continent was reopened it was inevitable that some rich people would desert the south Devon watering places in favour of more cosmopolitan resorts on the French and Italian Riviera, for fashionable tourist centres in Switzerland and on the Rhine, and also for the the spa towns of Germany and Austria.

The south Devon resorts also had to face increasing competition from new watering places much closer to home. On the Somerset coast Weston-super-Mare, Clevedon and Portishead all started to develop as summer seaside resorts. These resorts began to attract some visitors from Bath and Bristol who had previously been in the habit of travelling to south Devon for the summer sea-bathing season.[5]

New English rivals also began to challenge for the lucrative winter trade. The south Devon seaside resorts had been the first in England to be recognized as winter health resorts, but in the second quarter of the nineteenth century several other south-coast watering places began to aspire to winter resort status. Hastings, Dover and Ventnor all developed important winter seasons.[6] None of these new competitors could claim to be as warm in winter as the south Devon resorts, but all of them were much nearer to London, and this helped them to attract some visitors who might otherwise have wintered on the south Devon coast.

The south Devon watering places were extremely concerned at this growing competition from other English health resorts, and so in their guidebooks they made sweeping assertions about their climatic advantages over their rivals, particularly in respect of winter temperatures, shelter from cold winds and freedom from fogs. In 1832 a guide to Torquay devoted no less than 23 pages to a eulogy of the resort's climate, using carefully chosen statistics to back its claim that there was no other watering place in Britain which possessed so many advantages for invalids.[7]

The south Devon resorts were even more worried about the threat posed by foreign resorts, and they campaigned hard to persuade the invalid that they offered more hope of a cure than their rivals on the Mediterranean. In 1817 one local guidebook suggested that families should think twice before they were induced by 'novelty or the idea of cheap living . . . to seek the south of France'. It declared: 'Invalids will not find more real benefit than in the healthy town of Teignmouth, the enclosed vale of Dawlish, or the warmer region of Torquay'.[8]

It was, though, the disinterested testimony of medical experts which

eventually counted far more than the partisan propaganda issuing from
the local resorts. The opinion of Dr James Clark, a royal physician, proved
to be of particular importance. His book, *The Influence of Climate in the
Prevention and Cure of Chronic Diseases*, first published in 1829, was the first
serious attempt to make a scientific study of the effects of different climates
in the treatment of disease. He gave general praise to the health-giving
qualities of the 'soft and humid' air of the south Devon coast. Yet when
Dr Clark considered the merits of individual south Devon resorts, he
gave an unqualified recommendation to only one. Torquay, he stated,
'possessed all the advantages of the south-west climate to the highest
degree'. He recommended it as being exceptionally mild in winter, and
as having the additional advantages of being largely free from fogs and
being drier and more sheltered than its neighbours.[9] This commendation
from such a distinguished doctor helped Torquay to attract an increasing
share of the lucrative invalid trade. Other south Devon resorts received
less favourable reviews in this book. Dr Clark drew attention to defects
in their climates which he felt impaired their claim to be winter havens
for invalids. Dawlish he considered to be less dry and more exposed to
easterly winds than Torquay. Exmouth he suggested was 'damp and
subject to fogs', while Sidmouth he thought was inferior to all the other
south Devon resorts as a place of winter retreat because it was exposed
to currents of cold air from inland.[10] These unwelcome criticisms severely
damaged the profitable winter trade at those resorts.

In 1841 Dr A.B. Granville, a leading authority on health resorts,
published a book entitled *The Spas of England and Principal Sea-Bathing
Places*, which was the first to warn invalids that even a visit to Torquay
offered no guarantee of a cure. Guidebook publicity gave the impression
that Torquay was peopled with happy convalescents progressing well
towards full recovery, but on his visit to the resort in 1840 Dr Granville
discovered a town of death and despair, 'filled in general with respirator-
bearing people who look like muzzled ghosts'.[11] Dr Granville's book
described a resort living under the shadow of death, with the hotels
equipped with spitting pots and echoing to the sound of 'cavernous'
coughs, while ominously outside the only sound to be heard was the
'frequent tolling of the funeral bell . . . awful and thrilling to the rest,
who were trembling on the verge of their grave with symptoms of the
same devouring malady, consumption'.[12]

This was hardly the publicity Torquay had hoped for! At most resorts
invalids formed only a very small proportion of the visiting public and
their sufferings were rarely seen or commented on. But Torquay was

falling victim to its success in promoting itself as a health resort, for an increasing number of its visitors and residents were consumptives or victims of other life-threatening diseases. Unfortunately the restorative powers of the balmy sea air were not sufficient to save many of these invalids. In 1838 alone there had been 38 deaths from consumption at Torquay.[13] There was, though, at that time no real cure for tuberculosis and so, despite his alarming findings, Dr Granville still recommended Torquay to the invalid as 'the only asylum where he can hope for health'.[14]

While Dr Granville gave a measure of support to Torquay's claim to be the 'south-western asylum of diseased lungs',[15] he disparaged the claims of several other leading south Devon watering places to be considered as winter health resorts. Teignmouth, for example, he pronounced generally unsuitable for sickly people in winter, because it was exposed to cold easterly winds.[16] Exmouth he stated was battered by chilling gales in the inclement months, and he declared that 'neither it nor its climate can be recommended to very delicate invalids in winter'.[17] This adverse publicity caused many potential visitors to decide to winter elsewhere in England or abroad.

There was no possibility of a substantial increase in local demand to compensate for the loss of trade to other watering places at home and overseas. The Devon woollen industry had collapsed during the French Wars and while there was a revival after the return of peace it was only on a much reduced scale.[18] Shorn of its principal manufacturing base, Devon had become increasingly dependent on agriculture to provide its wealth, but now the rural community began to suffer hardship as corn prices fell in the aftermath of the war, ruining farmers and forcing down the rentals the landed gentry received.[19] The victory celebrations hardly seemed to have come to an end before rural Devon faced the prospect of recession, with market towns stagnating and the spectre of unemployment stalking the countryside. Exeter also fell victim to the post-war slump, for, with profits plunging and wages tumbling, the people of the region had less to spend on the range of goods and services the city provided. Exeter's foreign trade was also faltering. Although the return of peace meant that the city's merchants were free once more to buy and sell overseas, they were unable to recover their former share of trade with foreign markets.[20] The city faced hard times; at a time when many English towns and cities were mushrooming, the population of Exeter only increased from 23,479 in 1821 to 32,818 in 1851.

It is significant that in that period some of the strongest resort growth was taking place on English coasts backed by inland regions experiencing rapid economic development. Resorts like Blackpool, Southport and Rhyl grew rapidly because of the increase in the number of middle-class visitors from nearby areas of industrial expansion.[21] The south Devon resorts, however, lacked the advantage of a prospering hinterland, so they could not expect to enjoy similar increases in local demand for seaside holidays.

The south Devon seaside resorts were also at a disadvantage when steamship services were developed in the 1820s. This was a decade when steam packets started to transport large numbers of holiday-makers from London to Margate and Gravesend, from Liverpool to Rhyl, and from Hull to Cleethorpes.[22] Likewise on the north Devon coast, steamships gave an important boost to the tourist economy at Ilfracombe and at Lynton and Lynmouth, because sea transport provided the easiest way of reaching them from the expanding urban areas of South Wales and Bristol. The south Devon resorts, on the other hand, were difficult to reach by sea from the major centres of holiday demand, so steamships played only a comparatively small part in their development. Teignmouth was linked with Portsmouth and Plymouth in 1823 when the steam packet *Sir Francis Drake* began calling at the resort. But Portsmouth and Plymouth were themselves seaside towns, and neither was backed by a large urban hinterland, so few holiday-makers arrived at Teignmouth by this route and the service was soon withdrawn.[23] In 1831 a steam packet began operating regularly between London and Topsham, a small port on the Exe estuary serving Exeter. By the following year it was also calling at Exmouth to embark and disembark passengers. But the voyage from London to south Devon took 38 hours, which was twice as long as the coach journey, so not surprisingly steamer travel never became a really popular means of travelling from the capital to the south Devon resorts.[24]

Yet in this era of increasing competition from rival watering places, there was one development which enabled the south Devon resorts to retain at least part of the lucrative trade they had built up during the French Wars: road transport improvements made them somewhat easier to reach from distant parts of the country. Large sections of the main highways leading into Devon were reconstructed, with smooth surfaces, easier gradients and less steep bends. Of all the road works undertaken, none had more important advantages for the development of tourism than the opening in 1819 of the 'New Direct Road' over Salisbury Plain, which provided a much shorter route from London to south Devon.[25]

These road improvements made it possible to greatly accelerate coach services. In 1823 the 'Subscription' coach still took 23 hours to travel from London to Exeter. But horse-flesh was soon being strained to the limit as competing coaches slashed times in their efforts to provide the quickest service. By 1828 the 'Celerity', taking the new road over Salisbury Plain, was completing the journey between the two cities in only 19¾ hours.[26] By 1831 the 'Telegraph' had cut the travel time to 17 hours.[27] In 1837 the 'Devonport Mail' further reduced the journey time to only 16½ hours. Coaches from other parts of the country were also speeded up and many new services were introduced. By the mid-1830s 70 coaches from all parts of the country were arriving in Exeter every day.[28]

Roads leading to the south Devon resorts were also improved (see Map 2, p.66). In 1819 the turnpike road from Exeter to Exmouth was macadamized and soon afterwards the newly-turnpiked Exmouth to Sidmouth road was resurfaced.[29] A good turnpike road was made from Exeter along the coast via Starcross to Dawlish and Teignmouth. In 1827 the opening of the Shaldon Bridge across the Teign estuary provided the last link in a coast road linking Torquay with Teignmouth, Dawlish and Exeter. Another new turnpike was made to provide a good access route to Torquay from Newton Abbot.[30] Faster and more frequent coach services began operating on these roads. By 1828 coaches were running from Exeter four times a day to Teignmouth and as often to Exmouth. All the other leading resorts had regular coach services to and from Exeter, where they were timed to connect with services to London, Bristol and other distant parts of the country.[31]

The south Devon resorts had become much easier to reach, but only for those with ample purses. The high cost of travel still deterred many from making the journey. It has been estimated that in the 1830s a five-pound note barely covered the expenses of a coach journey from London to Exeter, after allowing for meals *en route* and tips for the guard, drivers and ostlers.[32] In an age when working men commonly earned less than a pound a week, such charges placed the south Devon resorts well out of reach for those with only limited means. It was hardly surprising that many holiday-makers still preferred to visit resorts located nearer to their homes rather than to make the expensive journey to the south Devon coast.

We have seen that the return of peace in 1815 was followed by an era of increased competition in the English holiday industry, which meant that it became much more difficult to attract tourists to south Devon. Our next task will be to consider how the development of the south Devon

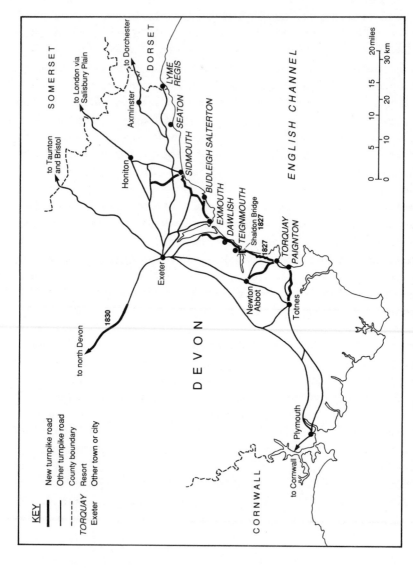

Map 2. Roads Serving the South Devon Resorts in 1835.
A growing network of turnpike roads was greatly improving access to the coastal resorts.

seaside resorts was affected in a period when most of them found that their visitor numbers were falling.

The population figures in Tables 5 and 6 show that the pace of development slackened at most of the south Devon resorts. A new watering place began to emerge at Paignton and the tiny resort of Seaton increased its population significantly, but nearly all of the older resorts grew at a more gradual rate between 1821 and 1841 than in the two previous decades. At both Teignmouth and Dawlish the population actually fell between 1831 and 1841. This slowing down of growth-rates was not confined to south Devon. Walton has shown that most of England's south coast resorts grew more slowly in the 1830s and 1840s than they had in the previous two decades.[33]

Torquay was a notable exception to this general trend, for it expanded dramatically at a time when many south Devon resorts were stagnating. In just 20 years from 1821 its population increased by a massive 210.8 per cent. In 1821 Torquay had only 1,925 inhabitants, but by 1841 it had become the largest watering place on the Devon coast with a population of 5,982. Contemporary reports confirm that Torquay was growing rapidly. In 1821 it was reported that Torquay had 'from a small village grown into a well-frequented watering place'.[34] By 1830 it was estimated that Torquay contained 'about 130 genteel and commodious houses, either occupied by resident gentry or as lodging houses'.[35] Thereafter building works multiplied, so that by 1843 Torquay had become a substantial town.

Torquay's rapid growth resulted mainly from the development of its winter season. In Torquay's early days the fine coastal scenery had been the principal attraction, and it had been in the summer months that its few visitors had mainly arrived. Yet by 1821 the growing resort was being 'much resorted to by winter visitants on account of its sheltered and warm position'.[36] The winter season there soon became far more important than the summer one. On 18 September 1828, at the time of year when most English resorts were bidding farewell to their summer visitors, it was reported from Torquay that its busy season was 'just commencing', that lodgings were 'filling rapidly' and visitors were 'numerous beyond precedent'.[37] By 1840 Torquay was firmly established as England's principal winter health resort. In that year Dr Granville visited Torquay and commented:

It is the very nature of the place to have, as it were, a permanent residentiary set of invalids, who hurry thither on the coming on of

Table 5   Population of the Principal
South Devon Resorts, 1821–1841

Resort	*1821*	*1831*	*1841*	*Increase 1821–1841*
Exmouth	3895	4252	5119	1224
Teignmouth	3980	4688	4459	479
Dawlish	2700	3151	3132	432
Sidmouth	2747	3126	3309	562
Budleigh Salterton	1706	2044	2319	613
Torquay	1925	3582	5982	4057
Seaton	489	600	765	276
Paignton	1796	1960	2501	705

Table 6   Percentage Growth-Rates of the Population of the
Principal South Devon Resorts, 1821–1841

Resort	*1821–1831*	*1831–1841*	*1821–1841*
Exmouth	9.2	20.4	31.4
Teignmouth	17.8	−4.9	12.0
Dawlish	16.7	−0.6	16.0
Sidmouth	13.8	5.9	20.5
Budleigh Salterton	19.8	13.5	35.9
Torquay	86.1	67.0	210.8
Seaton	22.7	27.5	56.4
Paignton	9.1	27.6	39.3

Source for Tables 5 and 6: Decennial Census.
Exmouth figures are for Littleham and Withycombe Raleigh parishes. Teignmouth figures are for East and West Teignmouth parishes. Budleigh Salterton figures are for East Budleigh parish. Torquay figures are for Tormohun parish.

winter, distribute themselves in all the houses and lodgings that can possibly be had, and there remain stationary and ensconced until the warm sun of June again permits them to run up to the metropolis, or return to their country-houses.[38]

It was not only invalids who resided there during the inclement months. Torquay's growing specialization as a winter resort also enabled it to attract many genteel visitors seeking good company rather than renewed health.

The older south Devon resorts gradually lost most of their winter trade. In 1817 the pattern of two distinct seasons was still sufficiently entrenched for one local guidebook to state:

> All our towns on the coast have their interchange of migrating visitors, which takes place about June, when the invalids who have wintered in the mild climate of the south, summer in their northern homes: it is at this time that our gay season commences.[39]

As late as 1826 Teignmouth claimed that 'the company often comes in November for the winter',[40] while two years later Exmouth was still boasting that by November it was 'very full, the lodging houses with little exception being entirely occupied'.[41] But the winter season at the older watering places declined in importance until it was a mere adjunct to the main summer season. Some was lost to resorts located in other parts of England and overseas; most was captured by their fast-developing local rival. When Dr Granville visited Torquay in 1840 he found that as a winter health resort it had 'almost monopolised . . . that reputation of superiority which, in years not long past, had been shared by three or four other sea towns not far removed from it'.[42]

Dr Granville also spent some time in Dawlish, Teignmouth and Exmouth, and his account of his visit provides a valuable assessment of their standing as seaside resorts in the period just before the railway reached south Devon. He found that, unlike Torquay, they had all declined in favour since the end of the Napoleonic Wars. Dawlish, for example, had been deserted by most of the fashionable society that had frequented it during the war years. He commented:

> Dawlish since the peace has made no progress. While Torquay, before nearly unknown, has since that period kept advancing, and taken at length the lead, becoming a sort of winter Brighton, and eclipsing all other Devonshire watering places—Dawlish has nearly stood still,

having few new lodging-houses, and being now distinguished only
by its tranquillity, its fine air, and fine coast.[43]

Teignmouth likewise was languishing after having flourished at the
beginning of the century. Dr Granville described it as 'poor and mean in
appearance'.[44] He noted that Exmouth had also lost trade, and suggested
that this was because medical opinion no longer considered it a suitable
place for a winter residence due to it being exposed to cold winds. Dr
Granville concluded:

> Although Exmouth has been considered the oldest sea watering place
> in Devonshire, and the genial nature of its atmosphere has formerly
> been much descanted upon, subsequent and longer experience has
> not confirmed those high commendations. The influx of strangers is
> much smaller than it was wont to be in former times, and invalids
> have gone in search of a more sheltered and more genial situation.[45]

At a time when the fortunes of most of the older south Devon resorts
were in decline, it is perhaps a little surprising to find a new watering
place beginning to emerge at Paignton. Why should a new seaside resort
develop there when others were losing their momentum? The answer lies
mainly in its close proximity to Torquay, for some of the holiday-makers
staying at that flourishing watering place began to make the short journey
round the bay to visit this pleasant coastal village. Paignton also had
another advantage: it was blessed with one of the best beaches on the
south Devon coast, pink sands sloping only gently towards the sea.

Torquay was making its reputation as a winter watering place, but its
satellite at Paignton began to develop as a summer sea-bathing resort. In
1821 Paignton had only 1796 inhabitants, most of whom earned their
living on the land. Tables 3 and 4 show that after growing only slowly
in the 1820s, Paignton began to expand in the 1830s as it took on a tourist
function. By 1832 a local guidebook could report: 'Paignton has much
improved within a few years, many new houses have been erected and
much attention has been paid to the accommodations for invalids'.[46] In
1753 Dean Milles had found Paignton 'unhealthy on account of some
marshes', with 'sickness enough in ye place to support two apothecaries'.[47]
Now, by a strange irony, Paignton had become another south Devon
health resort, where holiday-makers congregated in the search for renewed
health and vigour.

While some fashionable tourists had deserted the south Devon coast for alternative holiday destinations, the resorts still entertained a significant number of illustrious holiday-makers. In November 1828, for example, it was reported that eight titled visitors, including the Marchioness of Bute and the Countess of Guildford, were residing at Exmouth for the winter.[48]

Members of the royal family occasionally honoured resorts with a visit. In December 1819 the Duke and Duchess of Kent, together with their infant daughter, Princess Victoria, arrived at Sidmouth for the winter season.[49] The news that royalty was present caused an influx of visitors. It was soon reported that the resort was 'full of company'[50] and that 'it was expected by the inhabitants of Sidmouth that they were to have a gay winter under such illustrious patronage'.[51] Their hopes were dashed when the Duke of Kent contracted a chill while walking by the sea and died in January 1820.[52] In 1828 the Duchess of Clarence, later Queen Adelaide, arrived at Torquay for a fleeting visit,[53] while in August 1833 Princess Victoria had a brief stay at the same resort.[54] These royal visits received great publicity, but nothing could disguise the fact that the south Devon resorts had lost a significant proportion of the blue-blooded patronage they had enjoyed during the Napoleonic Wars.

Yet the south Devon seaside resorts still maintained a relatively high social tone. On the Lancashire coast some genteel holiday-makers were in retreat from resorts like Blackpool and Southport, which were being invaded by a growing number of artisans from nearby industrial districts, while further south at seaside resorts like Brighton and Margate, fashionable society was beginning to avoid the summer season, when more and more uncultivated holiday-makers arrived from London.[55] At the south Devon seaside resorts, however, the high cost of the long journey from London and other major centres of demand still acted as a deterrent to lower-class holiday-makers, and this made them attractive retreats for those who wished to leave their social inferiors far behind. Those members of the aristocracy and gentry who still holidayed there, found that they were joined by a growing number of visitors drawn from the professional and commercial classes. A survey of the visitors at Torquay in 1838 indicated the presence of 'eighty-two spinsters, nineteen medicals, twelve divines and two attorneys'.[56] These were not people drawn from the highest echelons of society, but many had social pretensions and arrived hoping for opportunities to mix in fashionable company. Certainly they were moneyed people used to a leisured lifestyle. Their affluence was indicated by the fact that they could often afford to holiday for several months at a time. For these visitors, the air of quiet gentility they found on this coast was an important attraction.

Nor were the south Devon resorts dependent solely on middle-class visitors to fill the gap left by the departure of some of the more fashionable patrons. In the years after 1815 they also developed their residential function, with many wealthy annuitants building second homes or retiring permanently there. Half-pay army and navy officers were well-represented, settling at the resorts after the restoration of peace. At Teignmouth, for example, they ranged from Viscount Exmouth, hero of the naval battle off Algiers in 1816, and Admiral Tobin, who had family connections with Nelson, down to Thomas Luny, a junior officer who built a house near the harbour and supplemented his income by selling marine paintings.[57] Retired East India Company officials began to take up residence on this coast and the watering places started to make extravagant claims about the peculiar advantages their climate offered this wealthy group. Many wealthy invalids also bought houses at the resorts and lived out long declines there.

Although there had undoubtedly been a decline in both the quality and quantity of visitors holidaying on the south Devon coast, the seaside resorts still tried to provide the same forms of entertainment that had proved so popular in the years when they had played host to the cream of society. Tradition was maintained; some members of fashionable society might have left for more exotic locations, but those who remained were reassured to find that most of the social institutions were still modelled on those that had been tried and tested at the eighteenth-century spas. Sea-water baths were still an important amenity at all the leading resorts and were also being opened at some of the smaller watering places. Torquay acquired its first bathing establishment in 1817[58] and Budleigh Salterton had a small bath house by 1838.[59] The company could also play cards at the assembly rooms, borrow the latest novel at the circulating library, or take the air on the promenades.

There were signs, though, that the assembly rooms were finding it difficult to maintain the same range and standard of facilities that had been available in the war years. In part this was due to a decrease in the number of visitors to support these expensive institutions. The public rooms at Exmouth, for example, had only 60 subscribers in 1819.[60] In part it was due to the change in social profile of the visiting public, for as some of the fashionables deserted the south Devon resorts, so those that remained went less often to assemblies, where they risked being outnumbered by middle-class visitors. But it was also the result of a nation-wide trend towards the privatization of upper-class leisure, with the gentry entertaining in the privacy of their own homes so that they would not be obliged to mix with their social inferiors at public places of entertainment.[61]

The social élite at the south Devon resorts began to retreat from the assembly rooms to the seclusion of their seaside houses, where they needed only to fraternize with carefully chosen guests. Private parties became increasingly popular at all the resorts. Those lucky enough to gain admission whiled away the hours with amusements very similar to those long in vogue at the assemblies, with conversation, cards, music, poetry and dancing all being popular. These exclusive gatherings were usually small, intimate affairs, but sometimes splendid balls and banquets were given for as many as 150 invited guests.[62] Mr Fish of Knowle House in Sidmouth, for example, each year invited a 'select company' to a 'grand banqueting rout', with a sumptuous dinner being served, while outside the 'grounds were handsomely illuminated and the fountains in full play'.[63]

Gradually the assemblies fell out of fashion. As late as 1826 splendid new Public Rooms were opened at Teignmouth,[64] but before long there were complaints that some fashionable people were not giving the new establishment their support, preferring instead to entertain in their private residences.[65] By 1840 the heyday of the public assembly was over. One local guidebook expressed sorrow that the Exmouth Rooms were not well attended and looked back nostalgically to 'days not long since past . . . when the gentry held it to be a pleasurable duty to meet in public, and set forth examples of courtesy and manners'.[66]

Circulating libraries still attracted some wealthy patrons, for they provided a far wider range of books and newspapers than could be found in most private houses. They also retained their function as a social rendezvous, where those out for a stroll along the promenade could rest awhile and enjoy good company. When John Mockett holidayed in Exmouth in 1835 he visited Ewen's Library every day on the pretext of reading the newspapers, but his real reason for going there was to 'meet with some friends from Kent and many others'.[67] Many subscribers obviously considered that the libraries' greatest treasures were to be found not on the bookshelves, nor in the columns of a newspaper, but in the snippets of information gleaned from pleasant conversations in the library lounge.

The proprietors of these libraries diversified into an ever-increasing

number of sidelines. Croydon's Library at Teignmouth had a billiard room
and also acted as an accommodation bureau and a theatre-booking
agency.[68] Ewen's Library at Exmouth kept a register of 'furnished and
unfurnished houses suitable for the reception of genteel families'.[69]
Wallis's Marine Library at Sidmouth sold lottery tickets and charged a
shilling admission to a camera obscura, a small room where, by means of
mirrors, the sea, promenade and passing company could all be seen in
miniature.[70]

The circulating library was a popular institution with the visiting
public, and with such a diverse range of functions it must have been an
interesting business to run, but unfortunately the financial risks involved
in acquiring and stocking one of these prestigious establishments were
considerable. Despite their attempts to obtain additional income, some
librarians experienced trading difficulties. At Sidmouth, for example, John
Marsh, proprietor of Marsh's Library, went bankrupt in 1820,[71] while the
Marine Library was closed in 1835 due to lack of support.[72]

Regattas continued to attract large crowds to the south Devon resorts.
These events were little affected by the reduction in the size of the
company holidaying at most of the watering places, for they also received
the patronage of the fashionable society of inland Devon. In 1824 the
Exeter and Plymouth Gazette reported that 'all the nobility and gentry' had
arrived at Torquay to join the 5,000 spectators for the annual regatta.[73]
At the Torquay regatta in 1834 John Mockett was 'highly delighted to
see all the equipages and fashionable persons from every part of the
county'.[74] Lady Sylvester attended a regatta at Dawlish in August 1824
and recorded her impressions in her diary:

> A very pretty public breakfast tastily laid out. Lady Mallet Vaughan
> was Lady Patroness. The day was very pleasant, not too hot, and the
> number of boats in the water rendered it a very pretty sight. We sat
> down to breakfast about 170, and the bands of music, company, smart
> carriages, etc., etc., made it a very cheerful, gay scene . . . There was
> a ball in the evening and a very good one.[75]

These formalized patterns of entertainment, with their strong links with
the past, and with a heavy emphasis on status, decorum and the dictates
of fashion, survived right through this period. Amusements like cures
had long been sought and sanctioned by a privileged class accustomed to
the traditional regimen of the spa. Although the market had widened,
and a growing number of professional, propertied and business people

had joined the company holidaying at the south Devon resorts, the new arrivals were keen to copy the sophisticated lifestyle of their social superiors.

The traditional holiday régime could not be preserved indefinitely. By 1843 the railway was rapidly advancing towards south Devon, and on the trains would come many new holiday-makers drawn from a much wider range of social groupings. Many of the new visitors would be middle-class families, unfamiliar with the conventions of the spa, but eager to sample the pleasures of a beach holiday. The old order would then face a serious challenge.

Six

New Openings: North Devon Resorts, 1816–1843

On the morning of 30 June 1817 Fanny Burney set off from Bath to travel to the little-known seaside resort of Ilfracombe. Fanny, a famous novelist and a leading luminary of select society, was leaving the citadel of high fashion for a distant outpost. Soon after nine she boarded the stage coach and travelled all day, reaching Taunton in time for tea. The coach was soon on the road again. After a short stop at Tiverton it travelled all through the night, swaying and bumping over stony roads as it crossed the moors. Not until mid-morning the following day did Fanny finally reach Barnstaple. It had taken the coach over 25 hours to cover a distance of approximately 110 miles! Still ahead was the prospect of a bone-shaking ride in a chaise over the twelve miles of ill-made road leading to Ilfracombe.[1] The length and discomfort of this journey serve as a reminder of the obstacles still standing in the way of any large-scale development of tourism at Ilfracombe and its coastal neighbours.

Any attempt to account for the advance of the north Devon tourist industry in the years which followed must focus on transport innovations. The period between 1816 and 1843 saw a whole series of improvements being made to both land and sea travel facilities to north Devon and this chapter will give them special attention. It will show that these transport improvements encouraged an influx of tourists, with resulting benefits for the holiday industry. At a time when the pace of progress was slackening at most of the south Devon seaside resorts, Ilfracombe, Lynton and Lynmouth, and Instow all grew substantially. This chapter will consider the physical development and character of these north Devon resorts. It will show that even though their principal asset was their distinctive holiday environment, they were not content to be different, but tried to provide some of the social amenities found at the fashionable spas and older south Devon seaside resorts.

A major programme of road construction was a key factor in opening north Devon to the tourist (see Map 3, p.78). The first essential was to make Barnstaple more accessible from the outside world, for this old market town controlled the main routes to the remote north Devon coast. For many years the main approach road from Taunton in the east had taken a detour via Tiverton before climbing over Rackenford Moor and then descending to South Molton and Barnstaple. This was a long and very slow road. But in 1826 a new turnpike was opened between Wiveliscombe and Bampton and this formed the last link in a more direct and much easier route from Taunton to Barnstaple.[2] Road access from the south was also improved. In 1827 the Barnstaple Turnpike Trust commenced work on a completely new road from Barnstaple along the Taw valley to Eggesford.[3] This was an ambitious project, for it involved completely re-routing the course of the road so that it ran along a low but marshy valley instead of over a series of hills. Work progressed rapidly and the turnpike was 'open to the public in good condition for travelling' by November 1830.[4] In the same month the Exeter Turnpike Trust opened a connecting turnpike running from Eggesford to Copplestone, where it joined an existing road leading to Exeter.[5] This meant that Barnstaple had finally obtained an almost level road link with Exeter. In a relatively short period land access to Barnstaple from other parts of the country had been greatly improved. The other essential need was for much better roads leading from Barnstaple to the coastal resorts.

Ilfracombe was easily the most important north Devon resort, so not surprisingly it was the first to be connected with Barnstaple by a new road. Sir Bourchier Wrey, lord of the manor of Ilfracombe, played a major part in the decision to improve land access to his resort. He had become one of the trustees of the Barnstaple Trust in 1827 and soon afterwards he chaired the meeting at which it was decided to build a new turnpike from Barnstaple to Ilfracombe.[6] The turnpike opened in 1829 and it at once won 'the admiration of all who travelled over it'.[7]

So by 1830 it was possible to travel on good turnpike roads all the way from Exeter to Ilfracombe. Dr Clark, the famous advocate of sea-air cures, then began to advise gentlefolk wintering at the south Devon resorts that they would find 'excellent summer residences for invalids' at Ilfracombe. In his books he pointed out: 'One objection to such a migration, which formerly existed in the badness of the roads, is now remedied by the formation of a new level line of road from Exeter to Barnstaple and Ilfracombe'.[8]

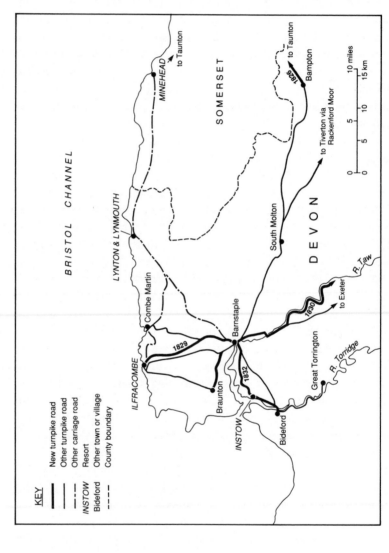

Map 3. Roads Serving the North Devon Resorts in 1835.
New turnpike roads had made it much easier to reach Ilfracombe and Instow, but the resort of Lynton and Lynmouth was still many miles from the nearest turnpike.

In 1832 the Barnstaple Trust constructed another new turnpike, which this time connected Instow with both Barnstaple and Bideford.[9] While Instow had for many years attracted a few local bathers, the lack of a road along the eastern shores of the Torridge estuary had made the village very difficult to reach. The new turnpike was principally intended to improve communications between Barnstaple and Bideford, but it passed through Instow and greatly improved access to the tiny estuarine resort. Instow was now well placed to tap the holiday demand from north Devon's two principal urban centres. 'Its easy distance from the towns of Barnstaple and Bideford, and the delightful roads which communicate with them, obtain for it a decided preference from the gentry of those vicinities,' declared the *North Devon Journal* in 1842.[10]

Roads over the moor to Lynton and Lynmouth were made only slowly. Most of the local traffic was by pack-horse or sledge.[11] It was extremely difficult to travel there in a wheeled vehicle. In 1823 Mrs Selwyn, a writer who had travelled the length and breadth of the country, complained bitterly about her journey in a horse-drawn carriage to Lynton: 'The drive from Ilfracombe to Lynton is through the worst of roads. It exceeded all we had met with . . . the horses being fatigued, the drivers gave them beer, two large jugs divided among the four'.[12]

The lord of the manor played an important role in the provision of better approach roads to Lynton and Lynmouth. An 1825 guidebook stated:

> A few years ago . . . the roads to it were impassable, even for carts
> . . . by the indefatigable exertion of the landed proprietor, Mr Lock,
> new lines of road were opened both here and in the immediate
> vicinity. Carriages then began, though with difficulty, to find their
> way.[13]

The ratepayers also helped to pay for improvements. The Lynton Vestry Minutes for the next decade contain several references to carriage roads being cut and bridges being constructed in the parish.[14] In the absence of any initiative from a turnpike trust, the local community was investing considerable sums in improving access to the resort.

Coach services to north Devon were speeded up once roads had been improved. By 1827 the 'North Devon' coach was running from London to Taunton and then over the new road to Barnstaple in 28¼ hours.[15] By 1831 a new light coach called the 'Subscription' was travelling from London to Exeter and then over the recently opened turnpike to

Barnstaple in 25 ½ hours.[16] In the following year the 'Royal Mail' began running from London via Taunton to Barnstaple in 24 hours.[17] This was the fastest coach time ever achieved between the capital and Barnstaple, but it was still substantially longer than the 17 hours needed for the coach journey between London and Exeter in 1832.

Travel to the coastal resorts also became easier. In 1819 a coach ran three times a week from Ilfracombe to connect with services leaving Barnstaple for London and other distant parts of the country.[18] By 1839 the coach service between Ilfracombe and Barnstaple had become a daily one.[19] By 1830 the track-way over the moor from Barnstaple to Lynton and Lynmouth had been sufficiently improved for a 'conveyance' to be able to run there three times a week.[20] Once the new turnpike was opened from Barnstaple to Bideford in 1832, the nascent resort of Instow had the advantage of being on the main coaching route between Barnstaple, Bideford and Plymouth. In 1838 it was reported that 'four mail coaches with numberless other stage coaches and carriages passed daily through Instow'.[21] With the introduction of these public-transport services to the north Devon resorts, it at last became possible for the tourist to contemplate a journey there without feeling that he or she was setting off on an arduous expedition into the unknown.

Developments in water transport were also of crucial consequence, for they made the north Devon resorts easily accessible by sea from important centres of holiday demand at Bristol and Bath, and from the expanding urban areas of South Wales. Sailing services on the Bristol Channel had been increasing, so that by 1819 one guidebook could report that from Ilfracombe packets were 'constantly passing to Bristol, Swansea and Milford'.[22] Sailing packets, though, were relatively slow and greatly dependent on the vagaries of the wind. It was the advent of the steamer which made possible a big increase in the number of visitors arriving by sea. In 1822 the *Duke of Lancaster*, a steam packet, started calling at Ilfracombe on her passages between Bristol and Cork.[23] In 1824 steam packets plying between Swansea and Bristol began embarking and disembarking passengers at Ilfracombe.[24] These early services were not very reliable, partly because of mechanical failure and partly because steamers were sometimes transferred to other routes in mid-season. In 1826, however, the steam packet *Glamorgan* began plying regularly between Swansea, Ilfracombe and Bristol. The *Exeter Flying Post* commented that this provided 'what had been so long desired; a certain and ready means of communication between the north of Devon, Wales and Bristol'.[25]

Ilfracombe benefited most from this revolution in sea transport. It already had a small harbour, and between 1824 and 1829 the existing stone pier was extended further out to sea to provide sheltered berths in deeper water. Smaller steamers could be accommodated in the improved harbour, but larger vessels still had to drop anchor offshore and put passengers ashore in small boats. These steamships made the resort accessible to many new visitors and gave a major boost to the small tourist industry. In 1828 T.H. Cornish remarked that the 'constant and rapid communication with Ireland, Wales and Bristol had wrought a most surprising change' with many 'families of distinction' arriving by sea.[26]

In a few short years major improvements in sea and road transport had placed Ilfracombe within reach for many more visitors. In 1831 the *North Devon Journal* commented: 'The establishment of a regular steam communication between Ilfracombe and Bristol, and the opening of the new road to Barnstaple, have rendered this remote but attractive spot easily accessible from every part of the country'.[27]

Steamship services also began to transform Lynton and Lynmouth's prospects as a seaside resort. The *Glamorgan* began calling at Lynmouth in 1830 on its passage between Bristol and Ilfracombe.[28] In the next decade packet steamers *en route* from Bristol to both Bideford and Hayle likewise began to call. Facilities for disembarkation were poor; the small tidal haven at the mouth of the Lyn was too small to accommodate the steamers, so they anchored offshore while passengers were landed in small craft. Lynmouth was a port of call for fewer packet steamers than Ilfracombe, but the small resort still benefited considerably from its new sea links with areas of holiday demand.

The tiny resort of Instow also began to be served by packet steamers. In October 1833 a group of north Devon businessmen decided that there was a need for a regular steam packet service between Bristol and the Torridge estuary. They formed a company and had the *Torridge* built at Bideford. In 1835 this steamer commenced a weekly service between Bristol and Bideford and called off Instow to land passengers.[29]

Steamships greatly reduced the cost of travel to north Devon. In 1832 the fare between Bristol and Ilfracombe on the steam packet *George IV* was 15*s*. 6*d*. in the best cabin and 8*s*. on deck. This compared very favourably with the fare of £1 15*s*. inside and £1 1*s*. outside on the 'Royal Mail' coach between Bristol and Barnstaple.[30] Not surprisingly sea travel became very popular with those who had to consider costs when making the long journey to the north Devon coast.

Price-cutting wars occasionally broke out between rival steamship companies and for a time sea travel to the north Devon resorts became even cheaper. In early August 1836, for example, fares between Bristol and Ilfracombe plummeted when two steamships battled fiercely for trade. The *North Devon Journal* reported from Barnstaple:

> So great is the competition between the *Star* and *Benledi* steam packets, which ply between Bristol and Ilfracombe, that notice was given yesterday that passengers would be conveyed from this town to Ilfracombe in a carriage for nothing and from thence to Bristol in a steamer for *one* shilling . . . this has greatly benefited the town of Ilfracombe by the immense number of visitors whom the extreme cheapness of the fare has attracted.[31]

Later in August the same newspaper reported from Ilfracombe: 'Not less than 500 or 600 passengers were landed here last evening from the two Bristol steamers'.[32] Never before had Ilfracombe experienced such an influx. Low fares were encouraging far more people to visit the little resort. Unfortunately for the tourist, the price war soon came to an end. The syndicate that owned the *Benledi* found the competition too fierce and at the end of the season gave up the Ilfracombe service. Fares then returned to their former levels, but they were still much lower than the cost of coach travel to north Devon.[33]

In June 1841 the Great Western Railway completed its line from London to Bristol and this gave a substantial boost to steam packet services between Bristol and the north Devon resorts. The combined rail and steamer trip for a time provided the quickest possible journey from the metropolis to the Devon coast. Seeking to take advantage of the increased demand, the Hayle Steamship Company at once ordered a powerful new paddle steamer, the *Cornwall*, which began operating between Bristol, Ilfracombe and Hayle in 1842. The *North Devon Journal* advised its readers:

> Parties left Ilfracombe at half-past twelve on Wednesday by the new steamboat *Cornwall*, being her first trip, and arrived at Bristol a little after six, in time for the seven o'clock train, and were at Paddington by eleven thirty, thus completing the journey within eleven hours.[34]

Passengers arriving by sea at the north Devon resorts had previously been drawn mainly from centres of demand adjacent to the Bristol Channel, but, following the opening of this new rail and sea link, the steamers also brought increasing numbers of passengers from London and the Home Counties.

The opening of the first sections of the Bristol and Exeter Railway also made it easier for holiday-makers from distant parts of the country to reach the north Devon resorts. On 14 June 1841 this railway was opened from Bristol as far as Bridgwater. Two weeks later the Great Western Railway opened the last section of its line from London to Bristol and this meant that there was a continuous broad-gauge link between London and Bridgwater.[35] The 'North Devon Mail' coach, which had been running via Salisbury to connect with the new London and Southampton Railway, was then re-routed to run to the new railhead at Bridgwater. Travel times were slashed. It had been taking at least 22¼ hours to travel by land from London to Barnstaple, but passengers could now leave Paddington on the 8.55 p.m. train and arrive at Barnstaple at 10.35 a.m., after a journey of only 13 hours 40 minutes. The *North Devon Journal* hailed this new service as a 'triumph of skill and enterprise', and indeed it was.[36] In July 1842 the next section of the Bristol and Exeter Railway, to Taunton, was opened and north Devon coaches at once began running to the new station. The combined train and coach journey time between London and Barnstaple was again reduced, this time by approximately an hour.[37]

In May 1843 the Bristol and Exeter Railway was extended to a temporary station at Beambridge, west of Wellington, and this new railhead at once became the focal point for coach services from all over Devon. It was now possible to catch the train at Paddington at 8.55 p.m. and arrive in Barnstaple on the coach at 8.45 a.m., after a journey of only 11 hours 50 minutes.[38] This was only one hour and 20 minutes longer than the combined train and coach journey from London to Exeter, so resorts on the north Devon coast could compete on almost equal terms with their south Devon rivals.[39]

Coach services multiplied between the north Devon resorts and the Bristol and Exeter Railway. In the summer of 1843 the 'Royal Mail' and 'Ruby' coaches both began running direct from Ilfracombe to the new railhead at Beambridge,[40] while two other coaches from Ilfracombe connected in Barnstaple with coaches running to Beambridge. At the same time some of the coach services running through Instow were also re-routed to run to the station at Beambridge. In July of that year the resort of Lynton and Lynmouth obtained its first proper coach service, when a light coach began running to the station at Taunton each day.[41] This was an interesting development. Land access to Lynton and

Lynmouth had previously been mainly from the west via Barnstaple, but from this time onwards a substantial number of visitors began to travel to the resort on the more direct route from the east.

The benefits of this improved access by land and sea were soon in evidence at the north Devon resorts. In June 1843 it was reported that Instow was 'completely filled', while at Ilfracombe visitors were said to be 'pouring in' because of the 'greater facilities of communication'.[42] In the following month it was reported that the season at Lynton and Lynmouth was one of the best ever, following the introduction of a 'daily means of access by rail and coach and almost as frequent by steamers'.[43]

Transport developments had made it possible for many more visitors to reach the remote north Devon coast, but what effect did this increased holiday demand have on the growth of the principal seaside resorts? Tables 7 and 8 show that the population of Ilfracombe and of Lynton and Lynmouth increased substantially between 1821 and 1841. By 1841 Ilfracombe's population had grown by 40.3 per cent to reach 3,679, while Lynton and Lynmouth's population had increased by 62.5 per cent, from a low base, to reach 1,027. They were still comparatively small resorts, but they had grown vigorously at a time when most of the leading south Devon seaside resorts, with the notable exception of Torquay, had been experiencing a period of only sluggish growth. The tables show that Instow had only a very small population in 1831, but that in the next decade it too began to grow, after it had been made accessible by road and had begun to develop its holiday function.

Contemporary accounts confirm that Ilfracombe was expanding and that it was beginning to provide the accommodation expected of a small but increasingly fashionable watering place. At the start of the period Ilfracombe was still a very small resort with few houses suitable for visitors. In 1817 Fanny Burney complained:

> The town itself has nothing, except its position, to recommend it: not a public building of any sort, not even a private house that is pretty, not a mansion that is spacious, not a cottage that is neat. The houses are built on a small scale, down, down, down to a smaller: and the one only street is scarcely ever broader than a lane, and in many places not wider than an alley.[44]

It was in the late 1820s that the construction of splendid villas and grand

Table 7   Population of the Principal
North Devon Resorts, 1821–1841

Resort	1821	1831	1841	Increase 1821–1841
Ilfracombe	2622	3201	3679	1057
Lynton and Lynmouth	632	792	1027	395
Instow	353	369	557	204

Table 8   Percentage Growth-Rates of the Population of the
Principal North Devon Resorts, 1821–1841

Resort	1821–1831	1831–1841	1821–1841
Ilfracombe	22.1	14.9	40.3
Lynton and Lynmouth	25.3	29.7	62.5
Instow	4.5	50.9	57.8

Source for Tables 7 and 8: Decennial Census.

terraces began in earnest as improvements in land and sea access made it possible for visitors to arrive in greater numbers. In 1832 the *North Devon Journal* commented on the rapid expansion of the resort:

> Ilfracombe within a few years past has been greatly enlarged by the addition of numerous commodious lodging houses and elegant terraces. It has become a place of fashionable resort to the affluent and to the valetudinarian.[45]

Lynton and Lynmouth also began to expand as transport improvements enabled more visitors to reach this remote resort. At Lynmouth the construction of a new road alongside the river in 1828 opened up some good sites for development, and in the next decade a line of fine lodging houses was erected.[46] Up at Lynton the old farming village was set back from the cliffs and nestled in a depression, so that the houses received shelter from the winter gales. The wealthy strangers who began to arrive were more concerned with obtaining fine sea views than with protection from the elements, so the new lodging houses and villas were erected on exposed sites along the cliff top where they could command fine marine outlooks.

Lynton and Lynmouth gradually took on the countenance of a small seaside resort. 'Many houses of tolerable appearance have within a few years been built for the accommodation of guests; there are also several respectable inns,' reported one traveller in 1830.[47] Not everyone welcomed the development. John Eagles, an artist, revisited Lynmouth in 1833 and was shocked to find that the 'simple thatched cottage' he had previously stayed in had been 'hotelified'.[48]

Instow also began to provide more accommodation for visitors. In 1828 a local guidebook confirmed that it was being used as a 'bathing place' by local people.[49] It was, though, the construction of the new turnpike linking it with Barnstaple and Bideford in 1832 which enabled it to develop a more important summer season and to capture most of the local trade formerly enjoyed by Appledore on the opposite side of the estuary. In July 1838 the opening of hot and cold sea-water baths and adjacent furnished lodgings were proudly announced. Dry sands, invigorating air and pleasant scenery were claimed as the resort's principal attractions.[50] Yet, while it was true that Instow was blessed with some natural advantages, they were not sufficiently outstanding for the resort to be able to attract substantial numbers of visitors from distant parts of the country, so most of its small clientele originated from within the county. Although for a time it enjoyed moderate success, it never grew to be more than a coastal village.

There are difficulties in considering the size and social composition of the visiting public at the north Devon resorts in this period. Arrival lists for Instow were never published in the local press, and usually they were inserted only infrequently for the other two seaside resorts.

The summer of 1827, however, was a notable exception to the usual dearth of arrival lists, for in that year the *North Devon Journal* regularly published lists for Ilfracombe and Lynton and Lynmouth. In the course

of a season lasting from May to early October, the newspaper recorded
a total of 1,033 people arriving at Ilfracombe, while in the same period
at Lynton and Lynmouth 695 arrivals were listed. These arrival lists
suggest that in 1827 both resorts still had only a small visiting public, for
even in August, at the peak of the season, neither of them ever had more
than a hundred new visitors listed as arriving in a single week.[51]

Only fragments of information about visitor numbers exist for the end
of the period. The decennial census taken on the night of 7 June 1841 is
of some assistance. It reveals that on that night there were only 62 visitors
present at Instow[52] and just 38 at Lynton and Lynmouth.[53] These figures
indicate that these resorts still had only a very small number of visitors,
though it should be pointed out that the census was taken quite early in
the main season and numbers would have increased significantly by
August. Unfortunately similar data are not available for Ilfracombe as at
that resort the census enumerators did not specially identify visitors.

The local press very rarely published arrival lists in the early 1840s.
Just two lists exist and both are for Ilfracombe in August 1842, the *North
Devon Journal* recording 236 arrivals in the first week of the month
and 202 in the third week.[54] These figures were approximately three times
larger than the average number of arrivals recorded each week in August
1827. They suggest that Ilfracombe's holiday-making population had
grown substantially following the major improvements in land and sea
access to the resort, although visitor numbers were much smaller than at
English seaside resorts located closer to major centres of demand.[55]

Some eminent members of society were holidaying on the north Devon
coast in this period. The arrival lists for 1827 show that 20 titled people
holidayed in Ilfracombe during the course of the summer, while in
the same period Lynton and Lynmouth had 15 titled visitors. Other
distinguished visitors at the two resorts included several generals and
admirals, two bishops, two Members of Parliament and a judge.[56]

It could be argued that the steamers, which in later years were to pose
a serious threat to the genteel atmosphere of these resorts, were in this
early period enhancing their social tone, by allowing wealthy and
fashionable influences from distant parts to percolate down to the north
Devon coast. From Bristol, for example, members of the Coutts banking
family and the Wills tobacco-manufacturing family often arrived at
Lynmouth and Ilfracombe by sea from Bristol for the summer season.
From South Wales came some prominent ironmasters like the Marquis
of Bute and the Earl of Uxbridge.[57] When in the 1840s the steamers began
to connect with the new train services at Bristol, they began to carry some

influential families from London to join the company holidaying at the north Devon resorts.

The case of Lynton and Lynmouth serves to show that the influx of visitors brought about great changes in the lives of the local inhabitants and that these changes were not always for the best. Early visitors to the twin villages had been impressed with the appealing innocence of country folk living close to nature and seemingly reflecting the virtues of a less avaricious age. At the beginning of the century one traveller had envied the local peasantry's remoteness from the 'bustle of the world and the cares of crowded life',[58] while another had remarked that 'their constant diligence and cheerful character claim the respect and attention of the higher classes'.[59] Sadly, as the tourist trade developed, the simple dignity of an earlier era was corroded by the grasping greed of a new commercialism, and before long the visitor found himself being accosted by local inhabitants touting for trade. Rival hoteliers began to squabble over potential patrons. In 1833 the proprietor of the Castle Hotel placed advertisements in the local press declaring:

> The practice of one of the other inns, in keeping persons constantly on the roads watching for carriages, with a variety of fabrications to induce families to go to the Valley of Rocks Inn, is entirely beneath the respectability of this establishment.[60]

The custom persisted and as late as 1851 one guidebook found it necessary to caution the intending visitor:

> At Lynton telescopes are employed at the rival houses for the prompt discovery of the approaching traveller. He had better therefore determine beforehand on his inn, or he will become a bone of contention to a triad of postboys, who wait with additional horses at the bottom of the hill to drag the coach to its destination.[61]

The first tourists to discover Lynton and Lynmouth had enjoyed spying on the lives of honest local rustics, but since then the roles had been reversed, for the inhabitants had become worldly-wise and scanned the road for unsuspecting tourists on whom to prey. As elsewhere on the Devon coast, the development of the tourist industry had brought considerable financial benefits, but only at some cost to the charming simplicity and sturdy independence of life in the seaside communities.

*

In 1816 the north Devon resorts were too small to provide many man-made entertainment facilities and they still relied almost entirely on their natural attributes to attract visitors. In the years that followed, however, the increase in the size of the visiting public encouraged some cautious investment in public buildings and artificial amusements. These were designed to meet the sophisticated needs of a leisured clientele accustomed to formalalized patterns of entertainment. There were few attempts at originality. Social activities at the north Devon resorts were modelled on time-honoured holiday rituals that had become fashionable at the spas over a hundred years earlier and which had for many years dominated life at the principal south Devon seaside resorts.

Bathing facilities were still the first essential at any fashionable watering place; so once Ilfracombe began to expand it set out to improve its provision, both for visitors who wished to bathe in the sea and for those who preferred to seek sea-water cures in the comfort of a bath-house. In 1819 one guidebook reported that Ilfracombe had many bathing machines available for the use of bathers.[62] By 1822 hot and cold sea-water baths were available 'for the accommodation of invalids'.[63]

An Ilfracombe guidebook of 1830 included details of the resort's bathing conventions:

> The hot and cold baths are on the Quay; and the sea-bathing for ladies is at Wildersmouth, where machines and bathing women are in attendance from six to eleven o'clock in the morning; after which they are directed to be drawn up.[64]

In this period bathing was still regarded as an aid to health rather than as a pleasure, and it was normal for bathing to take place early in the day. It is interesting to note that by this time bathing was segregated, and that the ladies had been allocated the best beach. Gentlemen still bathed nude, so modesty dictated that they take a boat trip to the secluded Crewkhorne and Rapparee beaches when wanting to take a dip.[65]

The growth of Ilfracombe soon encouraged further investment in improved bathing facilities. A group of local businessmen established the Ilfracombe Sea Bathing Company. In 1836 this company erected an elegant new bath-house, where both hot and cold sea-water baths were available. At the rear of the baths the company had tunnels cut through the cliffs to reach the previously inaccessible Crewkhorne Cove, where it allocated separate bathing beaches for ladies and gentlemen. An 1839 guidebook explained the rules:

The westward part is allotted to gentlemen, while the eastward is by
custom left to the ladies and is carefully guarded against all intrusion.
Machines and bathing women are in attendance, and every information respecting the proper time to bathe will be given at the
Baths.[66]

Sea-water baths were also provided at Lynmouth and Instow. In 1830
it was reported that Lynmouth had 'a bath-house of neat appearance,
lately erected, where hot and cold baths are prepared'.[67] In 1838 baths
were erected at Instow and the proprietor advertised that they were
'replete with every convenience for sea-water, hot, cold and shower
bathing'. Just in case these facilities were not enough to attract those who
had been accustomed to bathe at the spas, the advertisement added for
good measure that a 'chalybeate spring has also been discovered in a field
close by, on which its spirited proprietor intends shortly to erect a neat
pump room'.[68] Unfortunately Instow never grew sufficiently to warrant
the construction of this pump room.

Assembly rooms had long been a focal point of social life at the spas
and principal south Devon resorts, but it was only in the years after 1816
that Ilfracombe became the first and only north Devon resort with
sufficient visitors to warrant holding assemblies. It has already been
explained that on the south Devon coast the first assemblies were held in
rooms attached to inns. This was also the case at Ilfracombe. In 1817
Fanny Burney found that the small company had begun to assemble for
balls at the recently opened Sutton's Hotel.[69] By 1824 Ilfracombe had its
own purpose-built assembly rooms.[70] The Public Rooms, as they were
known, had a grecian-style facade and formed the centre-piece to
Coronation Terrace, a row of 'genteel houses' being built on the hill-side
overlooking the harbour. This elegant public building had a ballroom,
billiard room and reading room.[71] It satisfied the growing demand for a
fashionable meeting-place in which to dance, play cards, listen to music
and enjoy polite conversation.

Small circulating libraries were opened at the two principal north
Devon resorts. We have seen that these libraries had long been important
social institutions at the spas, and that in the years leading up to 1815
they had been opened at all the principal south Devon watering places.
In that period the visiting public at the north Devon resorts had been
too small to warrant the substantial capital investment needed to build
and stock one of these prestigious establishments. By 1817 Ilfracombe did
have a circulating library of sorts, but Fanny Burney ridiculed its 'poor,

little, mean' appearance and claimed that 'no one read there and its outward promise exhibited only toys and fruit'.[72] Fanny had been accustomed to the splendid libraries of Bath, and Ilfracombe was far too small a resort to provide similar facilities. She was herself the author of *Evelina* and two other successful novels, and this perhaps explains why she was so critical of a library that stocked very few books. By 1838 a circulating library had opened on the quay at Lynmouth and in such a small coastal village it was hardly surprising to find that it included a 'fancy repository' selling a varied selection of trivial souvenirs and that its owner supplemented his income by managing the bath-house and a lodging house.[73]

As Ilfracombe grew, so its library provision improved. In 1823 Banfield's Library opened and by 1830 claimed to have 'a good collection of books, drawings, music, stationery, &c.'.[74] By 1840 Ilfracombe had become large enough to support three competing libraries. Banfield's Library, the largest, boasted over 2,000 volumes and had a reading room which was 'comfortable and commodious' and contained 'a liberal supply of papers and periodicals, navy, army and share lists'.[75]

For many years visitors to spas and seaside resorts had been accustomed to find promenades where visitors could stroll, take the air and cast a critical eye over other holiday-makers, but at the beginning of this period this amenity had not been introduced at the north Devon resorts. When Fanny Burney visited Ilfracombe in 1817 she was disgusted to find that it had 'no walks for wet weather, either paved, gravelled or sandied'.[76]

Yet in the years that followed considerable sums were spent at Ilfracombe to provide first paths, and then a promenade, along the cliffs. By 1830 the resort had progressed sufficiently for its first guidebook to be able to boast of public walks commanding 'bold, rocky and extensive sea views', which were 'made and kept in repair by voluntary contributions'.[77] Public subscriptions also paid for the construction of Capstone Parade, the resort's first real promenade. This project was embarked upon in the winter of 1842 to provide work for some of the resort's seasonally-unemployed inhabitants, who were suffering hardship during a period of severe weather. When the Parade opened in September 1843 it was claimed that it offered some of the finest marine views in the country and afforded exceptional opportunities for those hoping to benefit from the remedial properties of the sea air. Ilfracombe boasted: 'Here the sick, infirm and convalescent at all times may saunter and inhale the soft sea breeze, the breeze of health'.[78]

The smaller resorts also obtained public walks in this period. At Lynton in 1817 a broad path was notched along the cliff face from the village out to the Valley of Rocks. The costs of construction were met by Mr Sanford, a wealthy summer resident. Known as North Walk, it became a popular promenade providing spectacular marine vistas.[79] In 1838 the tiny resort of Instow obtained its own public walk: 'a ten-feet gravel promenade, half a mile in length' running along the shore.[80] This promenade once again afforded fine sea views and enabled visitors to take full advantage of the beneficial sea breezes.

In July 1828 Ilfracombe staged its first regatta. Once again it was emulating the south Devon seaside resorts, where these annual events had become major attractions. Separate races were held for gentlemen's yachts, fishing boats and rowing boats. The *North Devon Journal* reported that the town 'was never known so full', with 'rank and fashion' crowding the cliffs to view the races.[81] The ball in the evening was attended by over 120 people, 'amongst whom were many of the most respectable residents of the town and neighbourhood, including a great display of youth and beauty, all appearing to be much gratified with the day's amusements'.[82] So successful had been the regatta that it was agreed that 'the races should be conducted another year on a more extended scale, so as to attract not only a greater number of boats, but also the attention of the numerous respectable families residing in the north of Devon'.[83] Subscribers promised to 'come forward with four times the sum' in the following year.[84] Better prizes attracted more entries and in August 1829 the regatta was 'witnessed by a numerous assemblage of spectators estimated at around 2,000, presenting a scene of animation and gaiety'.[85] Such support ensured a flourishing future for the Ilfracombe regatta which continued for many years as the resort's principal social occasion. The success of these regattas prompted Instow in August 1841 to begin staging similar events, albeit on a smaller scale, with hundreds assembling on the front to watch pilot boats and rowing boats competing on the Torridge estuary for substantial prizes.[86]

So by 1843 North Devon had in Ilfracombe its only fully-fledged seaside resort offering most of the diversions expected of a fashionable watering place. By a strange paradox, progress at Ilfracombe had involved looking back into the past and providing the social institutions that had long been fashionable at the spas and larger seaside resorts. It almost seemed as if the resort was afraid to assert its individuality, and that it preferred to play safe by adopting a holiday formula which had proved successful on the south Devon coast during the Napoleonic Wars.

North Devon also had in Lynton and Lynmouth, and Instow two small seaside resorts providing a limited range of social amenities, but still depending largely on their natural advantages to attract visitors. In 1838 Instow boasted of its new sea-water baths and its promenade, but it had few other facilities and marketed itself as a health resort, claiming that it was 'admitted by the Faculty to be the most healthy and therefore best-adapted residence for the prolongation of health'.[87] Lynton and Lynmouth had obtained sea-water baths, a small circulating library and a cliff walk, but picturesque scenery was still the resort's principal asset. Some tourists preferred natural attractions to artificial pleasures, but others were very critical of the lack of amenities at the smaller resorts and found that the small size of the company gave them insufficient opportunities to make the acquaintance of fashionable visitors. So while Thomas Cornish in 1828 was prepared to concede that Lynton and Lynmouth had 'peculiar beauties', he also warned potential visitors that 'even the ardent lover of the sublime and beautiful would not remain longer than a day' because of the 'absence of social intercourse'.[88]

The north Devon tourist industry had prospered in the period between 1816 and 1843 as improvements in land and sea transport had enabled more visitors to reach this remote region. In earlier years Ilfracombe and Lynton and Lynmouth had entertained only a small clientele originating mainly from inland Devon. The introduction of steamers had enabled them to cater for a regional market centred on the Bristol Channel, while the approach of the railway, and the development of connecting coach and steamer services, had allowed them to extend their catchment area and to attract a growing number of visitors from London and other distant parts of the country. Transport improvements had also made it possible for Instow to develop its holiday trade, but the natural advantages enjoyed by this resort were never sufficient to attract a national clientele and it relied for most of its custom on a limited number of visitors from its immediate hinterland. For a short time in the 1840s the advance of the railway meant that Ilfracombe and Lynton and Lynmouth were able to compete on equal terms with their southern counterparts for the patronage of the visiting public. Yet by the end of 1843 the railway was being extended towards south Devon and before long it would begin to draw tourists away from the north Devon coast.

Seven

The Railway Brings New Visitors: South Devon Resorts, 1844–1900

Crowds gathered in Exeter on the morning of 1 May 1844 to see the last section of the Bristol and Exeter Railway officially opened. From as far away as Torquay, people streamed into the city, all anxious to be present when history was made. Excitement mounted as the clock reached twelve-thirty and the first train was heard approaching. Cheers rang round the new station as the engines 'Sunbeam' and 'Castor' puffed in, together hauling a massive load of 21 carriages crammed with 800 passengers from Bristol and Taunton. Following closely behind was a train from London carrying Isambard Kingdom Brunel, the engineer responsible for the construction of the railway, together with numerous local dignitaries. This special had taken only 5 ¼ hours to travel the 194 miles from Paddington![1]

What a momentous day this was! Steam trains had at last reached south Devon and a new era had been ushered in. The railway would soon extend down to the nearby coast where it would revolutionize the tourist industry. For better or worse, holidays at the south Devon seaside resorts would never be the same again.

The period from 1844 to 1900 proved to be a time of major change at the south Devon coastal resorts. The railway brought many more visitors. Genteel holiday-makers had to rub shoulders with a growing number of new arrivals drawn from the middle-ranks of society. Working-class rail excursionists also began to make brief visits. Even though they arrived in much smaller numbers than at many more easily accessible English seaside resorts, they still from time to time managed to disrupt the air of quiet gentility which usually characterized the south Devon resorts. This chapter will consider how the south Devon coastal resorts responded to the challenge of catering for an enlarged clientele drawn from much wider social and geographical backgrounds. It will also show that, while this was an era of progress, at most of these resorts the rate of growth and the speed and nature of change were much less dramatic than at many English coastal watering places located closer to the principal centres of holiday demand.

This was an age in which increasing numbers of people found they could afford to visit the seaside. Great Britain had become a great manufacturing and trading nation, and prosperity was slowly filtering down the social scale. The ranks of the middle class were swollen by the expansion of white-collar occupations, particularly in commerce, banking and the civil service. By the 1860s these salary earners commonly enjoyed a fortnight's paid holiday a year, which provided them with the time and money to consider travelling to the distant Devon coast for an extended stay.[2]

Working-class wages also grew sufficiently to fuel a desire to escape for a few hours from the grim inland towns and to sample the delights of the seaside. While few members of the poorer classes were given holidays with pay, many of them were granted sufficient free time from work to make possible day excursions to the coast. The Factory Act of 1850 granted textile workers a Saturday half-holiday and in the years that followed other groups of workers campaigned successfully for the same privilege.[3] Following the Bank Holiday Act of 1871 most workers found that they were freed from their toil on certain specified days. Easter Monday, Whit Monday and August Bank Holiday became easily the busiest days of the year at the British seaside, for it was then that the bottled-up demand of the working classes was uncorked and a flood of day-trippers poured into all the coastal resorts within easy reach of their urban homes.[4]

'Increased intercourse with the more populous districts of England cannot but prove highly advantageous to the fair and lovely spinsters of Devon', declared the *Western Times* in its editorial on the opening of the railway to Exeter.[5] The editor had in mind the many single ladies resident in the county, but his comment was equally applicable to the seaside resorts. The arrival of the railway gave the beautiful Devon watering places the opportunity to attract many new admirers from distant centres of holiday demand. Passenger trains provided a much faster, cheaper and more comfortable mode of transport than anything that had gone before. These were immense advantages for anyone contemplating the long journey to visit watering places on the south Devon coast.

Travel times to south Devon were slashed. The fastest time achieved by coaches running between London and Exeter had been 16½ hours, but by May 1845 express trains were completing the journey in as little as 4½ hours. These trains travelled at an average speed of 43 miles per hour and were easily the fastest in the world.[6] They caused a sensation. Exeter, the gateway to the south Devon resorts, was at last within easy reach from the capital. Extra coach services were soon established to link the resorts with the new railhead. Torquay, for example, had previously found six coaches a day from Exeter to be quite sufficient, but by 1845 eight were needed to meet the increased demand.[7]

The cost of travel from London to Exeter was also substantially reduced, though it still acted as a deterrent to those with limited budgets. The average fare for an inside seat on a coach between London and Exeter had been £2 12s. 6d., with £4 14s. 6d. being charged on the mail coach. By the 1860s the first and second class rail fares between the same cities were £1 15s. and £1 5s. respectively, with a supplement of 5s. for travel on an express. Third class travel was not encouraged, for fares were for many years fixed at the maximum permitted rate of a penny a mile and this put the long journey from London well beyond the means of the working man.[8]

It was not long before work began to extend the railway to the coast. In July 1844 the South Devon Railway was authorized by Parliament. The company's prospectus stated that, while the main objective was to build a railway from Exeter to Plymouth, a coastal route would be taken to provide 'direct communication with all the favourite watering places on the south coasts of Devon'.[9] The main coaching traffic between Exeter and Plymouth had always been along an inland route, so this decision to take the railway close to the coast was of major importance to the seaside resorts west of the Exe.

The South Devon Railway was opened as far as Dawlish and Teignmouth on Whit weekend 1846. Imagine the excitement as the first trains made their way slowly down the side of the Exe estuary and then turned to run along the very edge of the sea towards the holiday resorts. For many of the Exeter citizens cramming the carriages this was a double first; their first ride on a train and their first visit to the seaside. The inhabitants of Dawlish and Teignmouth were equally excited. They massed at the stations to see the latest mechanical marvels steam in,[10] and to welcome an unprecedented number of visitors to their resorts. A report in the *Exeter Flying Post* captured the feeling of elation:

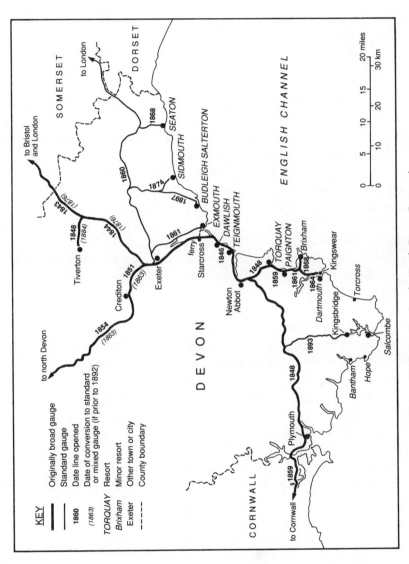

Map 4. Railways Serving the South Devon Resorts in 1900.
Resorts to the east of the Exe had been handicapped by the late arrival of the railway.

At the station at Exeter, from the hour of seven in the morning, it
was a most animated scene, the numbers continually increasing in
order to take the trip down. Indeed, such was the amount that
twenty-one carriages were required to contain them, and it is
computed that upwards of 1,500 persons went down by the morning
train . . . At Dawlish and Teignmouth bands of music were stationed,
flags floated from every tower and eminence, while from the bosom
of old ocean came the echo of the joy and hilarity that reigned on
land.[11]

The South Devon Railway also claimed to serve Exmouth. The trains
stopped at Starcross where a ferry was available to carry passengers across
the Exe estuary to the seaside resort. But the crossing by rowing boat
was inconvenient and time-consuming and was only used by a few
passengers.[12] So Exmouth received little benefit from the South Devon
Railway. It could only watch as trains ran along the opposite side of the
estuary taking holiday-makers away from it towards Dawlish and Teignmouth.

Torquay was the next resort to be connected to the growing national
rail network. Trains began running as far as Newton Abbot in December
1846, and from there a five-mile branch line to Torquay was opened on
18 December 1848.[13] The advantages of a rail link were soon demonstrated
as the resort enjoyed an exceptional winter season. On 8 February 1849
the *Exeter Flying Post* reported: 'This delightful watering place already
feels the beneficial effects of railway communication by the opening of
the South Devon Railway branch line. The town is well-filled with visitors
of distinction, scarce a lodging in the town being unlet'.[14]

The arrival of the railway at Torquay spelt the beginning of the end
for most of the packet steamer services to the south Devon coast. These
steamships had never brought many visitors to the resorts. In 1845
Torquay, which had become the main port of call, had been served by
three packet steamers: the *Zephyr* and *Queen* from London and the
Brunswick from Southampton. Yet only 2,896 passengers landed or
boarded from these three steamers in the whole of that year; a very small
total when compared with the 22,644 people estimated in the same year
to have travelled on the coaches running between Exeter and Torquay.[15]
Once the railway reached Torquay, the packet steamers found it even
more difficult to compete, for the trains provided much faster travel. As
the rail network spread along the coast, so most of the packet steamer
services petered out.

Paignton was the next south Devon resort to obtain a rail link. In 1857 the Torbay and Dartmouth Railway had been authorized by Parliament. On 11 July 1859 the first section of the new line was opened from the end of the Torquay branch line to a new station closer to the centre of Torquay. Three weeks later the railway was extended to Paignton.[16] So by 1859 four resorts west of the Exe were enjoying the benefits of being connected to the national rail network. The railway funnelled holiday demand into these resorts, and away from the watering places east of the Exe which still lacked a railway.

Dawlish and Teignmouth had benefited from being the first Devon resorts to be reached by railway, but, once the railway had been extended further west, the trains began carrying many passengers straight through these resorts and on to Torquay and Paignton. It is clear that all four resorts profited at the expense of other Devon watering places which were still without a railway. Yet it is also apparent that the benefits were not shared equally. Once the railway had reached all four resorts, its role in influencing demand flows lessened and other factors such as the natural and social advantages of particular watering places became more important in determining their share of the growing number of visitors arriving by train. So, once Torquay had a rail link, a large proportion of the increased demand flowed there because it was thought to offer important climatic and social advantages, even though most of the rail passengers had to travel through Dawlish and Teignmouth to reach it.

On 19 July 1860 the London and South Western Railway opened a railway from Yeovil to Exeter, which provided the last link in their line from London to Exeter. The new 171-mile line from Waterloo to Exeter was 23 miles shorter than the Great Western Railway's line from Paddington via Bristol to Exeter. It also had a different gauge. The LSWR operated on the standard gauge of 4ft 8½ in., whereas the GWR and its allies, the Bristol and Exeter Railway and the South Devon Railway, had a broad gauge of 7ft 0¼ in.[17] Competition was soon intense as the broad- and standard-gauge interests battled for the largest share of the holiday trade.

The arrival of the railway in south-east Devon held out a lifeline to the sinking economies of Exmouth, Sidmouth, Seaton and Budleigh Salterton. They had lost many of their visitors to those resorts west of the Exe which had been fortunate enough to obtain rail links, but the new LSWR line gave them reason to hope for better times. There was, though, still a serious obstacle standing in the way of improved trade. Whereas the South Devon Railway had deliberately taken its line close to the coast, the LSWR had been intent only on reaching Exeter and had followed an inland route. So small locally-sponsored companies had to take the initiative in constructing long branch lines from the LSWR to the coastal resorts. Branch lines were opened to Exmouth in 1861, to Seaton in 1868, to Sidmouth in 1874, and finally to the little resort of Budleigh Salterton in 1897.[18]

The watering places east of the Exe never benefited as much from the railway as did their counterparts on the western side of the estuary. To the west of the Exe both Dawlish and Teignmouth were on the main line, while Torquay and Paignton were easily reached on a comparatively short branch line. These resorts had direct services on GWR lines from London, the West Midlands and South Wales, and good connecting services from the North. The resorts to the east of the Exe were less fortunate. They were all on branch lines, and the LSWR line they connected with provided a good service with London, but not from other parts of the country. Travel to them from the Midlands and North was made somewhat easier in 1874, when the Somerset and Dorset Railway was extended northwards from the LSWR line at Templecombe as far as Bath, where it connected with the Midland Railway.[19] This, though, was a slow cross-country route, which usually involved changing trains several times, so it brought only comparatively small numbers of visitors to the seaside resorts of south-east Devon.[20]

Railway services to resorts west of the Exe were further improved in 1892. The GWR had extended its broad-gauge empire in 1876, when it had taken over both the Bristol and Exeter Railway and the South Devon Railway, but since then its broad gauge had become an anachronism and an obstacle to the through running of trains, as most of the remainder of the national rail network was standard gauge. In 1892 the GWR reluctantly decided that its remaining broad-gauge lines must be converted to standard gauge. In the course of a single frantic weekend in May the Company narrowed every inch of its 213 miles of broad-gauge track west of Exeter.[21] The *Torquay Times* thanked the GWR for relieving Torquay and its neighbours from that 'ostracism for which an exceptional gauge was responsible', and welcomed the announcement of a through train from Liverpool and fast trains from Scotland which it believed to be 'pregnant with great possibilities for the future'.[22]

In the last years of the century, through trains brought growing numbers of visitors from the North to the GWR resorts of Torquay, Paignton, Teignmouth and Dawlish. But the LSWR resorts of Exmouth, Sidmouth, Seaton and Budleigh Salterton remained difficult to reach from that area of expanding demand. Accidents of railway company alignment were helping to define the catchment areas of individual watering places.

When the railway first reached the south Devon coast there seemed little threat of an influx of excursionists. The South Devon Railway at first seemed reluctant to upset its wealthy patrons by carrying large numbers of poorer people. The Company decided not to organize any special trains to the seaside, but it did allow private individuals or organizations to charter a train. The first excursion train ever run on the South Devon Railway was organized by the Exeter Temperance Society which in July 1846 took a group from Exeter to Teignmouth at a shilling a head.[23] Trains were occasionally chartered by industrialists to take their employees to the seaside for a day as a reward for their efforts. One such outing took place in August 1854 when John Heathcoat took the workers from his Tiverton lace factory to Teignmouth for the day.[24] Similarly in August 1857 an Exeter iron founder hired a train to take his workforce on a day trip to Teignmouth, while in August 1858 an Exeter boot and shoe manufacturer took his employees on an excursion to Dawlish.[25] In this early period such events were the exception rather than the rule; few excursion trains ran on the South Devon Railway and the numbers of trippers carried were normally quite small.

Rail trips from inland Devon to the nearby coast became more popular from the late 1870s onwards, though numbers carried were still relatively small. The rail companies began to offer reduced day-return fares on regular services, and on bank holidays special trains sometimes ran from Exeter and other Devon towns to the nearby coast. Exmouth was usually the favourite venue for excursionists from Exeter, because it was the closest resort to the city and a day-excursion ticket cost only a shilling, which was cheaper than that to any of the other coastal watering places. So while from Exeter on Whit Monday 1890 3,000 went by rail to Exmouth for the day, only 400 went to Dawlish, 400 to Torquay and 1,500 to Teignmouth, where the Yeomanry Band was a special attraction.[26] Excursion trains ran only rarely from Exeter to Sidmouth or Seaton, for their shingle beaches were not as inviting to local trippers as the sandy beaches at resorts further west.

It was only in the final decade of the nineteenth century that excursion trains from far-off parts of the country began to arrive at the south Devon resorts in significant numbers. The introduction of more powerful locomotives and better-designed rolling stock improved the speed and comfort of rail travel and at last made long-distance day trips to the south Devon coast a practical proposition.[27]

The geographical origins of the long-distance rail excursions arriving at a particular resort were largely determined by the extent of the rail network of the company it happened to be served by. In the 1890s the resorts served by the GWR all started to receive excursion trains from London, the Midlands, South Wales and other distant parts of the GWR rail network.[28] On Whit Monday 1894, for example, it was reported that at Torquay 'cheap trains arrived from Wolverhampton and the Midlands, London, Swindon, Bristol, Taunton, Plymouth, Exeter and smaller places'.[29] The resorts served by the LSWR, on the other hand, received very few excursion trains from the Midlands and South Wales, because they would have had to follow a cross-country route over the railway networks of at least three different companies. The LSWR long-distance excursion trains to the south Devon coast originated chiefly from London and the majority of this traffic was directed into Seaton, simply because it happened to be the nearest south Devon resort to the capital.

It is clear that railways played a vital role in channelling both long-stay holiday-makers and excursionists into particular resorts. Their principal function, though, was to make it possible for increased numbers of people, drawn from a wider spectrum of society, to travel long distances to the south Devon coast. None of the south Devon resorts was created by the railway, but the scale and character of their development was in all cases strongly influenced by this new form of transport.

We have seen how the railway placed the south Devon resorts within reach for holiday-makers drawn from much wider social and geographical backgrounds, but we still need to examine the reasons why people living in distant parts of the country were prepared to undertake the long and expensive journey to the south Devon coast when there was a wide choice of seaside resorts located much closer to them.

It was still the promise of renewed health which lured many visitors. The south Devon watering places had well-established reputations as important health resorts. While a few leading medical authorities had questioned whether some of the resorts were suitable as winter retreats for invalids, it was still generally accepted that they all had salubrious climates which would benefit those who visited them. Chapter 9 will discuss the ways in which all the Devon resorts tried to give the impression that they radiated good health, but it will show that the threat of epidemic disease obliged them to make expensive public-health improvements to protect their reputations as health resorts.

The seemingly unspoilt coastal environment of the Devon coast also held a growing appeal for those obliged to spend most of their working lives in squalid factories or overcrowded offices in the expanding inland towns. Sadly, some of these natural assets were themselves being eroded as the trickle of holiday-makers became a steady stream and as holiday resorts steadily expanded and obliterated long stretches of fine coastal scenery.

The south Devon resorts also attracted those who were seeking havens of social decorum, where they could avoid the close presence of the lower ranks of society. Distance still insulated the south Devon coast from massive incursions of the working class. Elsewhere in England trains were transporting ever-increasing numbers of day-trippers to resorts close to their urban homes. Yet the railway also offered a means of escape to those who resented these intrusions by their social inferiors and who could afford to travel far beyond their reach, to the comparative seclusion of the south Devon resorts.

The south Devon resorts also appealed to those who wanted to avoid commercialized entertainment. In this period the mass of plebeian holiday-makers seemed to be happiest at crowded resorts dedicated to the pursuit of pleasure. There was, though, a discriminating minority who wished to avoid the noise and artificiality of man-made amusements and who were prepared to travel long distances to see superb natural scenery and to enjoy a wide range of outdoor recreations. Chapter 10 will show that the south Devon resorts set out to attract these people by boasting of their relative freedom from minstrel shows and vulgar catch-penny amusements.

A growing enthusiasm for beach holidays also had important consequences for the south Devon resorts. In earlier days the beach had only been visited for an early morning health dip and draught of salt water, or perhaps for an afternoon stroll. Fashions changed and by mid-Victorian times many visitors wanted to actually swim in the briny, and they became interested in a whole range of recreational pursuits associated with the sea and shore. With the growth of family holidays the beach became a natural playground. Children could make sand-castles, paddle or go shrimping, while parents could relax and quietly contemplate the ever-changing sea. Watering places with sandy beaches such as Dawlish, Teignmouth, Exmouth and especially the emerging resort of Paignton benefited from this shift of public interest. But the resorts of Sidmouth, Seaton and Budleigh Salterton lost trade because they had steep, shingle beaches. In the past these three resorts had relied on their genial climate to attract health-seeking visitors, but their beaches held little appeal for the middle-class families who formed an increasingly important part of the holiday market.

Having seen that the south Devon seaside resorts had some important natural and social advantages which made them attractive holiday destinations, we now need to consider why it was that, apart from Torquay and Paignton, they all failed to match the dynamic growth of many other English and Welsh seaside resorts.

In part it was due to their distance from London, which was still far and away the most important centre of holiday demand. Seaside resorts like Southend, Eastbourne, Bournemouth and Hastings were expanding rapidly because they were relatively easy to reach from the capital. But the cost of the long journey to the south Devon resorts still deterred Londoners with only modest means.

There were, though, some British seaside resorts which expanded rapidly despite being far away from the capital. Blackpool, Southport and Morecambe flourished because of the burgeoning demand from the prosperous industrial towns of Lancashire. Redcar and Whitley Bay sprang up to serve the towns of the Northumberland and Durham Coalfield. Weston-super-Mare's population soared because it was conveniently placed to serve Bristol. New Brighton was created to serve Liverpool, and Penarth to serve the needs of Cardiff. Cleethorpes and Skegness developed from tiny villages into important resorts because they were easily accessible by rail from the industrial areas of the East Midlands and Yorkshire. All these provincial watering places grew rapidly because they shared in the prosperity of nearby centres of trade and industry.[30]

The south Devon resorts, on the other hand, lacked the advantage of rapidly escalating demand from adjacent inland areas. The industry of inland Devon was steadily declining. The woollen trade, which had once provided most of the county's wealth, had dwindled so much that by 1881 only 1,200 people were still engaged in the industry. Numbers employed in other industries in inland Devon were extremely small when compared with the huge numbers working in the manufacturing towns of northern England.[31] Devon, the third largest among the English counties, had ranked fourth in terms of population until 1831, but had fallen to seventh by 1861 and then to ninth by 1881. The manufacturing and metropolitan counties were racing ahead; by 1901 Devon was less than half as densely peopled as England and Wales as a whole.[32] At a time when some provincial seaside resorts were expanding because of their proximity to inland areas of economic wealth and expanding populations, the south Devon resorts were handicapped because the region just inland from their coast was not as prosperous or as densely populated.

Another factor which eventually had an adverse effect on the fortunes of some south Devon seaside resorts was the continuing expansion of the railways; for while railways could channel holiday demand into a resort, they could also divert it elsewhere. The arrival of the railway had made it possible for more holiday-makers to visit the south Devon seaside resorts. Yet, as the railway extended its tentacles further westwards into Cornwall, it began to draw away some tourists who might otherwise have visited the south Devon coast. The railway opened up previously inaccessible parts of the Cornish coast and made it much easier to reach previously little-known resorts. Holiday-makers might, for example, decide to visit the winter resorts of Penzance and Falmouth, which could boast of even milder climates than the south Devon resorts; or the beach resort of Newquay, which had far larger stretches of sand than the south Devon watering places; or they could choose to stay at quaint fishing villages such as Looe and St Ives, with scenic attractions equal to any found on the south Devon coast. These emerging Cornish resorts began to take an increasing share of the English holiday market and captured some of the rail-borne tourist trade that otherwise might have been enjoyed by the south Devon resorts.

The population data contained in Tables 9 and 10 provide a barometer with which to gauge rises and falls in the fortunes of the principal south Devon seaside resorts. They show how different resorts responded to the arrival of the railway and to changes in the scale and nature of the demand for holidays.

The tables reveal the impact that the early arrival of the railway had on the development of Teignmouth and Dawlish. Between 1831 and 1841 the population of both resorts had actually fallen, due to the depressed state of their tourist industries. But in the following decade they both started to grow again, for they benefited from being the first Devon coastal resorts to be connected to the national rail network. Later in the century, when the benefits of rail transport were more evenly spread and they faced increased competition from other rail resorts, their growth

Table 9 Population of the Principal
South Devon Resorts, 1841–1901

Resort	1841	1851	1861	1871	1881	1891	1901	Incr. 1841–1901
Torquay	5982	11474	16419	21657	24767	25534	33625*	27643*
Exmouth	5119	5961	6049	6524	7224	9297*	10485	5366*
Teignmouth	4459	5149	6022	6751	7120	7006	7366	2907
Sidmouth	3309	3441	3354	3360	3475	3758	4201	892
Dawlish	3132	3546	4014	4241	4519	4925*	4681	1549*
Budleigh Salterton	2319	2447	2496	2897	2856	2636	2660	341
Seaton	765	766	809	1013	1221	1293	1325	560
Paignton	2501	2746	3090	3590	4613	6783	8385	5884

Table 10 Percentage Growth-Rates of the Population of the
Principal South Devon Resorts, 1841–1901

Resort	1841–51	1851–61	1861–71	1871–81	1881–91	1891–1901	1841–1901
Torquay	91.8	43.1	31.9	14.4	3.1	31.7*	462.1*
Exmouth	16.4	1.5	7.9	10.7	28.7*	12.8	104.8*
Teignmouth	15.5	17.0	12.1	5.5	−1.6	5.1	65.2
Sidmouth	4.0	−2.5	0.2	3.4	8.1	11.8	27.0
Dawlish	13.2	13.2	5.7	6.6	9.0*	−5.0	49.5*
Budleigh Salterton	5.5	2.0	16.1	−1.4	−7.7	0.9	14.7
Seaton	0.1	5.6	25.2	20.5	5.9	2.5	73.2
Paignton	9.8	12.5	16.2	28.5	47.0	23.6	235.3

Source for Tables 9 and 10: Decennial Census.
* *Boundary changes affect precise comparability of figures.*
Exmouth figures are for Littleham and Withycombe Raleigh parishes. Teignmouth figures are for East and West Teignmouth parishes. Budleigh Salterton figures are for East Budleigh parish. Torquay figures until 1891 are for Tormohun parish. In 1900 parts of St Marychurch and Cockington were added to Torquay thus increasing substantially the 1901 figure for Torquay.

rates slowed and for a time they even experienced a slight fall in population.

The tables show Torquay expanding rapidly to become a major watering place. Even when its older neighbours had been stagnating in the 1820s and 1830s, its increasing reputation as a winter health resort had enabled it to grow substantially. The arrival of the railway in 1848 gave a further boost to its tourist economy and encouraged vigorous new growth. By 1851 Torquay had a population of 11,474, which meant that it was the ninth largest seaside resort in England and Wales. By 1881 Torquay's population had reached 24,767, and it had improved its national ranking to eighth. In the later nineteenth century Torquay spilled out of the parish of Tormohun into the neighbouring parishes of St Marychurch and Cockington. In 1900 parts of the latter two parishes were included within Torquay, so that the 1901 census gave a much more accurate population figure for the resort. Table 9 shows Torquay beginning the new century with 33,625 inhabitants, which was more than three times the population of Exmouth, the next largest Devon watering place.

The tables also highlight the rise to importance of Paignton. This resort had been slow to develop a tourist industry, partly because in earlier times it had been difficult to reach, but also because its exposed position had rendered it unsuitable as a health resort in the period when a mild climate was considered all important. It grew in favour after it obtained a rail link in 1859, with its sandy beaches becoming an increasingly important advantage enabling it to obtain the custom of many middle-class families. The tables show its population surging from 3,090 in 1861 to 8,385 in 1901, by which time it had become the third largest resort on the south Devon coast.

The growth of Exmouth was also closely related to the expansion of the rail network in south Devon. Its population increased substantially in the 1840s, for in the early part of that decade its tourist trade benefited from the fact that it was the nearest south Devon resort to the Bristol and Exeter Railway. Exmouth grew very little in the 1850s because it lost trade to the resorts west of the Exe which had been connected to the rail network. The rate of growth quickened again after it obtained its own branch line in 1861. In the last two decades of the century Exmouth recorded large population increases, at a time when its beach was attracting many new visitors and it was also becoming increasingly important as a commuter resort for businessmen travelling by rail to work in Exeter each day.

Population growth at Sidmouth, Seaton and Budleigh Salterton was extremely limited because their holiday trade was adversely affected by the late arrival of the railway and also by the nature of their beaches. The tables show that Sidmouth hardly grew at all in the period between 1841 and 1871, and that its population actually fell between 1851 and 1861. After Sidmouth finally obtained a rail link in 1874, it experienced a period of moderate growth. By this time, however, holiday-makers wanted to spend more time on the beach and fine sands attracted more visitors than a mild climate, so the fact that Sidmouth's principal beach was steep and shingly proved to be a handicap which prevented major expansion. Seaton also suffered from the late arrival of the railway, only recording a net increase of 44 inhabitants between 1841 and 1861. Seaton was connected to the rail network in 1864, and a period of moderate growth ensued. At the end of the century this growth petered out, for the shingle beach had become a major drawback which deterred many potential visitors. Budleigh Salterton's population increased significantly in the 1860s, after access to it was improved by the opening of the railway from Exeter to nearby Exmouth. Yet in the years that followed its steep pebble beach began to prove a serious disadvantage. The resort experienced a decline in trade, with its population actually falling until it belatedly obtained its own rail link in 1897. These three resorts had all grown less than resorts further west which had benefited by obtaining rail links at an earlier date and also by having sandy beaches.

In considering the pattern of urban development at some of the principal south Devon resorts, we shall first consider the case of Torquay. This resort is a good example of the way in which the quality and pattern of building could be controlled by great landowners and their agents. The land in Torquay was mainly owned in large estates. This meant that usually roads were laid out and building plots planned in an orderly and attractive manner and that Torquay, for most of the period, escaped the piecemeal developments often found at English resorts where land holdings were fragmented.[33]

The Palk family owned the manor of Torre and their steward, William Kitson, exercised real power in Torquay, being elected as Chairman of the Improvement Commission, when this body was established in 1835, and then of the Local Board of Health which succeeded it in 1850.[34] William Kitson was primarily responsible for the superb planning of large parts of the resort, with its roads sweeping round the contours of the surrounding hills and the villas symmetrically arranged on the wooded slopes.[35] But the character of development was not determined solely by the landowner and his agent; the nature of the demand for houses was also critically important. At Torquay the developers had to meet the requirements of a substantial number of wealthy people, who were seeking large building plots offering both spectacular views and the opportunity to take full advantage of the sea air. The pattern of development also had to take full account of the physical constraints imposed by the hilly terrain. High planning standards were maintained and development carefully controlled while the Palks owned the estate, but heavy family debts forced its sale in the period between 1885 and 1894. So, at the very end of the century, Torquay at last began to experience the unfortunate consequences of piecemeal building by small-scale developers who had purchased individual freeholds.[36]

The Carys were landed gentry with an ancestral home on the site of the ancient Abbey of Torre. After the railway was extended further into Torquay in 1859, Robert Cary and his advisers realized that the opening of the new station would make the Abbey end of the town more popular, so they began to develop their land, building substantial houses suitable for the middle classes who were arriving in increasing numbers on the trains. They were not prepared, however, to see their private estate at Torre Abbey encroached upon, so they prevented any development west of Belgrave Road.[37] Robert Cary also began building 'better-class' properties at Babbacombe in the 1860s. Once again the advantages of development by a large landed proprietor were clearly to be seen. A magnificent promenade was constructed across Babbacombe Downs and fine detached houses and hotels were built along it. Inland from this the attractive Cary Park estate was laid out with a series of pleasant greens and broad avenues lined with large houses.[38]

The Mallock family of Cockington were considerable landowners at Torquay, but for many years they resisted the temptation to develop their land. In 1846 Charles Mallock succeeded to a secluded estate on the edge of a rapidly expanding resort. The opening of the railway to Torquay in 1848 was a strong incentive to development of the Chelston end of the estate, but he refused to allow any building there before 1865 and then only permitted the development of a limited number of sites.[39] When Richard Mallock inherited the estate in 1875, he decided to surrender much of Chelston and Livermead to the needs of the growing resort. The biggest expansion took place after 1882, when over 20 acres west of Torquay station were given over to building purposes. Yet Richard Mallock still prevented housing developments extending out to

Cockington Manor, because he had no wish to see his family home engulfed in urban sprawl.[40] In the later part of the century the Mallocks, like the Carys, had profited from the growth of Torquay, but both families had curtailed the expansion of the resort when it threatened to intrude on their privacy.

The case of Paignton illustrates the difficulties that could beset housing developments when a resort had no powerful landowners to oversee building schemes and use their influence to ensure that local government authorities were cooperative. In 1865 Mr W.R. Fletcher, a Birmingham businessman, purchased 60 acres of land adjoining the shore at Paignton with the intention of erecting villa residences.[41] He faced immense problems. At Torquay Mr Kitson, in his twin roles as steward of the Palk estate and Chairman of the Local Board, had been able to make sure that building developments were not hampered for want of public-health improvements. The situation at Paignton was quite different, for Mr Fletcher was regarded as an intruder and he encountered considerable opposition to his plans. In 1864 the recently established Local Board had constructed a sewer outfall to dispose of the resort's sewage, but this emptied onto the coastal marsh where Mr Fletcher hoped to build. For two years he unsuccessfully pressed the Local Board to stop polluting his land. Eventually in 1867 Mr Fletcher managed to persuade them that his development would greatly increase the rateable value of the resort, and at last they agreed to construct a new sewer outfall to carry Paignton's sewage out into the sea.[42]

Mr Fletcher also needed a reliable supply of pure water to supply his housing development. At Torquay the Local Board, under William Kitson's direction, had taken over responsibility for the supply of water in 1855, and in 1858 had brought in a good supply of water from a new reservoir on Dartmoor. Yet at Paignton the Local Board was reluctant to commit ratepayers to the expense of bringing piped water to the resort. Mr Fletcher himself had to take the initiative in establishing a private company, which built a small reservoir and in 1872 began supplying the resort with water.[43]

Mr Fletcher's problems were still not over, for the marshland he owned was frequently flooded during winter storms and the Local Board was not prepared to pay for sea defences. This difficulty was only overcome after Mr Fletcher's death, when in 1878 the trustees of his estate agreed to transfer a strip of sand dunes along the shore to the Local Board as a public open space, on condition that the Local Board built a sea wall to prevent flooding.[44]

As the obstacles to development were removed, so the resort began to expand towards the sea. In 1865 Paignton had still been a village grouped round the church and separated from the coast by marsh. By 1877 it was reported: 'A new town has sprung into existence on lands which were formerly only suitable for the growth of willows. The railway station is being gradually surrounded by streets and terraces possessing considerable architectural pretensions'.[45] The eventual success of the Fletcher housing development encouraged other small landowners to start similar schemes. Building works escalated on the marsh, until by 1885 it could be reported that there had 'sprung up, with almost mushroom-like rapidity, handsome villas and terraces of houses'.[46]

Development had started much later at Paignton than at Torquay; it was beset with far more physical difficulties and it lacked the advantage of local gentry to oversee the building schemes. There were also other major differences. Torquay was an exclusive winter resort where elevated sites with good views and warm, sheltered situations were sought after. Paignton, on the other hand, was a middle-class summer sea-bathing resort, so sites as close as possible to the beach were those most in demand and it was this that stimulated the expansion of Paignton across the coastal marsh towards the sea.

The case of Exmouth serves to show that genteel landowners did not always ensure that resort development was of a superior quality. At Exmouth almost all the land was concentrated in the hands of the Rolle family, who were old-established members of the Devon squirearchy, but they tended to grant leases without exercising proper control over the subsequent development. In 1850 the Board of Health inspector castigated the Rolle family for not having concerned themselves with the 'class or disposition of the houses erected' on their estate, with the result that properties were 'chiefly of the second and third class . . . built without much attention to regularity and uniformity of design'.[47] In order to meet the increased demand for accommodation after Exmouth obtained a rail link in 1861, some important new housing projects were begun. Many old courts and tenements were cleared in readiness for the building of Rolle Street. By 1875 this street was complete and houses were then erected on all the adjacent land.[48] In the absence of firm control from the Rolle estate, the local authority tried to regulate development at the end of the century, but met with only limited success. In 1895 the Exmouth Urban District Council found it was powerless to prevent the spread of houses across Wythycombe Marsh, despite the fact that this low-lying area was frequently flooded and was contaminated by sewage.[49]

Exmouth is an example of a resort where the landed proprietor failed to exercise proper control over development. Small developers were allowed to pursue their own interests without regard to the overall quality of the resort they were creating. The quality of development was generally inferior to that at Torquay, partly because there was less upper-class demand for housing at Exmouth, but chiefly because Exmouth lacked the large landowner's personal involvement in the planning process which so characterized the development of Torquay. By 1907 one travel writer was grieving over Exmouth's sprawling mass of mediocre housing, which he felt had clothed the resort 'with a sad shabbiness'.[50]

Sidmouth, in sharp contrast, is an example of a resort that was less blemished by Victorian brickwork, because it grew very little in the second half of the nineteenth century. There was little incentive to erect new houses. Property prices at Sidmouth depreciated by at least 25 per cent in the 1840s and 1850s, because the resort lacked a rail link.[51] The tardy arrival of the railway in 1874 provided some stimulus to development, but schemes were small in scale and the housing stock only increased by 219 between 1871 and 1901.[52] This was a matter of grave concern at the time. Yet in retrospect many consider this to have been a blessing. Sidmouth has retained many fine buildings from its Georgian and Regency heyday and these combine to give it an 'old-world' ambience which today is perhaps its principal attraction.

The emergence of several minor resorts on remote stretches of the south Devon coast was encouraged by a growing demand from those who sought to distance themselves from the artificial pleasures of larger watering places. Walton has stated that small resorts multiplied on remote English coastlines at the end of the nineteenth century, but that the new foundations were 'modest adaptations' of existing economies, 'with little new building beyond the occasional new hotel, villa or terrace of lodging houses'.[53] This was the experience at a number of coastal communities on the south-west coast of Devon.

Brixham was a fishing port which began to cater for a few visitors. Access had been improved by the opening of a branch line from the Torbay and Dartmouth Railway in 1868. It appealed only to a small number of holiday-makers who wanted to escape from the social and financial demands imposed by a stay in fashionable Torquay. It was frequented mainly by artists and others who could appreciate the scenery of Berry Head and find fascination in the activities of the fishing harbour.[54]

Some were less sold on its charms and regarded it as 'a sort of Devonshire Wapping with a Billingsgate smell'.[55] Tourism was still only a secondary function at the end of the century, when there were just four hotels and a number of lodging houses for the accommodation of visitors.[56]

Dartmouth was also late in developing a tourist trade. It suffered from the disadvantage of a rocky coastline which offered few facilities for bathers. Access by land to Dartmouth was difficult and this also deterred visitors. When the Torbay and Dartmouth Railway was proposed, the original intention was to build a line to cross the Dart and reach Dartmouth, but there was opposition from a local landowner. So when the railway opened in 1864, it terminated at Kingswear, from where steam ferries ran across the estuary to Dartmouth.[57] Proper access might have made Dartmouth fashionable, but, as it was, it catered for a small, select clientele attracted there by its river scenery and by the opportunities for boating and fishing. Even at the end of the century Dartmouth had only two hotels and Hope Moncrieff, the travel writer, described it as being 'less known as a health resort than as the station of the Britannia training ships'.[58]

Salcombe was an attractive coastal village blessed with exceptionally mild winters, so it might have been expected to develop as a health resort at an early date. In 1841 James Clark, a leading expert on health resorts, described it as 'perhaps the warmest place on the south-west coast', but he felt that there was a shortage of flat, sheltered ground, which meant that the genial climate was 'limited to too small a space to admit of Salcombe ever being the resort of invalids to any great extent'.[59] Difficult land access was another major obstacle to progress. Salcombe had to be reached by coach or steamer from Dartmouth or Plymouth, until in 1893 the GWR opened a branch line to Kingsbridge,[60] from where it was only a short steamer or carriage journey to the small seaport. Salcombe did not set out to attract sea-bathers; there were no bathing machines for the use of swimmers. It could, though, boast of fine scenery, excellent sea fishing and a sheltered harbour for yachtsmen. The biggest drawback was the lack of good tourist accommodation. A guide to Salcombe, published in 1884, frankly admitted that there was not a single hotel suitable for the 'quality' to stay at. Moncrieff wrote in 1899:

> The fashionable few have long loved this corner in secret. Now that Salcombe has lost its shipbuilding trade, it turns its serious attention to visitors and needs nothing but means of accommodation and access to make it a most popular watering place.[61]

He was to be proved right. After the advent of the car and motor coach had made travel there much easier, new hotels and boarding houses were opened and Salcombe began to attract many more visitors.

Some refugees from the crowds and commercial attractions of popular English resorts withdrew to really small and remote coastal settlements. Torcross was located to the south-west of Dartmouth, and had a few regular visitors who loved its peaceful atmosphere and its virtually deserted three-mile beach. It had just two hotels by the end of the century.[62] Hope lay to the west of Salcombe and again had a sandy beach. It was a small fishing village and an artist's paradise. Lodgings were only available at the Anchor Inn and at a few private houses.[63] Bantham, just to the north, was another seaside village with a good beach, but like Hope it had only one inn and was far from the nearest railhead.[64] These tiny coastal resorts were to remain havens of tranquillity until the motor car arrived.

The task of gathering information about visitors to the south Devon resorts is made a little easier for this period by the fact that local newspapers began to be published at many of the principal watering places and some of these included visitor lists on a more regular basis than had ever previously been the case. Only incomplete runs of visitor lists have survived, but these are sufficient to provide pointers as to the size of the visiting public, and also to changes in the holiday trade at different seasons and over long periods of time. The reader is reminded that figures obtained from these visitor lists should be treated with caution, for their accuracy depended on the policy of the editors towards visitors of lower social status and also the efficiency of the people who collected the returns, and these factors could vary over time and from resort to resort. Yet, if they are regarded solely as indicators of general trends, they can be a valuable source of information.

The visitor lists for Torquay make it clear that it was first and foremost a winter resort, though it did have a second season in summer. They show that in the winter months almost all of Torquay's houses were occupied by residents or let to visitors and the hotels were very busy, whereas each summer a significant proportion of the resort's accommodation was empty. In 1850, for example, the visitor lists for Torquay recorded 748 visitors for a week in early January as compared with 596 visitors for a week in early August.[65] The lists also indicate that Torquay's visiting public was growing. By 1890 the lists recorded 1,113 visitors for a week in early January and 650 visitors for a week in early August.[66]

The visitor lists for the other leading south Devon resorts show a very different picture. Summer was the busy season at these resorts, though they all retained a small but lucrative number of winter patrons. Teignmouth, for example, in 1850 had 341 visitors recorded for a week in early August as compared with 102 visitors listed for a week in early January.[67] Visitor numbers were relatively small and grew only gradually. In 1890 Teignmouth listed 584 visitors for a week in early August as compared with 164 for a week in early January.[68] Teignmouth was second only to Torquay in the numbers of visitors it listed, so it is significant that even in summer it consistently recorded far less visitors than Torquay which was principally a winter resort. Even allowing for some differences in the reliability of visitor lists at different resorts, it seems clear that the tourist trade of Torquay far surpassed that of any of the other south Devon resorts.

The numbers of staying visitors at the south Devon watering places seem extremely small when compared with those recorded at many of the popular seaside resorts located closer to the major centres of holiday demand. Ramsgate and Margate were both reported to be attracting up to 30,000 staying visitors at a time by the 1870s. Scarborough, Weston-super-Mare and Llandudno were each claiming a staying visitor population of 20,000 in the 1890s, while Southend claimed between 40,000 and 50,000 staying visitors at the height of the summer season in 1895. Blackpool was claiming as many as 70,000 staying visitors by 1884.[69] Such figures were often impressionistic rather than accurate, but even allowing for exaggeration at these resorts, and possible under-representation at the south Devon watering places, the visitor numbers at these other resorts were obviously far larger. The figures for the south Devon resorts even seem small when compared with the 3,409 visitors recorded on the visitor list at Ilfracombe at the peak of the summer season in 1900.[70]

How could the south Devon resorts flourish with only comparatively small numbers of visitors? The answer lies partly in the fact that they were catering for the quality and not the quantity trade. Their visitors were drawn mainly from the wealthier classes who spent freely while on holiday. Another reason for the success of the south Devon resorts was that their summer season was much longer than at many of the popular English seaside resorts and they also had the important advantage of a second season in winter. It should also be pointed out that the south Devon resorts did not derive all their income from visitors. They were also residential resorts enjoying the patronage of many wealthy people who had built second homes or retired there. Rich residents and long-stay visitors were present for most of the year and spent freely, so the south Devon resorts prospered even though their visitor numbers at the peak of the summer season were comparatively small.

Torquay was easily the most important resort in Devon. Its resort trade had many facets. It catered especially for invalids and enjoyed the reputation of being the leading English health resort for the treatment of lung diseases. So many consumptives went to live in Torquay that in 1872 the local Member of Parliament was referred to in the House of Commons as 'the representative of the pulmonary interest'.[71] Torquay also attracted the elderly. Many retired people bought houses in Torquay and spent their declining years there. It was also an extremely fashionable resort. By 1850 it had captured the major share of the aristocratic patronage formerly shared more evenly among the south Devon resorts. Some members of the nobility took up residence in the resort and many more arrived for an extended stay. These aristocrats formed the shining lights of a glittering company. Many pleasure seekers arrived each winter for an extended stay. The *Standard* in January 1872 described the winter season as 'brilliant', with dinners, dances, theatrical performances and concerts in abundance. The newspaper stated: 'The social atmosphere of Torquay is calculated to have a curative effect not much inferior to its physical atmosphere', and it suggested that this was its principal advantage over other invalid resorts such as Ventnor.[72] The resort also attracted summer visitors, who arrived seeking the simple pleasures of the seashore rather than the sophisticated amusements of a fashionable watering place. The secret of Torquay's success was that it appealed to so many different groups: it was at once a health and pleasure resort, a retreat for the elderly and a playground for the young.

Torquay was principally a winter resort, but the tourist interest was preoccupied with the need to promote the summer season. Torquay's main stock-in-trade had always been its mild winter climate and it was not generally considered to have many advantages as a summer sea-bathing resort. Dr Granville had not helped the development of a summer season when in 1841 he criticized Torquay's beaches and declared that the resort had 'no resources in the way of sea bathing'.[73] At this time the indoor bathing facilities were inadequate for a major resort. Hot and cold sea-water baths had been opened in 1817,[74] but the watering place had rapidly outgrown the capabilities of this tiny establishment. The resort eventually recognized that improved facilities were needed if more summer visitors were to be attracted. Subscriptions were collected and in 1857 new baths were opened which included a swimming pool as well as hot and cold baths.[75] The *Western Times* commented:

> Everything indicates the probability of Torquay becoming a summer as well as a winter watering place. Indeed now that the only requisite, a first-class bathing establishment is so satisfactorily supplied, we can conceive of no reason why it should not be so.[76]

The newspaper was mistaken. There was still one important factor making it difficult for Torquay to develop its summer season. The resort laboured under the drawback of being considered too hot in summer. The present generation of sun-worshippers would regard sunshine and high temperatures as distinct advantages, but Victorians prized pale rather than tanned skins and the medical profession advised invalids to avoid fierce sun and oppressive heat.

Torquay's tourist interest did its best to dispel this reputation for excessive heat. In 1859 one Torquay newspaper correspondent distorted the truth when he went so far as to claim that meteorological returns showed that 'as in winter it is the warmest, so in summer it is the coolest town in England'.[77] By 1885 the *Torquay Directory* was claiming: 'The old and utterly untrue impression that Torquay is very hot in summer has been exploded, and people find it is much cooler than almost any other place'.[78] This was wishful thinking. In fact Torquay's reputation for sweltering heat lingered on. As late as July 1900 the *Torquay Directory* reported: 'The fiction dies hard. It was only yesterday that we heard of a visitor from the Midlands being warned not to come to Torquay where he was certain to be roasted'.[79] Even at this late date, local guidebooks and newspapers were producing a mass of climatic statistics to try and convince potential visitors that summer temperatures in Torquay were actually lower than at many other English resorts. Times have certainly changed, for now the official guide presents the summer sunshine as one of the resort's chief assets.

Torquay remained principally a winter resort, but its summer trade did begin to increase in the later part of the century. For many years there had been a mass exodus in May, with many of the wealthy winter residents leaving to spend the summer elsewhere and the resort having its quiet season in the summer months. In the 1880s, however, the number of visitors in July and August began to increase. In June 1885 the *Torquay Directory* commented:

> With the advance of summer a considerable number of our villa residents have left town, some are indulging in the pleasures of a London season . . . others have hied away to the fjords of Norway, while many others have gone to Switzerland and Italy . . . The holiday folk will in a short time be streaming down in thousands to the western counties to spend a few weeks. It is a noteworthy fact that for several years past a considerable increase has been observed in the number of visitors who visit Torquay during the summer.[80]

At the very end of the century there were signs that some of Torquay's richest winter visitors were beginning to desert the resort and instead were wintering in Algiers, Luxor, Madeira, the Canaries and even in South Africa. Others were leaving for the Alps; a substantial part of Torquay's winter trade had been based on the reputation of its air as an aid in the treatment of tuberculosis, but fashions were changing and doctors were sending growing numbers of their wealthy consumptive patients to sanatoria in Switzerland instead of to Torquay. The 1901 edition of *Black's Guide to Torquay* accurately predicted that in the future the resort would have to rely increasingly on middle-class summer visitors and less on invalids and wealthy gentry who had hitherto been its main patrons.[81]

None of the other leading south Devon seaside resorts catered for either invalids or fashionable members of society on anything approaching the scale of Torquay, but all were quiet, decorous watering places entertaining comparatively small numbers of holiday-makers, and also providing retirement homes for a select group of affluent people who retired there after successful careers in business, the professions or the colonial civil service. While it was true that Exmouth, Teignmouth, Sidmouth and Dawlish had long ceased to play host to the cream of the English aristocracy, their visitor lists included the names of high-ranking army and naval officers, and leading members of the clergy, indicating that they were still being patronized by a 'good class' of visitor.

The south Devon seaside resorts all maintained a select, sedate character throughout the period up to 1900. Teignmouth, for example, was considered to be a particularly refined watering place. In 1899 a national guidebook described it as a 'highly respectable resort rather than a popular one', attracting 'many Anglo-Indians and other elements of good society'.[82] The same guide considered Exmouth to be another genteel

Plate 1. Different Lifestyles at Sidmouth, c.1830.

Plate 2. The Fashionable Health Resort of Torquay, c.1835.

Plate 3. The Sea-Water Baths at Dawlish, c.1830.

Plate 4.   The Ladies' Bathing Beach at Ilfracombe, c.1840.

Plate 5. Train Approaching Teignmouth, c.1850.

THE GRAPHIC, *March 5, 1870*

Plate 6. Winter Promenade at Torquay, 1870.

Plate 7. Tennis Outside the Woolacombe Bay Hotel, c.1894.

Plate 8. Swimming Gala at Ilfracombe Hotel Baths in August 1887.

resort with 'social advantages that would be an advantage to retired officers, Anglo-Indians and the like'.[83] Sidmouth had a smaller but even more select clientele who valued its tranquil atmosphere. Dawlish was also relatively quiet and staid. In 1899 a Ward Lock guide described it as having 'all the attractions of a small seaside holiday resort, without any of the disturbing influences or jarring noises that often mar the enjoyment of those who frequent the larger seaside towns'.[84] Paignton was yet another respectable and socially-aloof resort, as an article published in the *Paignton Observer* in 1885 made clear: 'Here you will find no rollicking horseplay or boisterous fun such as you may have been accustomed to on Ramsgate Pier or Margate Sands . . . Paignton prefers to be dignified and discreet'.[85] It is clear that the leading south Devon coastal resorts still aspired to gentility and were determined to defend their high social tone.

The influx of middle-class visitors gathered pace in the last two decades of the nineteenth century, but they were just as keen as their social superiors to maintain a due sense of decorum. Yet they did depart from the established pattern of holiday-making in two important ways. Firstly, the majority only stayed for one or two weeks, whereas upper-class visitors normally took much longer holidays. Secondly, many families were numbered among the growing number of middle-class arrivals. There had always been some families holidaying on the south Devon coast, but many of the established upper-class visitors had been elderly or infirm, whereas a high proportion of the new middle-class visitors were younger couples with children. These middle-class families usually visited the seaside in the summer because they wanted open-air holidays with most of their activities centred on the beach. So in summer the south Devon seaside resorts played host to a widening section of society, but in winter they still had a predominantly upper-class clientele.

In this period hardly any members of the working classes could afford the time and money to actually stay at the south Devon seaside resorts for a holiday, but the introduction of cheap rail excursion fares did allow some to make brief visits on day trips. We have already seen that distance from the major centres of urban demand protected the south Devon resorts from massive influxes of day-trippers. For most of the period working-class excursionists came mainly from the inland towns of Devon and were usually numbered in hundreds rather than thousands. It was only in the 1890s that some of the south Devon resorts also had to cope with the periodic arrival of rail excursions from far-off centres of population. Even then working-class day-trippers normally arrived in only moderate numbers and stayed for only a few hours. Some trippers from local towns were usually present on Saturday afternoons enjoying a half-holiday from their places of employment. More excursionists went there on Sundays, and more again arrived on bank holidays. Yet, even on a fine bank holiday in the 1890s, resorts like Dawlish and Teignmouth usually entertained only some 2,000 excursionists, while Torquay might have 3,000 present and Exmouth 4,000.[86] The largest number of excursionists recorded at a south Devon resort in the nineteenth century was 6,000 at Exmouth on August Bank Holiday 1897.[87]

These incursions were small in scale compared with the huge numbers flooding into popular English seaside resorts within easy reach from large urban areas. It has been estimated that at Margate in 1879 between 16,000 and 24,000 trippers were arriving by train every Sunday during the summer season.[88] Blackpool was entertaining up to 40,000 excursionists at a time by 1884.[89] Even the small adjoining seaside resorts of Redcar and Coatham were together playing host to as many as 20,000 trippers from the Teesside industrial area on bank holidays in the 1890s.[90] Such large scale invasions inevitably disrupted normal resort life and drove away some of the more genteel patrons.

The relatively small numbers of excursionists arriving at the south Devon seaside resorts posed much less of a threat to the established clientele and their brief visits usually passed off without any serious problems. Only when the trippers went bathing did their behaviour occasionally give rise to complaint. This problem first arose at Dawlish in the late 1850s when there were loud protests about the conduct of 'Exeter vagabonds' arriving on 'bathing trains'.[91]

It was Dr Miller, a leading Exeter medical practitioner, who was responsible for Dawlish being invaded by working-class bathers. He argued that the health of the poor of his city would benefit just as much from sea-bathing as did that of the rich, and he urged the South Devon Railway to make it possible for Exeter workmen to take their families for a dip in the sea. In August 1858 the Company reluctantly agreed to provide a six-penny return fare from Exeter to Dawlish, but took precautions to avoid offending the wealthy residents and visitors at the resort. The Company stipulated that the new cheap fare would only be available to those who travelled on the first train down and caught the first train back. This allowed the bathers a maximum of only one hour and ten minutes in Dawlish![92]

At first the sanctity of the Sabbath was preserved by not permitting the 'six-penny dip' concession on Sunday trains, but this irksome restriction was withdrawn after Dr Miller protested that that was the only day when most working men were free to visit the seaside.[93] These cheap fares proved very popular with the poorer inhabitants of Exeter and by 1859 as many as 350 were travelling on the Sunday morning train to Dawlish to bathe in the sea.[94] The established resort users were horrified to see some of these trippers strip off on the beach and rush naked into the sea:

> Through the liberality of the South Devon Railway Company the town was visited on Sundays by 300 or 400 bathers from Exeter; and they were conveyed down and back for sixpence . . . there were loud complaints of the very indecent conduct of the bathers by that train.[95]

Here then was an example of the way in which working-class excursions could be considered as 'improving' at the point of departure, but equally could be regarded as a threat by the resort which had to receive them.

Later in the century the normally quiet beaches at many other south Devon resorts were invaded at weekends and bank holidays by working-class bathers, some of whom entered the sea without regard to the bathing conventions of the day. On holiday at Seaton in 1871, the Revd Francis Kilvert saw a crowd of rail-trippers swarm onto the beach and stared in amazement at 'girls, with shoes, stockings and drawers off, wading in the tide, holding up their clothes nearly to their waists and naked from the waist down'.[96] On a Saturday afternoon in August 1887 one visitor to Torquay was shocked when 'a number of working men . . . whisked off their clothes and ran like savages to the sea'.[97]

Such behaviour by working-class bathers usually arose because these people lacked the money to hire swimming costumes and bathing machines, and were unaware of the regulations relating to the segregation of the sexes while bathing, rather than from any deliberate attempt to flout convention at the resorts. Nor was it only members of the working classes who inflamed debate over nude bathing. In Chapter 10 the bathing issue will receive further consideration and it will be shown that up until 1870, and even beyond that date, many 'better-class' male visitors obstinately persisted in swimming in the buff.

Sheer numbers of trippers, rather than wilful misconduct, occasionally caused problems at bank holidays for residents and long-stay visitors. William Miller described how on August Bank Holiday 1887 'the ordinary visitors at Teignmouth were nearly banished by the crowd which surged upon the promenade, the machines, the river; and ate and smoked upon the common and danced upon the pier'.[98] There were, though, only two bank holidays during the main summer season and at other times the number of day-trippers was generally far smaller. Even at bank holidays there was hardly ever any evidence at the south Devon resorts of the serious rowdyism, drunkenness, foul language and other forms of misbehaviour which from time to time occurred at Ilfracombe when parties of Welsh miners and metal workers disembarked from the excursion steamers.

Why were most of the trippers arriving at the south Devon resorts respectable, law-abiding people? The principal reason was that most came from closely-knit, long-established Devon towns and villages, so neighbours and work-mates knew each other well and could regulate each other's behaviour. The rough and unruly trippers who plagued so many British resorts in the later part of the century were usually unskilled young men emerging from the anonymity of London or the harsh environment of a heavily-industrialized area, and they preferred to take a short trip to the nearest seaside town rather than to make the long journey to the south Devon coast. When long-distance rail excursions began to increase at the end of the century, only artisans, clerical workers and other 'respectable' elements of the working population normally had the means and inclination to find the fare for the long day trip to Devon.

There was another reason why the south Devon resorts were usually untroubled by the hooligan element. Chapter 10 will show that the Devon watering places carefully avoided providing those types of commercial entertainment which might attract disorderly trippers. At Teignmouth, for example, it was admitted in 1888 that the town had its 'fair share of excursionists', but it was pointed out that they were those who sought 'quiet amusements' and that the resort was 'preferred by those who wished to spend a pleasant holiday without encountering any of the rough element so often met with on bank holidays in other places'.[99] So the south Devon resorts escaped most of the conflict between working-class trippers and established resort users that blighted so many other British coastal watering places in late-Victorian times.[100]

As the nineteenth century drew to a close it was becoming increasingly clear that the south Devon watering places, Torquay excepted, were failing to fulfil their early promise of greatness. Distance from the major sources of holiday demand was still an important limiting factor, for even though the arrival of the railway had made them more easily accessible, the cost of travel still filtered out many potential visitors and this meant that they could not keep pace with the explosive growth of many seaside resorts located close to major inland centres of population. Still more important as a factor limiting growth was the change that took place in the holiday requirements of English holiday-makers. The south Devon resorts had developed much of their early trade on the strength of their reputations as health resorts, but in the later nineteenth century the importance attached to seaside health cures gradually declined, so fewer people felt a pressing need to make the long journey to Devon. The mass of plebeian holiday-makers seemed happiest at crowded seaside resorts nearer to their urban homes, where they could enjoy commercial entertainment. Only a discriminating minority were attracted by the fine coastal scenery, select company and tranquil atmosphere of the south Devon resorts.

Eight

Recession and Revival: North Devon Resorts, 1844–1900

'Visitors are too few for our benefit,' complained the *North Devon Journal* in 1851; 'a railway to the north of Devon is our only hope of progress and of restoring the balance between the south and the north.'[1] The period of prosperity enjoyed by the north Devon seaside resorts had come to an abrupt end in 1846, when the railway reached the south Devon coast. Those south Devon seaside resorts with the good fortune to obtain an early rail link had captured a substantial part of north Devon's tourist trade, for travel to them had become much faster than to the north Devon watering places and it did not involve the discomforts of a long coach ride.

North Devon was still a sparsely populated region with small towns incapable of generating any substantial demand for seaside holidays, so the future prosperity of the coastal resorts depended on the provision of better land and sea links with areas of greater economic wealth. Just across the Bristol Channel were the rapidly expanding towns of the South Wales coalfield. Up the Channel was Bristol, where both trade and population would double in the second half of the century.[2] Further afield were the Midlands and London with a huge potential demand waiting to be tapped. The history of the north Devon resorts in this period is in large part the story of a struggle to obtain improved transport facilities, so that they could compete more successfully for visitors from those areas of burgeoning prosperity.

Lacking a rail link, the north Devon seaside resorts in the late 1840s became increasingly dependent on the steamers to bring in visitors. Frustration grew as these services often proved unreliable. There were frequent complaints that the steam packets only operated for a short summer season, and fears that they might not return again for the following year. In mid-September 1851, for example, there was a barrage of protests when the Bristol Steam Navigation Company suddenly discontinued its service from Bristol to Ilfracombe and brought the resort's season to a premature end. The *North Devon Journal* thundered:

> They put on their steamers to this place and take them off again without in the least consulting the welfare of the town, or indeed of their own passengers. The town is wholly emptied of its visitors through the mere caprice of a capricious company.[3]

Ilfracombe responded by establishing a committee to sell shares in the North Devon Railway, a company which proposed bringing a railway to the region. Shares worth £848 were purchased in the resort in a single week.[4] Exasperated by the failings of their steamer services, the north Devon resorts campaigned hard for a railway, in the hope that a more reliable, all-the-year-round form of transport would bring more visitors in the summer, lengthen the season and provide the opportunity to develop a winter trade.

Delay followed delay as railway politics obstructed the construction of a line to north Devon. As early as 1845 a local company had obtained an Act to build a railway from Exeter to Crediton, from where an extension to Barnstaple was proposed,[5] but rivalry between the major companies had delayed its construction. This was a battle of the gauges, with the Bristol and Exeter Railway and the GWR wanting a broad-gauge line, and the LSWR, which was planning to extend into Devon, fighting for a standard-gauge line. After a lengthy dispute the Exeter and Crediton Railway was constructed as a standard-gauge line and was completed in February 1848, but years of legal wrangling followed while the line remained closed and the tracks rusted. Eventually the railway was converted to broad gauge and was opened in May 1851.[6] Three more years were to pass before the North Devon Railway finally completed its extension of the line from Crediton to Barnstaple.[7]

The delay in the arrival of the railway had serious consequences for the tourist trade. The resorts grumbled about poor, short seasons and looked with envious eyes at the growing number of tourists travelling by train to the south Devon coast. Ilfracombe lamented: 'The extension of the rail to south Devon has given this town a mortal stab, it has felt its heart's blood oozing out . . . where the rail goes, there go the lodgers'.[8] Lynton and Lynmouth also complained bitterly about the scarcity of visitors, but predicted: 'As the railway approaches Barnstaple all obstacles

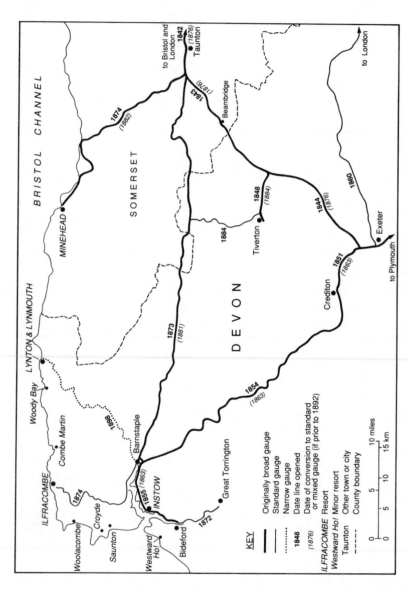

Map 5. Railways Serving the North Devon Resorts in 1900.
The North Devon resorts could only be reached by long, inconvenient branch lines.

to an early season will be removed, and then we hope to participate in the benefits which railway transit confers on our neighbours in the south'.[9] The railway from Exeter to Barnstaple finally opened on 12 July 1854, and at once began to bring new visitors to the region. Horse-coaches met the trains at Barnstaple Station and took the passengers on to the seaside resorts. At Ilfracombe it was reported: 'Within a week of the railway being open, this town was so full that there was not a lodging to be had'.[10] Soon it was claimed that Ilfracombe 'had never known so many visitors' and that 'parties waiting for lodgings . . . were obliged to sleep in attics or be content with half beds'.[11] In the past most tourists had departed with the last steamer of the season, but now they could stay on. In October and November of that year the local press rejoiced that at Ilfracombe an 'unprecedented number' of visitors still remained, 'testifying to the great benefit of the railway'.[12]

Yet the railway brought with it no cast-iron guarantees of future prosperity. On 29 October 1855 Instow became the first north Devon resort to be reached by passenger trains, for on that day the Bideford Extension Railway was opened from the North Devon Railway at Barnstaple to Instow and Bideford.[13] But it is doubtful if this line significantly increased the number of holiday-makers visiting Instow. To attract visitors from distant parts of the country, a seaside resort needed to have either an extremely mild climate, or large sandy beaches, or spectacular scenery, or a wide range of commercial amusements. Instow had none of these advantages, so it still catered mainly for a local rather than a national demand, and most of the arrivals by train were those who would previously have made the short journey by coach from one of the nearby towns. Indeed it can be argued that in some ways the railway actually limited the future development of Instow, for it enabled some of the resort's former patrons from Barnstaple and Bideford to travel to better-endowed resorts elsewhere on the Devon coast or even further afield.

The opening of the Bideford Extension Railway did provide the stimulus for an attempt to create the entirely new seaside resort of Westward Ho!. It was in 1863 that a business syndicate decided to begin constructing a watering place on the shores of Bideford Bay, recognizing that this previously isolated stretch of coast had potential for development now that it was only three miles from the railhead at Bideford.[14] Yet this was another resort where high expectations were never fulfilled, because the resort's natural attractions were insufficient to draw in large numbers of rail-borne visitors from distant parts of the country. In 1870 proposals were made for a railway actually connecting Westward Ho! with Bideford. In August the ceremony of 'cutting the first sod' was performed, but not long afterwards the scheme was abandoned when the contractor went bankrupt.[15] It was not until 1901 that Westward Ho! was actually linked to Bideford by rail and even then the line was not a financial success.[16]

Ilfracombe was determined to obtain its own rail link. Once the euphoria over the opening of the North Devon Railway had died down, the town's tourist interest began to point out that, while access to Barnstaple had been greatly improved, their resort was still over 12 miles from the railhead. The campaign for a direct rail link gathered momentum. In 1862 a group of local businessmen approached the LSWR for support in building a railway from Barnstaple to Ilfracombe.[17] The LSWR gave the scheme its enthusiastic backing. This company had opened its railway from Waterloo to Exeter in 1860 and had gained control of the North Devon Railway earlier in 1862, so it was well aware that an extension to this line must bring it extra business. In April 1863 the local promoters put their Ilfracombe Railway Bill before Parliament.[18] Hopes were dashed when the House of Lords rejected it on the grounds that the route chosen was not the best one between Barnstaple and Ilfracombe. Riots erupted on the streets of Ilfracombe and the disappointed promoters incited a mob of some 800 people to attack the houses of two opponents of the Bill.[19]

Another battle of the gauges then obstructed all attempts to build a railway to Ilfracombe. In 1863 the LSWR added an extra rail to the North Devon Railway, making it a mixed-gauge line on which its standard-gauge trains could operate, so it was anxious to ensure that any extension from Barnstaple to Ilfracombe should be standard gauge. Yet in the same year a broad-gauge railway was proposed from Taunton via Barnstaple to Ilfracombe. This Devon and Somerset Railway had the backing of the Bristol and Exeter Railway, and the GWR, but it was strongly opposed by the LSWR. In 1864 the Devon and Somerset Railway obtained an Act to build its broad-gauge line from Taunton to Barnstaple, but the proposed extension to Ilfracombe was thrown out by the House of Lords.[20] Long years of bitter dispute followed. The LSWR eventually won the day, for in 1870 the local company it supported obtained an Act to build a standard-gauge line to Ilfracombe.[21] The Barnstaple and Ilfracombe Railway opened on 20 July 1874. Banners proclaimed 'Waterloo to Ilfracombe' and the townspeople rejoiced.[22] They forgot for the moment that their new railway was at the end of a long and inconvenient branch line from Exeter.

There was, however, by this time an alternative railway route to north

Devon. The Devon and Somerset Railway had been opened from Taunton to Barnstaple in November 1873.[23] This broad-gauge line provided a more direct route to north Devon for passengers from Bristol, the Midlands and London. Unfortunately, for many years rivalry between the rail companies prevented trains on this line running through to Ilfracombe. The LSWR wanted to monopolize the Ilfracombe traffic, so it refused to allow the Barnstaple to Ilfracombe line to be made into a mixed gauge, which would have allowed broad-gauge trains to run over it. The Devon and Somerset Railway was equally determined to compete for a share of the passenger traffic to Ilfracombe, and so, shortly before the opening of the Barnstaple and Ilfracombe Railway, it began operating its own fast horse-coach service to Ilfracombe.[24]

So Ilfracombe, after being neglected for so many years, in 1874 suddenly found itself being served by two competing railway companies. The fastest LSWR train took 7 hours 18 minutes to complete the journey from Waterloo via Exeter and Barnstaple, while the journey by GWR from Paddington via Taunton to Barnstaple and then by horse-coach took only 18 minutes longer.[25] The new railway services had a sudden and decisive impact on the tourist trade at Ilfracombe. The summer of 1874 was a bumper one. All available accommodation was packed, and after several indifferent seasons the lodging-house keepers began to demand extortionate prices for their rooms.[26]

The arrival of the railway at Ilfracombe in 1874 further emphasized Lynton and Lynmouth's continuing isolation. The twin villages were by this time further from the railway than almost any other coastal resort in England. This isolation was undoubtedly a major obstacle to the expansion of their tourist trade. It did mean, though, that they attracted some discriminating visitors who were seeking a secluded haven well out of the reach of the railway.

Many visitors still arrived at the north Devon resorts by sea, even after the railway reached Barnstaple in 1854. There were undoubtedly certain advantages in travelling by steamer. It was, for instance, a much cheaper means of transport, with fares from Bristol to Ilfracombe in 1855 being only 8s. in the saloon or 5s. on deck, as compared with 18s. for a second-class rail ticket from Bristol to Barnstaple. It could also be quicker to travel to north Devon by sea. In 1855 the passage from Bristol to Ilfracombe was usually accomplished in seven hours, and times of as little as 4½ hours were recorded when the wind and tide were favourable. This compared quite well with the journey time by land, for it took 5 hours and 20 minutes to travel by rail from Bristol to Barnstaple and then at least two more hours to complete the journey to Ilfracombe by coach.[27]

Yet sea travel also had its drawbacks. Sea-sickness was a particular problem in bad weather.[28] Landing was difficult in rough seas, for harbour facilities were inadequate at Ilfracombe and almost non-existent at Lynmouth. The Bristol Channel also had an exceptionally high tidal range, which meant that for many years the timing of services had to vary each day according to the time of high tide.

Considerable efforts were made to improve landing facilities at some of the north Devon resorts. At Ilfracombe in 1873 a deep-water landing pier was built out from the harbour so that large steamers could land at any stage of the tide.[29] At the new resort of Westward Ho! work began in 1870 to build a promenade pier which could also be used to land passengers from steamers. Hopes were expressed that this pier would enable the resort to become 'easy of access to visitors from all parts of the country'.[30] Storm damage delayed its completion, but in July 1873 it was finally opened.[31] This pier was never a success. The flimsy structure was exposed to the full force of the Atlantic gales and they soon rendered it unsafe. It was finally demolished in 1880.[32] At Lynmouth, where steamers had to anchor in the bay while passengers were brought ashore in small boats, Parliamentary sanction for a landing pier was obtained on no less than five occasions. Yet, despite public meetings, petitions and newspaper campaigns organized by the business community, Lynton and Lynmouth never acquired good landing facilities, partly because of doubts about the financial viability of a pier, but largely because of opposition from some of the wealthy residents, who feared that a pier would enable large numbers of day-trippers to be landed.[33]

The importance attached to landing facilities was again shown at Woody Bay, just along the coast from Lynmouth. When at the very end of the century a speculator attempted to create another new resort at this remote bay, one of his first steps was to build a landing pier. The pier opened in 1897, alarming business interests at Lynton and Lynmouth, who feared that steamers would call at the new pier in preference to landing passengers by boat at Lynmouth.[34] Their fears were soon dispelled, for this pier had been built with more attention to economy than to durability and was soon damaged by a storm. It had to be demolished in 1902.

Sea travel to the north Devon resorts was significantly improved by developments further up the Bristol Channel. In 1867 a railway was constructed from Bristol to a projected new outport at Portishead. A pier was built at Portishead in the following year, and a low-water extension was added by the spring of 1870. These improvements rendered the steamer departures from Portishead virtually independent of the tides, so that departures could be at a fixed hour instead of having to be timed to leave at high water. They also speeded up the journey from Bristol to north Devon by cutting out the long, slow steamer journey down the Avon.[35] Most important of all, they made the north Devon resorts easier to reach from the Midlands, London and distant parts of the country. The service from Portishead to north Devon began in August 1869,[36] and by July 1870 the Cardiff and Portishead Steamship Company were advertising that their steamer *Ely* would leave Portishead at 1.30 p.m. each day, after the arrival of trains from Bristol, the Midlands and London, and would call off Lynmouth on its way to Ilfracombe. The fares were remarkably cheap: only 3*s.* single and 4*s.* 6*d.* return for the best cabin.[37]

In the early 1870s the principal north Devon resorts were still served by a number of steam packet services. Ilfracombe, for example, in 1873 was visited not only by a passenger steamer from Portishead every day except Sunday, but also by the *Bride* once a week *en route* between Bristol and Hayle, by the *Prince of Wales* one a week *en route* between Bristol and Padstow, and by the *Velindra* plying three times a week between Swansea and Ilfracombe.[38]

After the arrival of the railway at Ilfracombe in 1874, the packet steamer services to north Devon declined in number and importance. The service between Portishead and the north Devon coast, however, remained an important means of access. The cheap steamer fares encouraged many visitors from the Midlands and London to travel by train to Portishead and then to complete the journey to Lynmouth and Ilfracombe by sea.[39]

It was a railway company that finally put an end to the packet steamer service from Portishead. In 1885 the GWR took over the Portishead steamers, after buying up the Bristol and Portishead Railway, and at the end of the 1886 season it announced that it was terminating its steamer service to north Devon. In commercial terms the GWR's decision was easy to understand, for it had just leased the Devon and Somerset Railway, and it was negotiating to obtain the right to run trains through to Ilfracombe on the Barnstaple and Ilfracombe Railway, so it wanted to divert travellers to Ilfracombe from its steamers onto its trains.[40] It was, though, a grave blow for the north Devon holiday industry. In Ilfracombe the news that the Portishead steamer service was closing was greeted with dismay.[41] At Lynton and Lynmouth the news was received with stunned disbelief. As this resort still lacked a railway it had relied on this steamer service to bring in a substantial proportion of its holiday-makers. The

1887 season was a disaster in Lynton and Lynmouth, with hoteliers and lodging-house keepers complaining that they had been deserted by many of their regular visitors from Bristol and London.[42]

Yet sea travel to north Devon did not come to an end with the passing away of the Portishead steamers, for their place was taken by a growing number of pleasure steamers. A few long-stay visitors took advantage of these excursion steamers which, when operating in the summer months, still provided a cheap and convenient means of access from Bristol and South Wales. By far the most important function of these specialized vessels, however, was to bring in large numbers of trippers for brief visits. So the rapid development of the pleasure steamer trade was to have major implications for both the economy and the social tone of the leading north Devon resorts.

Day trips by steamer to the north Devon resorts were not a new innovation. As early as July 1843 the *Lord Beresford* had transported over 400 Welsh teetotallers from Swansea to Ilfracombe for a day visit.[43] Sea excursions from Wales had soon grown in popularity. Packet steamers, cargo vessels and even tugs had been released from their normal duties to ferry parties of excursionists across the Bristol Channel to both Ilfracombe and Lynmouth. The north Devon coast was often visible from South Wales and the return journey could easily be accomplished in a day.

Making the round trip from Bristol in a single day was a much more difficult proposition. As long ago as Easter Monday 1854 the fast paddle-steamer *Juno* had arrived at Ilfracombe with the first party of day excursionists ever to arrive from that city. Yet this trip had been fraught with difficulties, with delays caused by the tide and rough seas. Some of the 384 trippers had staggered ashore suffering from sea-sickness; all had faced the prospect of the long return journey after only three hours in Ilfracombe.[44] As late as the early 1870s it had still taken an average six hours for steamers to complete the 70-mile passage from Bristol to Ilfracombe. So only rarely had the north Devon coast been the destination for day trips from that port.

It was the introduction of a new breed of purpose-built pleasure steamers in the period after 1880 which transformed the excursion trade. Some of these fast, commodious passenger vessels operated from South Wales ports, often in conjunction with local railway companies. Others began running from Bristol, for these powerful steamers could often reach Lynmouth and Ilfracombe from that port in under four hours, which at last made a day excursion a practical proposition. For a time the Cardiff company of Edwards and Robertson led the field, but in 1888 the Campbell family moved the headquarters of their steamer business south from the Clyde to Bristol and began to compete vigorously for this lucrative tripper trade. The rivalry was intense with steamers not infrequently racing down the Channel. In the early 1890s P. and A. Campbell added a whole series of fine, new vessels to their fleet. Edwards and Robertson also spent heavily on new vessels, but their steamers were generally inferior in speed and quality and the company was forced out of business at the end of the 1895 season. From then on P. and A. Campbell dominated the excursion-steamer business and for many years their vessels were familiar sights at the north Devon resorts.[45]

Ilfracombe was the resort which attracted most of these steamer excursions. Some vessels called off Lynmouth to allow relatively small numbers of trippers to be landed by boat, but most of the steamers were bound for Ilfracombe, where the deep-water landing pier enabled large numbers of passengers to be disembarked. Sometimes at Ilfracombe there were as many as seven passenger steamers in the harbour at once. On August Bank Holiday 1890, for example, the *Waverley* and *Lady Gwendoline* arrived from Bristol, the *Velindra* and *Rio Formosa* from Swansea, the *Challenger* and *Privateer* from Neath and the *Bonnie Doone* from Cardiff.[46]

In 1894 the tradespeople of Lynton and Lynmouth renewed their demands for a landing pier, so that they could obtain a bigger share of this lucrative excursion trade,[47] and it was this threat of an influx of trippers that seems to have prompted a group of local gentry, to offer instead to give the resort a much-needed rail link. These wealthy residents, led by George Newnes, the publisher, formed a company which sought Parliamentary sanction for a narrow-gauge railway to connect Lynton with the LSWR line at Barnstaple.[48] Almost at once a rival syndicate led by Lord Fortescue, a north Devon landowner, produced proposals for a standard-gauge line from Lynton to the Devon and Somerset Railway at Filleigh.[49] This scheme was backed by the GWR, spurred into action by the fear that the LSWR might gain an advantage. It would have provided a much shorter route from London and the Midlands, and through trains could have operated on it, as there would have been no break of gauge. But the people of Lynton and Lynmouth decided to support the plan put forward by George Newnes' group, because they thought that it was more likely to be followed through to a successful conclusion. As a result it was the Lynton and Barnstaple Railway that was given the Royal Assent in June 1895.[50] The line finally opened on 11 May 1898 amidst general rejoicing.[51] Lynton and Lynmouth at last had a railway, but only a narrow-gauge line at the end of a long, roundabout route from Exeter.

While the north Devon seaside resorts had to entertain a considerable number of steamer excursions, rail excursions to them were far fewer than to the south Devon coastal watering places. In part this was due to the late arrival of the railway, for some of the south Devon resorts had begun to receive excursion trains long before Ilfracombe and Lynton obtained rail links. It was also due to the fact that when railways were eventually built to the north Devon coast they were extremely long branch lines. This meant that the north Devon resorts attracted far less day-trippers from Exeter than most of the more easily accessible watering places on the south Devon coast. At the end of the century, when some of the south Devon resorts became the destination for rail excursions from far-off parts of the country, the north Devon resorts received very few long-distance excursion trains because it took at least two hours longer to reach them.

We have seen that transport improvements gradually made the north Devon coast more easily accessible, but an important question still needs to be asked. Why was it that in the later nineteenth century a growing number of holiday-makers chose to make the long and expensive journey to north Devon, when there were many holiday destinations that were much easier to reach from their urban homes?

The answer is to be found principally in the pages of several important Victorian books, for in this period a number of authors sang the praises of Devon's relatively unspoilt natural environment. The spectacular scenery had for many years attracted a few discerning tourists to this remote coast, but in the second half of the nineteenth century the region was fortunate enough to be made the setting for two major Victorian novels which invested the landscapes with a new enchantment. Charles Kingsley's *Westward Ho!* directed attention to the coast of north Devon while R.D. Blackmore's *Lorna Doone* focused interest on the moorlands overlooking the sea. Between them these two authors played a major part in publicizing the scenic charms of north Devon, just as Scott drew attention to the attractions of the Scottish Highlands and Hardy did the same for those of Wessex. Meanwhile Philip Gosse, the eminent naturalist, was writing a string of books enthusing over the advantages of Ilfracombe as a centre for the fashionable new hobby of marine biology, while Charlotte Chanter, an amateur botanist living in Ilfracombe, published a book describing her experiences in collecting ferns along the north Devon coast which triggered off a local craze for collecting these delicate plants.

Chapter 10 will discuss the significance of these authors and their books and will show that they awakened national interest in the natural attractions of north Devon.

Other holiday-makers made the long journey to the north Devon coast because they had been led to believe that the maritime environment there was unusually salubrious and might improve their health. In Chapter 9 it will be shown that the leading north Devon seaside resorts all claimed to offer invalids a good chance of a cure. While they failed to obtain recognition as winter watering places, they had more success in their attempts to promote themselves as summer health resorts.

Population figures show how closely the north Devon tourist industry depended on the provision of improved transport facilities, for the two principal seaside resorts only grew at times when the promise of better land or sea access triggered off economic investment, or when the actual introduction of a new service led to an increase in the number of visitors. Tables 11 and 12 present the population statistics for the principal resorts in the period between 1841 and 1901. What is immediately apparent is that the growth of Ilfracombe and of Lynton and Lynmouth came to an abrupt halt after the railway reached some of their competitors on the south Devon coast in the late 1840s and began to draw away some of north Devon's tourist trade. At a time when Torquay, Teignmouth and Dawlish were expanding quite rapidly, the population stabilized and even fell very slightly at Ilfracombe between 1841 and 1851 and at Lynton and Lynmouth in the following decade.

Ilfracombe only began to grow again in the 1860s, in a period when the resort was being served by an increasing number of packet steamers and also when substantial building works were taking place in the confident expectation that the resort was about to be linked to the national rail network. The belated arrival of the railway at Ilfracombe in 1874 was followed by a period of sustained growth, so that by 1901 the town had a population of 8,557 and ranked third among the Devon resorts after Torquay and Exmouth.

Lynton and Lynmouth's failure to match Ilfracombe's growth can be largely attributed to the delay in the arrival there of the railway. The difficulties of access proved a severe handicap and as a result the resort grew very little in the period up to 1881. Its population then began to increase again as proposals for both a pier and a railway encouraged financial investment in new hotels and houses. Lynton and Lynmouth

Table 11   Population of the Principal
North Devon Resorts, 1841–1901

Resort	1841	1851	1861	1871	1881	1891	1901	Incr. 1841–1901
Ilfracombe	3679	3677	3851	4721	6255	7692	8557	4878
Lynton and								
Lynmouth	1027	1059	1043	1170	1213	1547	1641	614
Instow	557	626	614	647	657	677	634	77

Table 12   Percentage Growth-Rates of the Population of the
Principal North Devon Resorts, 1841–1901

Resort	1841–51	1851–61	1861–71	1871–81	1881–91	1891–1901	1841–1901
Ilfracombe	−0.1	4.7	22.6	32.5	23.0	11.2	132.6
Lynton and							
Lynmouth	3.1	−1.5	12.2	3.7	27.5	6.1	59.8
Instow	12.4	−1.9	5.4	1.5	3.0	−6.4	13.8

Source for Tables 11 and 12: Decennial Census.

started the new century with a population of only 1,641 and yet ranked second among the north Devon resorts.

The case of Instow serves as a reminder that resort growth did not automatically follow the acquisition of improved transport facilities, if a watering place's natural attractions were not sufficiently outstanding to persuade holiday-makers to make the long journey from distant centres of population. Tables 11 and 12 show Instow to be a resort which failed to live up to its early promise. Prior to the arrival of the railway the resort had been expanding, as more visitors from local towns arrived on the improved roads. In 1850 one guidebook reported: 'A great many new buildings and lodging houses have sprung up here within the last seven years'.[52] Hopes were high when the Bideford Extension Railway opened in 1855, but it failed to give a further boost to trade. The tables show that Instow's population actually fell slightly in the decade in which it obtained a rail link and that it had a net population increase of only eight between 1851 and 1901. At the end of the century Instow remained a comparatively small watering place which was being overtaken by some of the newer, better-endowed seaside resorts springing up elsewhere on the north Devon coast.

Topography exercised an unusual level of control over the urban development of both Ilfracombe and Lynton and Lynmouth. The upland coast at these two resorts was in some respects a negative factor restricting the number of sites suitable for building on. Yet in other ways it acted as a stimulus to development, for it gave rise to picturesque scenery and this meant that there was a strong demand for building plots with good views.

Development at these two resorts was also affected by the policies of the principal landowners. The Wreys were lords of the manor at Ilfracombe and the Lock-Roes were lords of the manor at Lynton and Lynmouth. Both families were content to sell off pieces of land for building whenever the opportunity arose, and both families failed to exercise control over subsequent development.

As the largest landowners were not prepared to enforce high planning standards, the quality of development was largely determined by the nature of the demand for houses. At Lynton and Lynmouth those seeking holiday accommodation or second homes were principally affluent people with high expectations and this encouraged building speculators to erect some fine houses on large plots of land. Ilfracombe had even more prosperous patrons and this led builders to construct many prestigious residences. In the later part of the century, however, Ilfracombe began to entertain an increasing number of middle-income families and this gave the incentive for the construction of many smaller detached and semi-detached villas.

The actual rate of development at the two resorts was largely determined by estimates of the likely level of demand for accommodation. Building booms occurred after transport links had been improved, or when there was at least the prospect of better travel facilities, while slumps occurred at times when inadequate transport links made it difficult to attract visitors.

At Ilfracombe in the late 1840s and 1850s the lack of a direct rail link discouraged investment and there were very few additions to the housing stock. The resort only began to expand again in the 1860s, when it was

confidently expected that a railway would soon be built and that this
would enable many more visitors to arrive. Many fine villas and terraces
were erected on sites commanding coastal views. In a decade of prestigious
developments, two projects are worthy of special mention. At Torrs Park
an estate company began leasing sites for development, and magnificent
villas, four or five storeys high, were soon dotting the slopes.[53] Meanwhile
on a prime seafront site at Wildersmouth, the Ilfracombe Hotel was
opened in 1867. This sumptuous 210-roomed hotel was owned by a
consortium of local businessmen and their massive investment represented
a considerable act of faith in the imminent arrival of the railway.[54]
Confidence that the town would be provided with improved transport
links collapsed in 1869 and for a time building operations in the town
ground to a halt.[55]

After the railway finally arrived in Ilfracombe in 1874, the increased
demand for holiday accommodation stimulated vigorous new growth.
The resort developed along a new axis extending from the railway station
through Torrs Park and then towards the harbour. Wilder Road was
completed in 1883 and was soon flanked by many large hotels and
boarding houses. The strong demand for lodgings and retirement homes
prompted many new housing developments. Some of these projects were
small in scale with landowners selling plots piecemeal to builders. There
were also some large estate developments, particularly at Wildercombe
Park and Chambercombe Park. Ilfracombe expanded rapidly, so that by
the end of the century development had reached the edge of the uplands
overlooking the town and was beginning to overflow into the
neighbouring valleys.[56]

At Lynton and Lynmouth the difficulties of both land and sea access
seriously limited visitor numbers and this meant that the resort grew
hardly at all in the period between 1844 and 1884. In 1885, however,
reports that both a railway and a landing pier were about to be built
triggered off a flurry of both hotel and house construction. The Tors
Hotel was opened at Lynmouth in 1886, while up at Lynton the
Kensington, the resort's first boarding house, opened in 1888.[57] These
transport proposals came to nothing but George Newnes kept hopes alive
by opening a cliff railway in 1890.

The stimulus for much larger-scale development at Lynton and
Lynmouth came in 1890 when George Newnes announced his intention
to obtain an Act to build a landing pier.[58] Several previous proposals for
a pier had come to nothing, but the business community was confident
that, with the rich publisher's backing, a pier would at last be built and

would usher in an era of great prosperity, so they began to invest heavily in property developments. Much of old Lynton was completely rebuilt and the town began to expand towards the Valley of Rocks.[59] The price of land soared, so that in May 1891 the local newspaper predicted: 'In future building land at Lynton will be sold by the inch'.[60]

Lynton and Lynmouth's building boom ended in March 1892, just as suddenly as it had begun, when George Newnes announced that he had abandoned his plans to build a pier.[61] This change of mind was in part prompted by the fact that he had decided to build a house in Lynton and so no longer wished to make the resort easier for trippers to visit. His decision had grave consequences. Land and property prices collapsed, builders went bankrupt and many workmen were obliged to leave their home town in search of employment elsewhere.[62] These heavy losses made local businessmen extremely cautious and it was only after the railway finally reached Lynton in 1898 that the resort began to expand again.[63]

A number of minor resorts began to spring up on the north Devon coast in the later part of the nineteenth century. Like the new small watering places in south Devon, they were all located in relatively remote districts and catered for those wishing to avoid crowds and noise.

The principal Devon seaside resorts had all evolved from pre-existing settlements, but Westward Ho! is an example of a holiday resort that was created on a previously uninhabited stretch of coast. It was in 1863 that the Northam Burrows Hotel and Villa Building Company was formed, with the object of establishing a new resort at Northam Burrows on the shores of Bideford Bay. 'The recent publication of Mr Kingsley's charming work *Westward Ho!*' had, proclaimed the prospectus, 'awakened public interest in the romantic and beautiful coast of north Devon'.[64] The foundation stone of the Westward Ho! Hotel was laid in February 1864 by Lord Portsmouth, the company chairman, who assured potential investors that visitors would soon be flooding in and that he hoped to see a 'second Torquay' rise up.[65] The hotel commenced trading in 1865 and expensive villas soon proliferated around it.[66] Hot and cold sea-water baths were opened in 1866 and bathing machines soon appeared on the beach,[67] as the new watering place made its bid for recognition as a national health resort.

A carefully orchestrated publicity campaign was mounted, but Westward Ho! seemed to be dogged by misfortune and it failed to attract the visitor numbers that investors had hoped for. While the resort was claiming that many invalids had there been 'raised from a bed of sickness to robust health',[68] alarming reports were beginning to circulate about the risk to health caused by the lack of a proper sewerage system.[69] In 1875 a local health official had to admit that there had been deaths caused by 'well water polluted by the products of putrefying sewage'.[70] Such adverse publicity tended to deter those already concerned about their health.

Despite the provision of a golf course and a large swimming pool for more active holiday-makers, Westward Ho! enjoyed only modest success. Problems mounted as the sea encroached on the pebble ridge protecting the resort, eventually sweeping several houses into the sea. Villas and roads were neglected and the tourist trade began to decline as an air of depression settled over the resort in the final years of the century. Westward Ho! was only to achieve national renown after the Second World War, when huge holiday camps were opened there; a far cry from its origin as an exclusive health resort catering for the gentry.[71]

A change of fashion led to a trio of tiny watering places emerging on a previously undeveloped stretch of the Atlantic seaboard to the north-west of Barnstaple. This region was exposed to the full force of westerly gales and had not been considered suitable for resort development earlier in the century, when the medical faculty had been stressing the importance of sheltered locations. In the late nineteenth century, however, with the gradual decline in the importance attached to climatic cures and the growing vogue for family holidays, this coast's extensive sandy beaches began to attract a new generation of holiday-makers. Transport improvements also encouraged the development of a tourist industry, for access to this remote region was made somewhat easier by the opening of the Barnstaple and Ilfracombe Railway in 1874.

The first new resort to emerge on this barren coast was at Woolacombe. In 1888 it was reported that an hotel and several lodging houses had recently been erected overlooking the magnificent beach and a large estate was being laid out for development.[72] Woolacombe grew rapidly. In 1896 a guidebook stated: 'About eight years ago a farmhouse and two workmen's cottages were the only buildings in this township. Now it possesses a really first-class hotel . . . there are numerous terraces of private boarding houses as well as shops and a post and telegraph office, and the place is growing yearly'.[73]

The same guidebook noted that just to the south at Croyde Bay another tourist development had been commenced with some boarding houses being built facing the sands. It also advised that further south again development had been taking place overlooking another fine beach at

Saunton Sands: 'It is only within the last few years that any buildings for the accommodation of visitors have been erected at the Sands. Now the place boasts a very good hotel, also numerous private boarding houses'.[74]

By the end of the century there were suggestions that some holiday-makers were beginning to desert Ilfracombe to stay at these new beach resorts on the Atlantic coast, just as some visitors were leaving the traditional health resorts on the south Devon coast for the newer sandy-beach resort of Paignton. Woolacombe, Croyde Bay and Saunton Sands were to attract growing numbers of visitors in the twentieth century as 'bucket and spade holidays' became increasingly popular.

Woody Bay on the Exmoor coast was the setting for another attempt to establish a new resort on a virgin site. Colonel Lake, a wealthy solicitor, purchased the Woody Bay estate in 1885[75] and immediately began making plans to develop an exclusive watering place. Woody Bay had few of the attributes which the Victorians normally expected of a seaside resort. The beach was very limited and was composed mainly of shingle, while the approach to it, down a steep valley, was extremely difficult. There was little there to appeal to invalids or families, or indeed to working-class excursionists. Yet Woody Bay could boast magnificent wooded cliffs plunging down into a secluded bay, and the promoter was confident that the fine views and tranquillity would attract a high-class clientele.

Large sums of money were needed to develop a resort in such unfavourable terrain and Colonel Lake was soon demonstrating that he had access to seemingly unlimited funds. Woody Bay was on an extremely remote stretch of coast, so his first task was to make it easier to reach by both land and sea. He invested large sums on new approach roads along the cliffs[76] and, as already noted, he constructed a pier to enable steamers and private yachts to land passengers. He used his influence to persuade the directors of the Lynton and Barnstaple Railway to open a station in remote country at Martinhoe Cross, solely to serve his new resort.[77] In 1894 he made a golf course which he hoped would attract wealthy patrons.[78] Good accommodation for visitors was also a priority and Colonel Lake again spent freely to provide two hotels and five superior lodging houses.[79] By 1900 work was almost complete on a third hotel adjoining the railway station.[80]

Just when it seemed that Woody Bay was well on the way to becoming a successful resort, all development came to an abrupt end. In November 1900 Colonel Lake was arrested and charged with embezzling his clients' funds to finance his scheme.[81] He was sentenced to twelve years in prison and the estate had to be sold off to pay off some of his debts.[82] Woody

Bay was purchased by Charles Bailey, a wealthy gentleman with an adjacent estate at Lee Abbey.[83] He had no wish to see a busy holiday resort growing up close to his family home, so he at once called a halt to all development. Thus ended an ambitious attempt to create an entirely new resort, which for a time had been perceived as a very real threat to nearby Lynton and Lynmouth.

Clovelly, on the other hand, is an example of a coastal settlement where the landed proprietors deliberately prevented the growth of a large resort. The New Inn was entertaining a few nobles and distinguished prelates by the 1840s,[84] but there were no hotels or large lodging houses in the village. The lords of the manor resided at Clovelly Court and they were determined to ensure that the visual charm of this quaint fishing village was not obscured by building developments. It could be argued that distance from the rail network also helped to prevent the growth of an important resort, but the village was easily accessible by sea and might have become as popular as Lynton and Lynmouth if the landowners had been prepared to allow development. In the late nineteenth century Clovelly was sometimes the destination for excursion steamers, but it was still not a residential resort, for it had only two inns and there were no large houses or hotels where visitors could stay.[85] Whereas at most of the Devon resorts the landowners were prepared, and often eager, to offer up their estates for development, at Clovelly the landed proprietors were determined to preserve their residential amenity, instead of seeking to profit from the sale of land for building. They ensured that Clovelly remained a picturesque but somewhat primitive place for a day visit, instead of becoming an over-built resort in which to stay.

To the east of Ilfracombe was Combe Martin, a coastal farming village, which at the end of the century began to take on a new function as a small seaside resort. There was no business syndicate or wealthy speculator to promote development, so early development was tentative and small in scale. In 1884 one guidebook roundly condemned it: 'It consists of a shabby main street over a mile long which is quite devoid of interest and is at times none too sweetly odorous'.[86] But, while Combe Martin's beach was shingly and it had few advantages as a sea-bathing resort, it did appeal to those who were seeking peace and seclusion, for it was far removed from the railway. By 1889 it had a few lodging houses and had begun to attract a limited number of visitors, who used it as a centre from which to tour Exmoor.[87]

*

While there were some who measured progress in terms of acres swallowed up by urban expansion, there were others who feared that over-development would 'kill the goose that laid the golden egg'. In their rush to make a quick profit, developers tended to forget that it was scenic beauty which attracted a substantial proportion of the region's visitors and the tourist industry might suffer if areas of outstanding beauty were obliterated by buildings.

Ilfracombe's coastal vistas were suffering most at the hands of the developers. In 1873 a letter appeared in the *Ilfracombe Chronicle* complaining that 'destroyers' were inflicting irreparable damage on the resort: 'Is it not a crime, under cover of improvement, to disfigure the natural beauty of the place? Ilfracombe of old, the resort of artists, tourists and lovers of anything beautiful, will ere long be spoilt'.[88]

Even Lynton and Lynmouth's superb scenery was not immune from the threat of urban expansion. In 1886 proposals for a small housing development on the previously unspoilt Tors estate prompted one travel writer to warn the inhabitants to be wary of 'the speculative builder, with his levelling mania, flattening, smoothing, and parading all around, raising stucco terraces and marine crescents, hideous to look upon, turning each seaside resort into one monotonous uniformity of common-place'.[89] The warning went unheeded and two years later another travel writer lamented on the way that both Lynton and Lynmouth were being developed:

> The hand of man is doing its usual fatal work on one of the loveliest spots our country had to boast of. Flaring notices everywhere proclaim the fact that building sites are procurable through the usual channels, this estate and the other has been laid out.[90]

The same writer noted with horror that the advanced guard of builders had already begun operations at Woolacombe. He was appalled that even on those remote shores the developer was 'pursuing his ravages' with villas 'run up in a night and christened with some crack-brained name early the next morning'.[91]

Visitor numbers fluctuated from year to year at the two principal north Devon seaside resorts, but in the later part of the century the general trend was upwards. The numbers recorded on visitor lists for a peak week in early August rose at Ilfracombe from 631 in 1860 to 3,409 in 1900,[92] and at the much smaller resort of Lynton and Lynmouth from 175 in

1860 to 410 in 1890.[93] The visitor lists for Ilfracombe highlight the impact made by the arrival of the railway, for the number of visitors recorded in a week in early August jumped from 1,139 in 1873 to 1,674 in the following year,[94] when the resort had just obtained the benefits of a rail service. At Lynton and Lynmouth the onerous task of preparing visitor lists had been abandoned by the time the railway opened in 1898, but press reports suggest that the arrival of the railway led to a significant if not dramatic increase in the number of visitors.[95]

Here an important point needs to be made! Increases in a resort's visitor numbers did not guarantee the long-term prosperity of individual businesses. Seaside resorts tended to assume that success in attracting more tourists would inevitably be followed by a golden era for all connected with the holiday industry, but this was by no means always the case. In 1896 the *Ilfracombe Gazette* pointed out that at Ilfracombe an increase in the number of holiday-makers was always followed by an upsurge in building, and 'as the accommodation increases, so the influx of visitors must increase in equal ratio to ensure every house shall be kept filled'.[96] In the same year the *North Devon Herald* pointed out that, while at Lynton and Lynmouth holiday-makers were arriving in greater numbers than in former times, there were still many empty rooms in the resort because 'the accommodation for visitors has increased in greater ratio than the number of visitors'.[97] So there was always concern at these resorts at times when bad weather, the loss of a steamer service, or a change in holiday habits, threatened to halt the rise in visitor numbers.[98]

This was not a problem peculiar to north Devon. New hotels and lodging houses mushroomed up at seaside resorts everywhere whenever trade was good, so there always seemed to be an insatiable demand for more and more visitors to fill the new accommodation. There is a lesson here for all involved in the present-day tourist industry.

Ilfracombe was Devon's busiest summer seaside resort. The 3,409 visitors shown on the visitor lists as staying there at the height of the summer season in 1900 were many more than those recorded at any of the south Devon watering places. Yet the visitor lists also reveal that at this resort visitor numbers dropped substantially on either side of the August peak. Ilfracombe was by this time attracting a higher proportion of less affluent visitors than any other Devon resort and many of these people had just one or two weeks holiday with pay each year, which they usually had to take at a fixed time in late July or in August. So while Ilfracombe was extremely busy for a few short weeks, its summer season was significantly shorter than at the south Devon watering places.

Lynton and Lynmouth was also a summer resort. Yet, while this resort had far fewer summer visitors than Ilfracombe, it did benefit from a longer season, because nearly all of its visitors were drawn from an affluent class who could afford to take a long holiday and were not obliged to holiday at the peak of the season.

Winter visitors were few in number on the north Devon coast. Potential visitors seem to have been deterred by the threat of cold weather. The very word 'north' did and still does conjure up an impression of bitterly cold winter weather which is not entirely borne out by the climatic statistics. Visitor lists for that season were usually a catalogue of empty lodging houses and hotels, either because there were no visitors there at all or because there were too few to justify the effort of recording them.

Ilfracombe battled hard to increase its winter trade. Business interests in the town were particularly jealous of Torquay's long winter season. A 'season extension campaign' was organized and statistics were published purporting to show that Ilfracombe was actually warmer than Torquay in the winter months.[99] Torquay challenged the accuracy of these figures and suggested that Ilfracombe's temperature figures were inflated by keeping the thermometers 'in what was practically a summer-house and not a screen'.[100] In January 1891 the *Ilfracombe Chronicle* declared: 'We must keep the fact of the mildness of our climate to the front in the hope that we shall reap our reward in an increased number of winter visitors'.[101] A few weeks later a freak blizzard left the resort covered with snow drifts up to eight feet deep![102] Ilfracombe's strenuous efforts to attract a large winter clientele were largely unsuccessful and it remained essentially a summer resort.

The visitor lists for Ilfracombe and for Lynton and Lynmouth sometimes give the place of residence of visitors, thus providing valuable information about the geographical extent of their catchment areas which is not available for any of the south Devon seaside resorts. They show that in an era when Blackpool, Weston-super-Mare and many other well-known English seaside resorts catered mainly for a regional market,[103] the two leading north Devon resorts had a national catchment area. Only a relatively small proportion of the visitors for whom a place of origin was recorded came from Devon and an unusually high proportion came from distant parts of the country. It is possible that the owners of holiday accommodation were more inclined to record the place of origin when their visitors had the prestige value of being from a far-off town, but, even allowing for some imbalance in the preparation of the lists, they still provide convincing proof that these resorts were attracting holiday-makers from all parts of the country. It is particularly interesting to find that London was a major centre of demand. Visitors from the capital steadily increased until by the 1880s over 30 per cent of those for whom a place of origin was recorded gave London as their home. Significant numbers were also arriving from the Home Counties, from the towns of southern England and from the North of England.[104]

Yet, while both Ilfracombe and Lynton and Lynmouth attracted many visitors from distant parts of the country, they also had a strong contingent of visitors from districts within easy reach of the steamship services starting from Bristol and Portishead. The visitor lists always contained the names of many Bristolians. Substantial numbers of holiday-makers from Bath and the towns of the West Midlands were also recorded. It is significant that the numbers of visitors recorded from both the Avon district and the West Midlands dropped significantly after the closure of the Portishead service in September 1886.[105]

An unusually high proportion of the visitors arriving at Lynton and Lynmouth were wealthy, long-stay patrons. The resort attracted a select clientele who regarded its remoteness as an advantage rather than a disadvantage, because it was said to be 'far from the reach of the cheap tripper, the niggers, and the thousand and one annoyances of an ordinary watering place'.[106] We have seen that the resident gentry opposed most of the schemes for improved land and sea access. They argued: 'Lynton and Lynmouth have a certain status peculiarly their own . . . those visitors who cannot afford to avail themselves of the present mode of conveyance . . . should seek elsewhere a cheaper watering place. We can afford to lose them'.[107]

Distance from the major centres of population also helped to preserve a relatively high social tone at Instow and Westward Ho!. Instow was a middle-class resort, with its small clientele being drawn mainly from Barnstaple, Bideford and rural north Devon. Westward Ho!'s visitors were drawn mainly from the upper ranks of society and came from all parts of the country. Like Lynton and Lynmouth, Westward Ho! tried to attract rich visitors by boasting of its select clientele. 'Accommodation is scanty, being mainly occupied by the families of captains, colonels and knights at arms, Anglo-Indians and other persons who find here congenial society', reported one guidebook in 1899.[108]

Ilfracombe lacked the quiet gentility of Lynton and Lynmouth and Westward Ho!, but for most of the period it remained a staid and even strait-laced resort. Ilfracombe played host to many wealthy families. But, as the century progressed, the resort also had to entertain growing numbers of lower-middle-class visitors from the Bristol area, who took advantage of the cheap fares on the steamers. As early as 1869 one visitor complained: 'Bristol and Clifton turn this beautiful watering place into a Margate and vulgar people arrive in shoals'.[109] In fact these new arrivals posed no real threat to Ilfracombe's sedate atmosphere. The vast majority were respectable, upwardly-mobile men and women, seeking to gain status by a short stay in a resort patronized by people from the upper ranks of society. These new arrivals were generally accepted, for they were anxious to emulate the life style of their social superiors and quickly adapted to the time-honoured holiday routine at the resort. In 1871 an article in the *Standard* described some elements of the new social mix:

> The world of Ilfracombe fashion is a slightly miscellaneous one. First and foremost comes the Bristolian contingent . . . then we have a truly formidable array of elderly spinster ladies . . . they swarm prolifically over the rocks and hills, distribute tracts to the thoughtless . . . give tea parties, devote themselves to religion, talk scandal and call it charity . . . London professional life has contributed its quota, so what with young men and old maidens and matrons . . . we are as pleasantly diversified an assemblage as one could wish.[110]

This preponderance of ladies among the visiting and resident population was not confined to Ilfracombe. The Devon seaside resorts were all regarded as safe havens for spinsters living off annuities, for widows with independent means, and for women whose husbands were serving their country overseas. Many younger women also holidayed there, often arriving in search of husbands, realizing that these fashionable resorts were ideal marriage markets in which to display their charms. Women were also strongly in the majority among the servant population. The census enumerators' returns show an unusually high ratio of female domestic servants at all the Devon resorts, with many women from the rural hinterland being attracted there to work in the hotels and lodging houses, and many female servants from distant parts of the country accompanying their employers when they took up residence on the Devon coast.

In the 1880s growing numbers of lower-middle-class holiday-makers arrived in Ilfracombe, and to accommodate them the resort became the first in Devon to open a considerable number of boarding houses.[111] Visitors had previously been faced with the choice of either paying for the meals and facilities of a full-blown hotel, or of renting accommodation in a lodging house. The new boarding houses were a compromise between the two. They provided full board at moderate prices, but they were usually unlicensed and had fewer amenities than hotels. They certainly did not provide the private suites of rooms found in good hotels and lodging houses, for this was a less expensive and more gregarious mode of holiday-making.[112] The first boarding houses in Ilfracombe were opened by lodging-house keepers, who began providing meals for their visitors and then expanded, either by acquiring adjoining properties or by building extensions. The Collingwood, for example, was created in the 1880s by an energetic landlady who gradually purchased all four lodging houses in Collingwood Terrace and converted them into a boarding house with 60 bedrooms. The Crescent Boarding Establishment was built up by another enterprising lady until by 1890 it had 50 bedrooms.[113] The success enjoyed by these establishments encouraged the amalgamation of other terraces of lodging houses into boarding houses and also prompted the construction of purpose-built establishments, such as the Granville Temperance Boarding House, which was opened in 1890.[114]

Fears were voiced in the final decade of the nineteenth century that Ilfracombe's social tone was declining. At the end of the 1893 season the *Ilfracombe Gazette* commented that 'while the number of visitors arriving in the town far exceeded that of any previous year, the status of the tourist was somewhat below the average, in short the masses predominated over the classes'.[115] Quality was being diluted by quantity, for, while Ilfracombe's visitors still included many people with independent means and many more with professional occupations, by this time the lower-middle class were arriving in rapidly growing numbers.

Far more seriously, for those who valued a high social tone, Ilfracombe in the later part of the century had to cope with a substantial increase in the number of working-class trippers arriving on day trips. Many of the town's more genteel residents and visitors viewed with horror the growing number of excursion steamers.

What a change in attitude had taken place! The first day-trippers from Wales had been greeted at Ilfracombe with enthusiasm. When on a July morning in 1843 the *Lord Beresford* had steamed into Ilfracombe harbour bringing over 400 Welsh teetotallers on a day visit from Swansea, the inhabitants had turned out in large numbers to greet them and had even hired a band to entertain them.[116] Likewise in August 1845, when big groups of trippers had arrived at Ilfracombe on the *Lady Charlotte* from Cardiff and then the next day on the *Swift* from Newport, the local people had rejoiced at the arrival of so many strangers. The *North Devon Journal* noted that 'a large number of the inhabitants had gathered to give a welcome to the visitors' and that the excursionists had been 'loudly cheered on departure'.[117] Again at Whitsun 1846, when the *Lord Beresford* from Swansea and the *Bristol* from Neath had arrived packed with teetotallers, the cliffs had been 'lined with people waiting to greet them'. The residents had even organized a festival to entertain the crowd of trippers.[118]

The warm welcome afforded to the early steamer excursionists from Wales owed much to the fact that their visits were usually organized by temperance groups, Sunday schools, friendly societies or other worthy institutions. The participants were usually well-behaved and were well-received, for many of the local inhabitants supported the organizations that had brought them. After the arrival of two steamers packed with trippers from Wales in July 1848 the *North Devon Journal* commented:

> It is pleasant to reflect on the change the power of steam is producing in the habits of society, for instead of spending their money and their time in the brutal sports of bygone days, the labouring classes are induced to take pleasure trips from one country to another, as is manifest from the frequency of excursions from Swansea, Neath and other places on the Welsh coast to Ilfracombe during the present summer.[119]

Unfortunately the arrival of an excursion steamer at Ilfracombe soon became a matter for real concern, for sometimes the trippers behaved in ways that outraged the more refined visitors. In June 1849 the local correspondent of the *North Devon Journal* reported that 'over 400 of the human swarm of Swansea' had invaded Ilfracombe and, after disturbing the peace by racing donkeys down the main street, they had scandalized the town by their behaviour on their return to the steamboat:

> Many of them went on board drunk; and what shocked our townspeople more . . . there were women—that ever we should have to write—women who were tumbled aboard in a state of—we cannot write that name of shame—a state not to be mentioned.[120]

While such events were the exception rather than the general rule, they occurred sufficiently often to cause anxiety whenever an excursion steamer called. The *North Devon Journal* not infrequently praised parties of trippers for 'enjoying themselves with great decorum' or for 'doing honour to themselves by the propriety of their conduct', but it could not forget the 'intemperate indulgences so conspicuous in past visits'.[121]

The main problem with the Welsh trippers was that they came from an alien class and culture and had a very different lifestyle from that of the long-stay visitors. Daniel Benham encountered some of these excursionists when holidaying at Ilfracombe in 1852 and his reaction was probably typical of that of many members of the select company staying at the resort: 'When we got into the town we found it full of Welsh people, an excursion party from Swansea, and they seemed as wild as their own mountains and as haggard looking as their smelting furnaces could make them'.[122]

As the visits by excursion steamers from Wales gradually increased in frequency, there were more reports of disturbances at Ilfracombe. In August 1864 the *Prince of Wales* and *Henry Southan* arrived from Port Talbot with 750 trippers made up of iron workers and their womenfolk. 'Seldom has a rougher lot of excursionists visited Ilfracombe', commented the *North Devon Journal*. 'The great majority of them, both men and women, became drunk before leaving and by their noise and violence created quite a stir'.[123] On Whit Monday 1874 the *Velindra* arrived from Swansea with over 400 'Welshies', including 'an extensive mixture of the very rough element', many of whom were very drunk.[124] Even these excesses paled into insignificance when compared with the outrageous behaviour of a party of 400 'miners and smelters' who arrived on the *Velindra* from Swansea on Bank Holiday Monday 1877. They arrived in a drunken state, knocked over the toll gate at the end of the pier and rushed past without paying. Then they rampaged through the town, attacking innkeepers, bread boys and market people. Extra constables were sent for from as far away as Barnstaple and Exeter, but the police were powerless in the face of such a large body of hooligans.[125]

Ilfracombe had better harbour facilities than any other north Devon resort, so it was obliged to play host to most of the excursion steamers and was more exposed than any other north Devon resort to the risk of offensive conduct of this kind. Yet the impact of these trippers on sedate Ilfracombe should not be over-exaggerated. In the 1870s there were only some 20 visits a year by excursion steamers and these were usually confined to Easter, Whitsun, August Bank Holiday and summer Saturdays. Serious disturbances were comparatively rare, and the most common complaint levelled against the Welsh trippers was that they ill-treated the donkeys.[126] Some residents regarded their visits as an annual curse, but most expressed the view that 'the amount of money they leave behind them more than counterbalances any little annoyance they may cause'.[127] It was only in the final decade of the nineteenth century that working-class excursionists began to invade Ilfracombe in larger numbers and on a much more regular basis. Some trippers arrived by train, but these originated principally from inland Devon and there were never any serious complaints about their behaviour. Powerful steamers brought growing numbers of trippers from Bristol, but the rougher element from that city normally only travelled as far as Weston-super-Mare and those travelling on to Ilfracombe were in general relatively well-behaved. It was the rapid rise in the number of steamer excursions from Wales which caused real concern, for these vessels were known locally as 'floating beer-shops' and their passengers were not infrequently drunk and disorderly. In 1896 Sir Cameron Gull, the local Member of Parliament, demanded in the House of Commons that 'respectable people shall not be annoyed by the sight of drunken men, and women too, landing from the steamers'.[128] The fear was that the influx of Welsh trippers would cause long-stay visitors to desert the town, perhaps for the south Devon watering places, as those resorts hardly ever experienced such rowdyism and drunkenness.

Ilfracombe was not the only British seaside resort having to face an invasion by working-class trippers. Excursionists had long been able to flood into coastal watering places near to the big centres of population, but at the end of the century rising wages and improved transport facilities enabled a growing number of young and unruly trippers to pour into 'respectable' seaside resorts such as Llandudno and Bournemouth, which had previously been insulated by distance from rough and rowdy excursionists.[129]

On August Bank Holiday 1893, 3,200 excursionists were landed by steamer at Ilfracombe and it was estimated that a further 2,300 trippers arrived by rail and road, making a total of some 5,500 excursionists present for the day.[130] This was an exceptionally large number for Ilfracombe, but much greater influxes were frequently experienced at many other British watering places. Weston-super-Mare, for example, was much closer to both Bristol and Cardiff, and in 1890 it had to entertain over 22,000 excursionists on Whit Monday, while a further 21,000 invaded the resort on August Bank Holiday Monday.[131] Set against such figures, tripper numbers at Ilfracombe seem relatively small. Numbers were growing though and while publicans and café owners welcomed the fillip to their trade, many people feared that the resort's social tone was being lowered.

The task was to find a way of assimilating the trippers, without upsetting the wealthy residents and without losing the valued patronage of the staying-visitors.

At English seaside resorts such as Scarborough, Margate and Blackpool the solution arrived at was to introduce social zoning, with the working class and 'better classes' being encouraged to use separate parts of the sea front and beaches.[132] Ilfracombe, though, was too small a resort to be able to segregate its visitors into different areas. While there was no official resort policy on this contentious issue, the solution adopted by many of Ilfracombe's wealthier patrons was to introduce their own form of social segregation, but by time instead of by geographical zoning. They began to confine their visits to the early and later parts of the season, and avoided July and August when the town was invaded by the excursionists. In 1899 one observer remarked: 'Of late years the tendency has been for Ilfracombe to be overrun with trippers brought in summer on the Channel excursion boats. Spring and autumn are its more select seasons'.[133]

The principal concern at Ilfracombe was to preserve the Sunday peace. Commercial self-interest demanded that the resort should entertain day-trippers on weekdays, but nearly everyone agreed on the need to prevent excursionists arriving on Sundays. The sanctity of the Sabbath was one of the cornerstones of Victorian middle-class life, and it was considered vital to keep it as a day of rest. So when the railway opened in 1874 the sabbatarian lobby ensured there was an agreement between the company and the town that no trains would be allowed to run to the resort on Sundays. When this expired in 1894 there was still a strong pressure group lobbying against Sunday trains and the company agreed to continue the ban.[134]

Yet the main threat to the Sabbath peace was not from rail excursionists, but from the trippers arriving on the steamers from Wales. The perceived threat became much more acute after the Sunday Closing Act came into force in Wales in 1881, for this encouraged many hard-drinking Welshmen to go on steamer excursions on Sundays in order to obtain alcoholic drinks. The Ilfracombe Local Board responded to local concern by passing a bye-law banning excursion steamers from entering the harbour on Sundays. In 1899 the Sabbath peace was again endangered when the Court of Quarter Sessions held that the local authority had no legal right to enforce such a ban, for they were not the owners of the harbour. Sabbatarians at once mounted a vigorous press campaign. The *Ilfracombe Chronicle* declared: 'It will be a thousand pities if the quiet Sunday, which is approved so much by visitors to Ilfracombe, is spoilt in the summer months by steamer traffic'.[135] The manorial authorities, who were the owners of the harbour, soon succumbed to public pressure and announced that the ban on Sunday steamers would continue.[136] So Ilfracombe, although increasingly exposed to the visits of trippers during the week, successfully excluded them on Sundays.

Lynton and Lynmouth also faced the threat of an influx of sea-borne trippers, but there the danger was largely averted by the opposition of the local gentry. It has already been shown that wealthy residents defeated no less than five different campaigns to build a pier, which would have made it much easier for steamers to land day-trippers. When there was once again talk of a pier at the very end of the century, one rich summer resident explained just why he was opposed to the scheme:

> Good-class visitors will not be attracted . . . the hordes who may come will desecrate this beautiful place and spend absolutely nothing, and will drive away people who like myself have dwelt among them for five months. Pandering to cheap trippers has been the ruin of most of the south-coast watering places.[137]

The opposition of the wealthy élite ensured that no pier was ever built and so Lynton and Lynmouth escaped the large-scale influxes of excursionists which caused serious conflict at so many British seaside resorts.

Lynton and Lynmouth's social élite also successfully prevented the risk of any large scale invasions of rail-borne trippers. In building the Lynton and Barnstaple Railway, George Newnes and his fellow directors must have been aware that the slow, circuitous journey via Exeter would place the resort out of reach for a long-distance day trip, and that, in any case, the change of gauge to a narrow-gauge line at Barnstaple would prevent the through running of excursion trains. The directors all lived in or near the resort and they were more concerned with preserving its exclusive character than with maximizing the profits from their railway. When the railway opened in 1898, and many people might have been expected to make the rail trip to Lynton, only 207 travelled there on Whit Monday and 397 on the August Bank Holiday.[138] The resort had been successfully protected from large influxes of trippers.

Some of Lynton and Lynmouth's tradespeople were therefore delighted to hear, in the very year that the Lynton and Barnstaple Railway opened, of another narrow-gauge railway scheme that planned to bring large numbers of day-trippers to the resort. The proposed Minehead and

Lynmouth railway was sponsored by two Welsh railway companies. A new pier was to be built at Minehead in Somerset to enable day-trippers from Wales to be landed before being taken on a narrow-gauge line to Lynmouth. George Newnes was less than pleased! Faced with the threat of competition for his new railway and the prospect of an influx of excursionists into the resort that he had made his home, he declared that he 'did not see why people who had built residential homes should be driven away by Cardiff speculators'[139] and immediately led the local gentry in opposing the scheme. This railway would have provided a much more direct link with the rest of the country, because it would have connected with the GWR line from Minehead to Taunton. It would also have obliged the twin villages to play host to large numbers of Welsh trippers. The resident gentry, without considering the interests of the rest of the inhabitants, decisively rejected this chance, and due to their strong opposition at a public inquiry the whole scheme was dropped.[140] This group of wealthy gentlemen were trying to determine the way that their resort would develop, by preventing it being invaded by large numbers of trippers.

By the end of the nineteenth century the leading north Devon seaside resorts had achieved their principal ambition. They had at last become reasonably easy to reach from distant parts of the country. Yet by no means everyone was happy with the new state of affairs. In the early days there had been general agreement that the improvement of land and sea transport would confer great benefits on the resorts, but many rich residents and genteel visitors had changed their opinion and had come to lament the fact that these formerly remote and exclusive watering places had been opened up to lower-middle-class holiday-makers and to periodic invasions by working-class day-trippers. Too late it was realized that inaccessibility had in some ways been an advantage, for it had given these resorts a strong romantic appeal and had safeguarded their high social tone. Greater accessibility was in fact making these watering places that much less attractive to those who valued seclusion and select company.

We have seen that both Ilfracombe and Lynton and Lynmouth had tried to limit the influxes of day-trippers. Quite early in the twentieth century these resorts finally abandoned their efforts to stem the swelling stream of 'lower-class' visitors, for with the advent of motor coaches it became much easier for these people to travel there. Instead the north Devon resorts started to actively encourage visits by members of the working classes, for it became apparent that, with the rise in real wages and the more general provision of holidays with pay, some of these people at last had sufficient money and time to be able to actually stay for a week in a boarding house and while on holiday they could be relied on to spend freely in the cafés and shops. Henceforth each north Devon resort would have to perform a balancing act, trying to retain as many of its affluent long-stay patrons as possible, while at the same time welcoming shorter visits by the 'common herd'. The eventual success or failure of these watering places would be determined by their ability to reconcile the needs and aspirations of holiday-makers drawn from very different social backgrounds.

Nine

Health at the Devon Resorts, 1844–1900

'Beware lest you find death where you seek health!' declared the *Lancet* in 1859.[1] This sombre warning, in an article entitled 'Death at the Seaside', was aimed at a public conditioned to regard a visit to a coastal watering place as a sure way of restoring good health. The rise of holiday resorts on the English coast had been stimulated by the general desire to escape from insanitary, disease-ridden inland towns to more salubrious locations by the sea. Yet as the seaside resorts began to expand, so they too were confronted with health problems similar to those their visitors thought that they had left behind. By the mid-nineteenth century the danger of epidemic disease threatened many English coastal resorts.

The principal stock-in-trade at the Devon seaside resorts had always been good health, so their tourist trade was particularly at risk if outbreaks of disease occurred. Over the years they had built reputations as specialized health resorts and they claimed to have unique healing powers. In the period after 1844 the promise of renewed health still lured many people to the Devon coast, so the resorts faced ruin if it was thought that holiday-makers actually risked their lives by visiting them.

Countless guidebooks and medical treatises still painted an alluring picture of the south Devon seaside resorts' natural health-giving advantages. Some publications even tried to identify watering places which were especially advantageous in the treatment of specific diseases. An authoritative book by Dr Shapter, a distinguished Exeter physician, entitled *The Climate of the South of Devon and its Influence upon Health*, can serve as an example. This book, first published in 1842 and reissued in 1862, recommended Sidmouth's mild air to consumptives and in cases of 'overwrought intellect', while Exmouth's bracing winds were said to make it 'particularly serviceable as a resort for weakly children and those of a scrofulous constitution'. Torquay and Dawlish were, the author considered, 'peculiarly suitable during the winter to persons labouring under chest complaints'. Finally he recommended Teignmouth's equable climate as being ideally suited for restoring the health and strength 'of those who may have suffered from the climates of the East or West Indies'.[2]

The north Devon watering places likewise continued to boast about their natural healthiness. An 1853 guidebook to Lynton and Lynmouth announced that, because of the 'rare purity of the air', there was 'no place in England so healthy'. As proof of the resort's salubrity the author, a local doctor, pointed to the lack of cases of consumption among the inhabitants and stated that most of them lived to an 'extreme age'.[3] The infant resort of Westward Ho! made similar claims for the healing properties of its salubrious sea air. In 1871 one journalist was told: 'Many ... sent to Westward Ho! as a last resort have, against all expectations, recovered'.[4]

Ilfracombe tried particularly hard to convince both the aged and infirm that it had unique natural advantages as a health resort. In an era long before the restrictions of the Trade Descriptions Acts, the titles of such guidebooks as *Ilfracombe: The Healthiest Devonshire Watering Place*[5] and *Ilfracombe: The Healthiest of All English Watering Places* illustrate the nature of the claims being made about Ilfracombe's superiority as both a summer and a winter health resort. The latter book, which was published in 1867, boasted that Ilfracombe's winters were extremely mild and were ideal for 'invalids, waifs and strays from the heat of India, worn-out clergymen ... and to all people, whether young or old, whose ailments arise mainly from want of stamina and general lack of tone'.[6]

With so many books praising the healthy natural environment at the Devon seaside resorts, it is hardly surprising that the sick and infirm still congregated there, in the hope that they would benefit from breathing the restorative sea air, dipping in the sea and living in a salubrious environment far removed from the diseases of inland towns.

It was certainly true that in their earlier days the Devon seaside resorts had been able to claim freedom from many of the health hazards besetting rapidly expanding urban centres. The Devon resorts had grown up in relatively sparsely-populated rural areas, so at first both the sea water and the sea air were relatively free from pollution and drinking water could be obtained from uncontaminated sources.

Yet as the resident populations of the Devon seaside resorts began to grow, so too did their sanitary problems. The increase in the number of holiday-makers placed additional strains on already inadequate systems of water supply and sewage disposal. Sewage was being produced in ever-growing quantities. It was no longer acceptable to allow it to collect in cesspools or alternatively to let it trickle across beaches into the sea. Well water was being polluted by seepage from these cesspools. The sea water was likewise being contaminated by raw sewage. At the same time the formerly pure sea air was being fouled by the stench and germs from open cesspits and from the noxious waste matter uncovered by each retreating tide. The greatest risks to health occurred in the summer months; for in dry periods there were frequent water shortages and in hot weather refuse decomposed rapidly, creating additional health hazards at just the time when resort populations were swollen by an influx of visitors. For many years the Devon resorts had projected an image of radiant well-being, but now there was a growing risk that the glow of good health would be replaced by the shadow of death.

The great cholera epidemic of 1849 finally destroyed the myth that the Devon coastal resorts were immune from the ravages of inland disease. This disease was usually contracted by drinking water contaminated by the faeces of infected people. Cholera was highly contagious, rapid in onset, distinguished by acute vomiting and uncontrolled bowel movements. It frequently terminated in death.[7] Panic spread at the prospect of a visitation, for Devonians remembered how the disease had rampaged through the county in 1832,[8] carrying off 1,901 victims.[9] Before the year was out, cholera would again sweep Devon and this time two of the seaside resorts would suffer major outbreaks.

It was in late August 1849 that the pestilence reached Torquay, a resort thronged with visitors and an ideal breeding ground for the scourge, but also a health resort with a reputation to defend. The town faced the spectre of ruin if the news leaked out and the tourists fled. At first the local press kept a conspiracy of silence, but on 5 September the *Torquay Directory* broke the news that cholera was present in the town and had already claimed three lives.[10] Other newspapers tried to refute the story, with the *Exeter and Plymouth Gazette* declaring that it was 'a matter of regret that so much stir and alarm should have been occasioned by a local paper, when fright is so efficacious in inducing the symptoms of the malady . . . several medical men assert there are no decided cases of Asiatic cholera as yet'.[11] Despite these reassuring words the disease spread, many died and the news could no longer be suppressed. Panic set in and at the end of September the Torquay registrar wrote to advise the General Board of Health that 'the part of the town where the deaths have occurred is almost wholly deserted'.[12]

Cholera also visited Ilfracombe that September and there too attempts were made to minimize the damage to the holiday industry by discounting the reports of an outbreak. At first the *North Devon Journal* asserted: 'The rumours are in many cases pure invention'.[13] But the death roll increased and soon it had to be admitted that there was 'consternation amongst the townspeople as well as among the visitors'.[14] Ilfracombe's holiday trade was devastated and in October a local official wrote in despair:

> The visitors have deserted the town causing a loss computed at not less than eight to ten thousand pounds. If something is not done before May next, it will be the means of ruining a great many.[15]

As their seasons slumped and panic spread, Ilfracombe and Torquay both petitioned the General Board of Health requesting that they be granted the powers of the Public Health Act of 1848, so that they could deal with the emergency. Exmouth had escaped the outbreak, but feared the consequences of any further epidemic and also sought to adopt the new Act. This Act had created the General Board of Health and it had also made it possible for townships to apply for permission to establish a Local Board of Health if at least a tenth of the ratepayers so wished. On receipt of a petition the General Board of Health sent an inspector to report on the sanitary state of the district and, if he recommended the application of the Act, then approval was given for the establishment of a Local Board.[16]

Thomas Rammell was the inspector sent to examine the sanitary state of these three Devon resorts. His subsequent reports described atrocious sanitary conditions, with totally inadequate sewage systems, contaminated water supplies and streets choked with refuse. A horrifying picture completely at variance with the hygienic image the resorts were trying to project. Thus, while the *Stranger's Guide* was proclaiming that at Exmouth 'all the helps to convenience and health, which the improved distribution of water, light and drainage have given to society, are here fully enjoyed',[17] the reality was very different. Thomas Rammell's report on Exmouth contained evidence castigating the town as the 'dirtiest place in the whole county', with a poor water supply mainly derived from a few wells, 'accumulations of filth', defective sewerage and a high death rate. The inspector registered surprise at finding so many 'pestiferous abodes in a town resorted to by invalids for the recovery of health'.[18] Conditions in

Torquay were similarly criticized, with an escalating population and consequent overcrowding being blamed for an increase in disease and a spectacular rise in the death-rate.[19] The state of Ilfracombe was likewise found to be 'decidedly low', with badly polluted water supplies, inadequate sewers, the equivalent of a thousand cart-loads of refuse strewn about the streets, and the harbour 'a large open cesspit'.[20] Once these damning reports were published, all three resorts were given permission to establish Local Boards of Health, so that they could begin to make much needed sanitary improvements and try to restore their tarnished reputations.

The Local Government Act of 1858 strengthened and greatly extended the powers of Local Boards and this eventually encouraged most of the other leading Devon seaside resorts to seek the right to manage their own affairs.[21] While the principal reason for applying to set up a Local Board was still the need to improve public health, the ratepayers at the resorts were aware that Local Boards had now been given the authority to regulate social behaviour as well as to deal with environmental health, and they could see considerable advantages in being able to deal with human as well as sanitary nuisances. The petition of the inhabitants of Dawlish, for example, stated that they sought these new powers not only to improve the sewerage system and to clean up the beach which had become the 'great depository of the filth of the town', but also to prevent 'indecent bathing'.[22] Local Boards were established at Teignmouth in 1859, at Dawlish in 1860, at both Sidmouth and Paignton in 1863, at Lynton and Lynmouth in 1866, at Westward Ho! in 1867 and at Seaton in 1877. At a time when many much larger inland Devon communities were content to leave their sanitary improvements, and much of their general administration, to the local Poor Law Union, the Devon seaside resorts had obtained their own strong local authorities so that they could control their own destinies.[23]

These Local Boards were soon busy making a whole range of public-health improvements. They busied themselves in laying new sewers. They appointed inspectors of nuisances, who were expected to identify and eliminate dangers to health arising from crowded hovels, choked sewers, filthy pig sties and a multitude of other sanitary problems. They employed scavengers to collect refuse and to clean and water the streets. Most important of all, each Local Board engaged a local doctor to act as medical officer of health, so that they could have professional advice on how to improve the sanitary state of their resort.[24]

While the Local Boards treated the provision of proper sewerage systems as an urgent priority, they at first seemed reluctant to commit their ratepayers to the additional burden of paying for improved supplies of water. Some of the reasons for this hesitancy can be found by examining the social composition of these bodies. Their members included not only hoteliers, publicans, shopkeepers and builders, all of whom had a vested interest in promoting the holiday industry, but also an 'economy faction' made up of farmers and some local residents, who had little to gain from an expansion of tourism and often stood for election with the declared intention of keeping rates down to a minimum. This latter group usually recognized the essential need for improvements to the sewering of the resorts, but argued that small watering places with only a limited number of ratepayers could not be expected to find the large sums needed to construct a reservoir and to provide a piped supply to every house.

Yet a growing awareness of the links between polluted water and disease soon caused those involved in the tourist industry to press for major improvements in the quality and reliability of the water supply. They were backed by those inhabitants who attached more importance to good health than to reducing the rates. This growing body of opinion demanded that drinking water should be obtained from uncontaminated sources situated some distance from the resorts. They also complained bitterly about shortages of water in the summer months, just when the seaside resorts were crowded with visitors and water was most needed to flush the new sewers and to cleanse the streets.

Some local authorities responded to this mounting pressure by themselves bringing in improved supplies of water. At Torquay the Local Board in 1855 purchased two small and totally inadequate water undertakings owned by the Palk and Cary families[25] and three years later opened a new reservoir on Dartmoor, providing the rapidly expanding resort with a plentiful supply of piped water.[26] At Ilfracombe the Local Board in 1860 opened its own reservoir, which for the first time provided the resort with a piped supply.[27] At Teignmouth the Local Board in 1871 started constructing a large new reservoir,[28] following complaints that in the busy summer season an existing reservoir was only capable of supplying the resort for some fifty minutes a day.[29] At Dawlish, where the inhabitants had for many years depended on water drawn from wells and a polluted stream, the Local Board in 1880 opened a reservoir and began providing a piped supply.[30]

The inhabitants at the other Devon seaside resorts relied on some of their leading citizens to set up private water companies and bring in a piped supply. At Exmouth a local solicitor in 1855 constructed a small waterworks and promised that water would be 'turned into the town three times a week'. When this supply proved unsatisfactory, the Exmouth District Water Company was formed and in 1867 it opened a large new reservoir which was capable of supplying the whole resort.[31] At Lynton and Lynmouth the ratepayers in 1866 persuaded a group of wealthy residents to create a private water company, when it became clear that their new Local Board would only have the financial resources to pay for the work of sewering the resort.[32] At Paignton in 1872[33] and at Westward Ho! in 1880,[34] speculative builders set up private companies to provide a supply of piped water, when they found that the lack of a safe supply of water was an obstacle to their plans for development. At Sidmouth[35] and Seaton[36] the residents were happy for the lords of the manor to provide a supply from their private waterworks. Yet eventually most of these private water undertakings were taken into public ownership,[37] often following complaints that their owners were unable or unwilling to meet the needs of the expanding resorts and were more interested in private profit than in the improvement of public health.

At Lynton and Lynmouth, for example, agitation for public control of the waterworks began in the 1870s, once it was realized that the Lynton Water Company was no longer owned by local people with a genuine interest in the resort, but instead had been sold to a group of outsiders. In October 1876 the Local Board offered to buy the undertaking, but their bid was flatly rejected.[38] Dissatisfaction swelled. In February 1887 there were alarming reports that the tank storing the filtered water contained 'muck as high as a man's knees besides numerous fish'.[39] At the peak of the summer season in 1890 there were complaints that the Company's small reservoir was unable to meet the demand and that 'lodging-house keepers were running hither and thither in search of water'.[40] Feelings ran high about a Company which had just paid its shareholders a 10 per cent dividend,[41] but could not adequately supply the resort. Public pressure finally obliged the Local Board to begin moves to try and purchase the water undertaking. After a long and costly legal battle with the Company,[42] the Local Board in December 1892 finally acquired the water utility on a long lease.[43]

By the end of 1902 Sidmouth and Westward Ho! were the only two important Devon seaside resorts where the waterworks were still operated by private enterprise. At all the other leading Devon resorts, the water undertakings were operated by the local authority. This high level of local government responsibility for the supply of water was not found everywhere in the country. Indeed it has been shown that of the 22 English seaside resorts which had borough status in 1902, only 12 owned their own waterworks.[44] So, while elsewhere in England some of the largest and most prosperous seaside resorts were content to leave water utilities in private ownership, on the Devon coast many relatively small watering places had decided to take on the heavy financial burden of operating a water undertaking, because they were specialized health resorts with reputations to defend.

In the late-nineteenth century the Devon seaside resorts became increasingly concerned about another grave risk to health. Earlier in the century the main priority of the new Local Boards had been to take sewage away from the inhabited areas, so all the leading resorts had run sewers across the beaches and simply allowed the untreated effluent to flow into the sea.[45] This had been a cheap and easy method of disposal. Yet it soon became apparent that this was a far from ideal solution. While it put an end to the practice of allowing sewage to collect in cesspools or to trickle into a convenient stream, it only transferred the health hazard from one location to another, for it meant that the sea water, which had long been promoted for its therapeutic properties, was being badly polluted and those bathing in it were far more likely to contract a disease than to be cured of one. The growing number of complaints of foul sea water, and of sewage-strewn beaches, eventually obliged the leading Devon resorts to consider remedial action.

Torquay's headlong expansion meant that it was the first Devon resort to suffer serious coastal pollution, and also the first to recognize the need to instigate a scheme aimed at improving the quality of the bathing water and the shoreline environment. In 1850 the bay at Torquay had been fancifully described in a local publication as an 'illimitable ocean bath of spotless purity'.[46] In fact three sewers were already spewing their contents straight across the main beach.[47] Bathers were obliged to dip in diluted sewage, while at low tide the stench on the shore was overpowering. Conditions became so bad that in 1875 it was agreed that the Local Board should embark on a major £65,000 improvement. Long tunnels were bored, old outfalls were intercepted and a new main was laid to an outlet north of Hope's Nose, where it was hoped that the tide would sweep the effluent well clear of the main beaches. This major engineering project was completed in 1878 and attracted considerable publicity.[48] It had the effect of focusing local attention on the need to extend sewer outfalls below the low tide mark, to points where tidal currents could carry the raw sewage further out to sea.

Other Devon seaside resorts were soon emulating the example of their leading rival. Dawlish, for example, in 1888 constructed a new outfall into deep water, after first having made a detailed study of the problem of sewage disposal in the sea. The Local Board used floats to determine the direction of tidal currents, consulted leading engineers and studied successful schemes at other seaside resorts before deciding where to locate the new outlet.[49] By the end of the century all the principal Devon resorts had constructed new sewer outfalls to points below the low-tide mark, in the hope that the tide would carry away the offensive matter.[50] Their efforts were only partially successful. Nothing could prevent some of the evils expelled at one point from washing up further along the coast.

The modern tourist would be astounded to find guidebooks expounding on sewage disposal and water treatment at his or her favourite resort; but late-Victorian seaside publicity gloried in sanitary achievements, which were thought to be the hallmark of an enlightened watering place. Early tourists had been enticed by claims of miracle cures, but many of their late-Victorian counterparts preferred to be given scientific proof of a pure water system and technical reassurances about sewage disposal. Devon resorts had always claimed better health as a principal attraction, but attention now began to shift from the natural assets of sea air and water to man-made health improvements. Sewerage systems and water-filtration plants became the subject of earnest examination in many guide books. The *Illustrated Guide to Ilfracombe*, for example, was an 1885 publication which devoted its opening chapter to a detailed description of the resort's drainage, waterworks and refuse collection. It delved deeply into the murky depths of filter beds, sewer ventilating shafts and free-flowing drains.[51] What a contrast with modern guidebooks featuring sun, sand and seductive bathing beauties!

Many guidebook writers allowed local bias to outweigh their professional judgement when they enthused over the sanitary state of their resort. Dr Slade-King was, in 1875, the author of *Ilfracombe: The Healthiest Devonshire Watering Place*, a book which praised the town's efficient sewerage system and the 'excellent' water.[52] Only three years later, typhoid swept through the prestigious Ilfracombe Hotel, and Dr Slade-King, in his official capacity as Medical Officer of Health for the resort, was obliged to report to the Local Government Board that he attributed the outbreak to 'sewer gas poisoning' caused by serious defects in the sewerage system.[53] While typhoid was still present, W. Walters published his *Ilfracombe: A Health Resort*, in which it was once again claimed that the town benefited from all the latest improvements of 'sanitary science'.[54] Some of the worst health hazards were remedied with the reconstruction of the waterworks in 1880 and the laying of new sewers in the following year. Local residents, though, were still calling attention to the failings of both the water supply and the sewerage system,[55] when in 1885 the *Illustrated Guide to Ilfracombe* was making extravagant claims for the excellence of the town's sanitary arrangements.[56]

Resorts also began to compete for trade by claiming the lowest death-rate, much as they now vie to top the sunshine league table.[57] In 1877, at a time when the average mortality-rate for England and Wales was 20.8 per 1,000,[58] Torquay boasted of its low death-rate: 'In spite of the additional deaths that must always occur in any places resorted to by invalids, it is yet one of the lowest in the Kingdom, not averaging more than 16 per 1,000 the year through'.[59] This comment called attention to a pitfall in interpreting death-rate statistics, for as a seaside town became famous as a health resort, so it attracted more sick and aged visitors, and inevitably its mortality-rate rose.

Higher standards of public health soon led to claims for even lower death-rates. In 1890 Seaton proudly announced a death-rate of only 13.8 per 1,000.[60] This compared very favourably with the national rate, which by then had fallen to 18.9 per 1,000.[61] In 1893 Exmouth asserted that 'in the table of mortality Exmouth stands lowest amongst a score of the most fashionable and frequented watering places',[62] while in the following year Sidmouth crowed it was 'one of six English watering places with the lowest death-rate'.[63] But all these boasts were to be topped by Lynton and Lynmouth's puffed-up claim that in 1899 it was the 'healthiest spot in the country' with a 'phenomenal death-rate' of only 9.7 per 1,000.[64]

So whereas in the early days the promises of miraculous recoveries from life-threatening diseases had been sufficient to entice visitors, by the late-Victorian era many holiday-makers were less gullible and when choosing a resort they expected to be provided with scientific data about the pureness of the water supply, technical evidence of a flawless sewerage system and statistical evidence of a low death-rate. The Devon seaside resorts had begun life trading on their natural advantages, stressing the therapeutic qualities of both their sea air and sea water, but they ended the nineteenth century giving more publicity to the sanitary achievements of their progressive local authorities.

By the end of the nineteenth century it was becoming apparent that fewer invalids were haunting the Devon coast in search of an elusive panacea. In part this was because less and less sick people believed that a visit to the seaside would restore them to full health. In part it was due to a marked improvement in the standards of medical treatment, which meant that fewer invalids felt the need to seek natural cures at the seaside. Yet conversely more physically-fit visitors were arriving at the coastal resorts seeking to ward off illness by experiencing the benefits of a seaside holiday.

The Devon watering places then began to worry that their well-established reputations as specialist caterers for the sick and infirm might frighten away fit and active visitors, who perhaps would not want to spend their holidays in the company of large numbers of seriously-ill people. Torquay, long famed as a national sanatorium, was most at risk if healthy visitors decided to avoid those resorts where it was likely they would encounter depressing scenes of death and despair. As early as 1877 one Torquay guidebook tried to allay the fears of prospective guests:

> And first let us assure those who meditate coming to Torquay, that they need not fear coming to a town of respirator-wearing invalids, as in smaller places. The general population is quite large enough to dilute the ailing members to scarcely observable proportions.[65]

The Devon resorts began to employ a new marketing strategy. While they still tried to attract the old and infirm, by publicizing the advantages of their mild maritime air, they now attached more importance to persuading younger and more robust holiday-makers that the Devon coast offered fine fresh air, good beaches and varied opportunities for wholesome exercise: an ideal combination for those seeking to maintain healthy constitutions. This stress on the preservation rather than the restoration of good health was also apparent when guidebooks claimed that the Devon watering places were models of sanitary excellence where visitors were safe from all risk of dangerous epidemics. So the century ended with the Devon watering places still marketing themselves as health resorts, but with their emphasis steadily shifting towards the prevention rather than the cure of disease.

Ten

Recreations at the Devon Resorts, 1844–1900

The Devon seaside resorts in the second half of the nineteenth century made a virtue of their dullness. Recreational opportunities were principally of an improving nature, designed to satisfy the Victorian desire to engage in instructive and uplifting activities. The growing middle-class clientele were representatives of an industrious breed who felt guilty about squandering time, even when on holiday. Indolence was regarded as a sin; salvation lay in a range of edifying and healthful pursuits which would exercise both mind and body, and thereby 'redeem idleness from the charge of being idle'.[1]

Attitudes had certainly changed! In the early days amusements at the Devon resorts had tended to be frivolous in character, providing pleasure for genteel patrons accustomed to frittering away their time and money at the spas and other centres of fashion. The sophisticated diversions of the assembly rooms, circulating libraries and theatres had since fallen out of favour, but a new range of more serious recreations had developed, most of which were conducted out in the open rather than in public buildings.

This enthusiasm for improving recreations was not peculiar to the Devon coast. Everywhere in England the Victorian middle classes were keen to take part in leisure activities which would provide educational opportunities and prevent them dissipating their growing amount of free time.[2] Yet it was perhaps at the Devon seaside resorts that the demand for 'rational recreation' was strongest. Many of their visitors had made the long journey to Devon in order to distance themselves from the 'cheap and cheerful' entertainments provided at seaside resorts within easy reach of the urban masses. They arrived seeking recreations which would enhance both their intellectual and social status.

Marine biology is a classic example of the type of improving pursuit favoured by many Victorians when on holiday at the Devon seaside. Here was a leisure activity which was both intellectually stimulating and physically invigorating, and one which could also be spiritually uplifting for those seeking evidence of God's handiwork in nature. Here was an interest which gave a new meaning and purpose to a holiday by the sea, for the marine air could still be inhaled while scientific discoveries were made and religious theories about the Creation evaluated.

The Victorian craze for marine biology originated on the Devon coast.[3] The varied rock formations and warm, sheltered waters nurtured a rich diversity of animal and vegetable life unequalled perhaps in any other part of Great Britain. Shell collecting had long been a fashionable pursuit at the Devon seaside resorts, but in the mid-nineteenth century attention began to shift from the shells to the form, habits and development of the creatures that lived in them.

It was Philip Gosse who popularized marine biology. Gosse had travelled widely in the Americas, but it was in Devon that he made his reputation as a leading naturalist. In 1852 he made lengthy visits to both Torquay and Ilfracombe in search of renewed health, but found instead the wonder-world of the tidal rock pool. He observed, sketched, dissected and classified the living organisms he found and then wrote books describing his discoveries. It was Gosse who first opened the eyes of the British public, so that in the tidal pool they perceived exciting beauty where before they saw only dull ugliness.[4] In the preface to his book, *A Naturalist's Rambles on the Devon Coast*, published in the following year, he declared: 'Few, very few, are at all aware of the many strange, beautiful or wondrous objects that are to be found by searching on these shores, that every season are crowded by idle pleasure-seekers'.[5] Amongst a whole stream of books soon issuing from Gosse's prolific pen were two further volumes recommending the Devon coast to the naturalist. *Seaside Pleasures: Sketches in the Neighbourhood of Ilfracombe*, enthused over the natural advantages of the north Devon coast,[6] while *Land and Sea* had long sections on both Torbay and Ilfracombe.[7] His books triggered off a new interest in rock-pool life and set in motion an invasion of the Devon coast by an army of amateur collectors.

The new pastime swept into vogue at all the leading seaside resorts, but Ilfracombe was recognized as its principal centre. Many of Ilfracombe's visitors set up aquaria in their lodging houses so that they could observe at close quarters the creatures they caught. From there one visitor wrote in 1867:

It is not very much use in coming to Ilfracombe unless you have some little taste for natural history. Socially it is everything here. You are hardly fit to live unless you know something about anemones. Nearly every house I suppose has got its aquarium.[8]

Sadly this new hobby had unforeseen consequences. The Devon tidal pools were stripped by an army of well-meaning collectors. Amateur enthusiasts were not entirely responsible for the plunder. Professional collectors soon realized that they could exploit the escalating demand and severely depleted the marine population, often taking as many as 'ten-dozen anemones in a single tide'. They opened shops in the principal resorts with their 'sea-weedy odours' attracting customers to examine their 'array of pans and dishes in front of the door, all crowded with full-blown specimens'.[9]

By 1865 Philip Gosse was expressing dismay at the ransacking of the Devon rock pools:

> Since the opening of sea-science to the million, such has been the invasion of the shore by crinoline and collecting jars, that you may search all the likely and promising rocks within reach of Torquay, which a few years ago were like gardens with full-blossomed anemones and antheas, and come home with an empty jar and an aching heart, all being now swept as clean as the palm of your hand.[10]

For Gosse this was a personal tragedy. Through the medium of his books he had unwittingly encouraged the ravaging of the submarine gardens he so loved.

The Victorians were insatiable collectors, so some visitors looked beyond the treasures of the Devon seashore and focused acquisitive eyes on the ferns to be found just inland. Here once again was the opportunity for the development of an 'improving' recreation, for expeditions after these feathery-fronded plants offered a happy association of fresh air, exercise and instruction, which could refresh and restore both body and mind. Here too was a hobby which owed much to the county's rich natural environment, for a profusion of rare ferns flourished in the moist maritime air.

It was Charlotte Chanter, wife of the vicar of Ilfracombe and sister of Charles Kingsley, who first drew public attention to the diversity of ferns found in Devon. Her book *Ferny Combes* appeared in 1856 and described an expedition in search of ferns which she had undertaken with her

husband. Together they had toured the north Devon coast from Lynmouth to Clovelly before crossing Dartmoor. Charlotte's object in writing
her book was not merely to give an account of the many ferns found in
rural Devon, but also to lead the collector into little-known byways and
beauty spots, where she believed they would obtain 'innocent amusement
and their restoration to health under the soothing influences of a rambling
tour'.[11]

Charlotte Chanter had concentrated mainly on the flora within easy
reach of the north Devon coast, but in the early 1860s other enthusiasts
published comprehensive accounts of the many ferns to be found near
Torquay, Sidmouth and Seaton.[12] Then in the 1870s Francis Heath, a
leading authority on ferns, published two books singing the praises of
Devon's 'unrivalled forms of fern-life'[13] and describing the county as the
'veritable paradise of the fern lover'.[14] This flood of books established
the county as the principal place of pilgrimage for fern collectors and
brought many new visitors to the Devon seaside resorts.

These authors failed to realize that their books would inspire the pillage
of the natural world they revered. This was an age when rare birds and
beasts were shot to be stuffed and displayed in grand mansions, when
uncommon anemones were plucked out of their marine environment to
be exhibited in home aquaria, and it also became the era when scarce ferns
were ripped out of Devon combes to be replanted in domestic ferneries.
Charlotte Chanter and her fellow writers gave precise information as to
the location of rare ferns and encouraged their readers to uproot the plants
and carry them home. Just as Gosse advised marine biologists to use
hammers and sharp knives when looking for specimens,[15] so Francis
Heath advised pteridologists to use chisels and garden forks to aid their
searches.[16]

Professional collectors cashed in on the craze and further depleted the
stocks of already rare species. They opened commercial ferneries catering
for the visitors who wanted to acquire uncommon ferns without the effort
of searching for them. By 1870 Edmund Gill, of the Victorian Fernery
at Lynton, was advertising himself as an 'experienced collector' who could
'supply any quantity at one shilling a dozen and upwards'.[17] At Ilfracombe
three dealers sold ferns.[18] James Dadd was the most successful. He set
up his business as early as 1858 and by 1879 had over ten thousand
ferns available for sale in his fernery.[19] In 1890 an article in the *Ilfracombe
Gazette* suggested that he had stripped the neighbourhood of all its finest
ferns:

Armed with a basket, trowel and a few short sticks . . . he has gone
over nearly every inch of hedgerow in north Devon, and the choice
species and varieties of the fern which had previously adorned their
banks have been carefully removed and replanted in the Langleigh
Fernery.[20]

Just as some holiday-makers sought to imbibe a quick dose of scientific
knowledge as they dabbled in rock pools or identified ferns in remote
combes, so others hoped to absorb a measure of literary culture by visiting
north Devon to see the landscapes portrayed so vividly in R.D. Blackmore's *Lorna Doone* and Charles Kingsley's *Westward Ho!*.

'Each town, each hamlet, hill or heath is associated either with *Lorna
Doone* or with *Westward Ho!*,' wrote a visitor to north Devon in 1887:
'Kingsley and Blackmore . . . have stamped out the individuality of their
genius on districts so rich in all the materials for romance.'[21] These books
were written by men who had grown up in Devon and were steeped in
local traditions. Both writers had a remarkable ability to evoke the spirit
and life of the region and to weave round local legends distinctive new
myths. Their romantic epics gripped the public imagination and made the
nation much more aware of this remote region.

Charles Kingsley wrote *Westward Ho!* in 1854 while staying at Bideford.
Local men were still relating tales of the Devon men who had sailed with
Drake and Grenville, and Kingsley used some of these stories in
his novel.[22] *Westward Ho!* invested the north Devon coast with the
glamour of Elizabethan adventure. It caught the imagination of the British
public and was a huge success. Tourists anxious to identify more
closely with this romantic story began to arrive in the region in growing
numbers.

While staying at Lynton in 1865, R.D. Blackmore began collecting local
stories about a gang of outlaws known as the Doones, who were said to
have terrorized the surrounding district. Blackmore's pen converted
shadowy figures of West Country legend into seemingly real presences.[23]
Lorna Doone was first published in 1869 and became so popular that by
1880 it had reached its seventeenth edition. Tourists invaded Exmoor to
seek out the remote landscapes so affectionately described in his novel.

Lynton and Lynmouth benefited most from the growing popularity of
Lorna Doone, with visitors using the little resort as a centre from which
to explore the Doone country. The novel was particularly successful in
the U.S.A. and by the end of the century a substantial number of
Americans were booking into Lynton and Lynmouth's hotels. In 1901

the *North Devon Herald* commented on the impact that this novel had had on the resort's trade:

> Blackmore's accident has been the means of converting what we proudly call the English Switzerland from one of England's least-known beauty spots into a prosperous tourist's resort, where for four or five months in the year the Devonshire accent is now little more conspicuous than the American.[24]

Sadly this was yet another case of authors unwittingly encouraging environmental damage, for as tourists arrived in increasing numbers to visit the districts described in these two novels, so inevitably they threatened the peace and rich natural habitat of previously unspoilt districts. Charles Kingsley was particularly dismayed when he heard that the success of his novel had given the incentive for the creation of the entirely new resort of Westward Ho! at Northam Burrows. In a letter written in 1864 to a director of the company building the new resort, he expressed his horror at the construction of a holiday complex on one of his favourite stretches of the coast:

> How goes on the Northam Burrows scheme for spoiling that beautiful place with hotels and villas? I suppose it must be, but you will frighten away all the sea-pies and defile the Pebble Ridge with chicken bones and sandwich scraps.[25]

Listening to music was another improving recreation favoured by the Victorians, so it was hardly surprising that all the principal Devon seaside resorts rang with the sound of band music. Bands were not a new attraction. For many years military bands had given occasional performances at the resorts, particularly during the Napoleonic Wars when many army units were garrisoned along the coast.[26] But it was in the second half of the nineteenth century that outdoor concerts really surged in popularity. Music had become the principal pleasure of the middle classes,[27] so they expected to find a good band whenever they visited the Devon coast. Any attempt to pander to popular taste was frowned upon. Music was expected to be of a highly respectable and inspirational nature.

Most of the Devon resorts at first tried to meet the demand for music by forming their own bands. These local bands were usually brass, for the instruments were easy to master and were ideally suited to playing out of doors.[28] Public subscriptions were collected to finance the purchase of instruments, a bandmaster was appointed and then recruitment and training began. Torquay, for example, had its own band of local performers by the 1840s. After failing through lack of support, it was reformed in 1850 and by 1853 was 'enlivening the town on stated evenings'.[29]

Unfortunately the musical renderings of the amateur town bands were often unacceptable to sophisticated audiences and so it was that most of the leading resorts eventually began to engage professional bands, usually made up of German or Italian musicians, to entertain their visitors. These groups usually performed during the main season and hence were known as the 'season band'. Torquay could afford to offer a substantial financial guarantee which would attract a talented group. So in 1871 Torquay was able to secure the services of an excellent band of Italian musicians, which for many years performed regularly in the town.[30] Smaller resorts often found difficulty in raising sufficient subscriptions from local businessmen to be able to afford the services of a quality band. They then had to make do with inferior groups of musicians, and what was worse they had to give them freedom to supplement their income as best they could.[31] The result was that these bands employed over-zealous collectors who pestered visitors for contributions. So it was not surprising that they often had to face fierce criticism. This was a patriotic age and some jingoistic Englishmen were quick to criticize foreign musicians, particularly when they gave indifferent performances and yet continually demanded money.

The case of Ilfracombe serves to illustrate the problems faced in trying to obtain the services of a good season band. Whilst there was general agreement that the town needed to provide musical entertainment, there was continual controversy about the quality and behaviour of the performers and the 'band question' bedevilled the town for many years.

Ilfracombe was one of the first Devon resorts to experience the pleasures and pains of a foreign band. As early as 1843 a wandering band of German musicians had arrived in the resort and played to the visitors.[32] From 1855 onwards a Mr Mark and his band of seven German musicians provided musical entertainment, returning as 'regular as the swallows' for the summer season each year.[33] George Henry Lewes formed a poor opinion of this band whilst staying at Ilfracombe in 1856. He claimed that it played only four tunes; 'never anything else and always pitilessly out of tune'.[34]

Discord jangled through the quiet resort in the summer of 1863 when this German band arrived as usual in June, but found that a group of English musicians were already playing in the town and were not prepared to give way.[35] The two bands battled for the financial support of the wealthy sojourners. The Germans had a favourite 'pitch' on Capstone Parade which they were determined not to share with their rivals. It was claimed that, once there each day, they prolonged 'their medley of nursery tunes to any length, for the sole purpose of preventing the English band from playing choice selections from the popular operas'.[36] Sometimes both sides tried to drown out each other's performance, 'which of course made the sound most discordant'.[37] The situation went from bad to worse with the foreign band being accused of using 'very base and German-like means' of overcoming their rivals, such as 'employing a travelling nuisance to commence playing at the time the English were performing in the High Street'.[38] The real victims were the holiday-makers who each day were subjected to this dire cacophony.

It was not only the two groups of musicians who clashed; the band issue split the town. Some inhabitants instituted a press campaign to drive out the 'execrable German band who have hitherto almost scared away visitors by their discordant noise and unintelligible jargon'.[39] Other residents defended the foreign musicians as 'a very respectable band . . . cheerfully welcomed and kindly encouraged by the higher class of society to come again'.[40]

Musical battles between rival bands were to be a recurring source of irritation at Ilfracombe. From 1876 Herr Klee's German band arrived regularly from Bath for the summer season, but it frequently had to face competition from rival bands of itinerant musicians. In 1876 one visitor wrote:

> The old and the new season bands, in close proximity, play against each other might and main. The effect on the ordinary ear is painful, but to the practical and cultivated musician it is simply unbearable.[41]

These clashes damaged Ilfracombe's tranquil ambience and caused wide-spread disquiet.

Ilfracombe's bands were also criticized when they badgered holiday-makers for contributions. In 1892 one visitor grumbled: 'It becomes rather a nuisance to be asked at your apartments twice a week to patronise the band, and then when out on the parade to have a box thrust before you with a like request'.[42] Yet these musicians could hardly be blamed for collecting so persistently. Whereas some of the leading south Devon resorts had band committees which collected subscriptions and engaged season bands for fixed financial guarantees, the band at

Ilfracombe depended almost entirely on the money it could collect. There were also complaints about Ilfracombe's failure to provide sheltered accommodation for the season band and its audience when inclement weather prevented outdoor performances. In the 1880s some of the town's business community were looking with envy at Paignton, which had a new pavilion where the band could play on wet days, and at Torquay, which had a new Winter Garden where its Italian band could perform indoors during the winter season. The Ilfracombe Local Board was caught in the crossfire between the resort's Improvement Committee, which largely represented the tourism interest and was pressing for a winter garden, where visitors could find both shelter and musical entertainment even in winter, and the 'economist' faction, who were equally determined to resist any scheme which would increase the rates. Finally in 1888 the Local Board resolved to celebrate Queen Victoria's golden jubilee by constructing the Victoria Pavilion on the sea front. This 'long glasshouse', with its potted palms and fish tanks, became a musical mecca where the visitors could sit or stroll up and down while the band played. At the same time a bandstand was provided at the start of Capstone Parade, and the season band played there regularly in fine weather.[43]

Ilfracombe had been one of the first Devon resorts to recognize that a season band was an essential requisite at a fashionable watering place, and yet paradoxically this was an amenity which inspired countless complaints and at times seriously jeopardized the resort's attempts to provide improving entertainment. Most of the problems were caused by the town's reluctance to accept the financial responsibility for providing a good band. Only in 1903 when the Urban District Council resolved to use ratepayers' money to subsidize its season band,[44] could the resort at last hope to provide the standard of musical entertainment expected by its more discriminating visitors.

Even when down by the shore, visitors to the Devon resorts were expected to engage in serious and respectable pursuits. In 1887 a travel writer described the restricted and restrained activities on the shore at Teignmouth:

> Visitors occupy themselves in various ways. Some are bathing; others, from the seats on the promenade, are quietly viewing the bathers and all that goes on. Others are reading a newspaper or books from a circulating library . . . Others are fishing, rowing or sailing about in boats. Others are listening to the musical band, which indeed is heard pretty well over the whole place, otherwise peaceful.[45]

Only the children could cast off their inhibitions and enjoy the innocent pleasure of building sandcastles and the thrill of standing barelegged in a sandpit surrounded by the incoming tide.

The preoccupation with personal improvement led to sporting activities playing an increased part in the holiday routine. Earlier in the century the advocates of 'rational recreation' had encouraged the English public to take up pursuits which exercised the mind rather than the body. In the period after 1850, however, moral reformers increasingly advocated participation in organized sports, which they believed would develop the desirable qualities of self-discipline, courage and fairness.[46] There was also a growing recognition that physical health could be improved by taking vigorous exercise, particularly at the coast where the sea air conferred additional benefits. So it was that yachting, cricket and hunting, the outdoor recreations favoured by genteel visitors in earlier times, all enjoyed a revival on the Devon coast and socially-acceptable visitors were encouraged to take part. But, in addition to these male-dominated pastimes, new outdoor sporting opportunities were introduced which both sexes could participate in. The emphasis was firmly on self-improvement, partly by developing physical fitness, partly by enhancing the social status of the participants. The working classes were effectively excluded from these select sports by the high cost of equipment and by the substantial subscriptions that had to be paid to join the clubs.

'Archery is pre-eminently attractive in as much as it furnishes the means of enjoyment to ladies as well as to gentlemen . . . and is a most graceful and health-giving amusement', commented the *Exeter Flying Post* in 1856 after an early tournament at Teignmouth.[47] Here then was a sport which provided moderate exercise in the fresh air. It came into vogue on the south Devon coast in the early 1850s[48] and by the end of the following decade most of the leading Devon seaside resorts had their own societies and staged annual tournaments.[49]

As the century progressed, more outdoor games were introduced. By the 1870s croquet was being played by both ladies and gentlemen at all the principal Devon watering places.[50] This select and sedate sport was soon overtaken in the popularity stakes by the much more energetic sport of tennis. Exmouth staged a tennis tournament in 1881, only four years after the first competition was organized at Wimbledon.[51] The Exmouth tennis tournament soon extended over a week and became an annual event which attracted players from all over the country. Ladies had their own competition, though their cumbersome costumes made playing difficult.[52] Clubs were soon formed at all the leading Devon coastal resorts[53] and a game of tennis soon became an important part of the holiday for many visitors.

Golf deserves a special mention, for Westward Ho! claimed to be its English cradle. This exclusive sport had originated in Scotland and exiles from that country had previously played at Manchester and Blackheath, but the club at Westward Ho! was probably the first to be formed by English players.[54] Its formation owed much to a chance visit by General Moncrieff, a member of the famous St Andrews Club in Scotland, to his friend the Revd Gossett, Vicar of Northam. General Moncrieff saw the huge expanse of sand dunes bordering the shore and declared: 'Providence obviously intended this for a golf course'.[55] The vicar began playing golf, and so many of his friends joined him that in 1864 a meeting was called 'to arrange the preliminaries of the fine Scotch game of golf in the Burrows of Northam'. The meeting resolved to form a club to be called the North Devon and West of England Golf Club.[56]

By a happy coincidence it was in 1864 that work began on adjoining land to construct the totally new resort of Westward Ho!, so the development of the golf club progressed hand in hand with the rise of the watering place. This close association was symbolized by the fact that the first club house was a bathing machine hauled up from the beach and relocated by the first tee.[57] Tournaments were staged at Westward Ho! from 1866 onwards and soon attracted players from all over the country.[58] The resort became such a mecca for golfers that in 1899 one travel writer warned: 'You can live at Westward Ho! without being connected with the army or navy; but you may as well stay away if you are no golfer'.[59] Westward Ho! owed much of its trade to this passion for golf, but such was the popularity of the new sport that by the end of the century all the principal Devon seaside resorts had their own links.

Westward Ho! also had the honour of being the birthplace of ladies' golf. Sixty-six women had joined the new ladies' club by the time it held its first tournament in June 1868. The *Exeter Flying Post* commented: 'The fair sex are to be congratulated on having added this outdoor amusement to the few hitherto allowed them'.[60] Later in the same year a second ladies' club was opened at Instow. In October the *North Devon Journal* reported: 'The Ladies' Club lately instituted at Instow had its first prize meeting on Saturday last on the excellent ground on the sand-hills and was attended by all the members and their friends'.[61] In the following year the ladies of Paignton formed a club and began playing this new sport.[62] These ladies' clubs were all in existence well before a ladies' club was established in 1872 at St Andrews, the home of golf.[63]

At the end of the century the cycling craze swept the Devon seaside resorts. As early as the late 1870s a few cyclists were to be seen pedalling along the coastal roads,[64] but the penny-farthings of that period were cumbersome and costly. Technological improvements soon transformed this new sport. By the 1890s bicycles had pneumatic tyres, and chain-driven rear wheels equal in size to the front wheel. Mass production made these new safety bicycles a relatively cheap and easy form of conveyance for visitors. At first it was thought unseemly for ladies to perch on a saddle, but by the 1890s the introduction of women's bicycles and more practical clothing enabled them to take up the sport.[65] The seaside promenades were relatively flat and well suited to cycling but the hilly interior was much less favourable terrain. Pedal-pushers refused to be daunted and soon began to explore Devon in increasing numbers.

At first cycling was looked on simply as another recreation promoting physical fitness, but by the end of the century it was clear that the bicycle was also becoming an instrument of change. It was opening up parts of the Devon coast remote from railways, which previously had only been accessible to those who could afford a horse and carriage. The bicycle heralded a new era of personal freedom for many tourists, who at last could plan their itineraries without recourse to railway timetables.

Sea-bathing gradually became an enjoyable pastime rather than an unpleasant ordeal. In the 1840s the majority of bathers were still being dipped under the waves by attendants, in the hope that they would benefit from the therapeutic properties of the sea water. In 1846 one gentleman visitor to Teignmouth wrote: 'The women attached as guides to the bathing machines are the most horrid-looking creatures I ever beheld —good heavens, to be dipped by one of them and soused like a condemned puppy or kitten! The idea is dreadful'.[66] This dipping ritual gradually fell from favour and by the 1860s bathers were being encouraged to actually swim in the unfamiliar element.[67] Doctors still advocated sea-bathing, but recommendations of the curative qualities of the sea water were gradually qualified, whilst the benefits of swimming, as a healthy form of exercise, were stressed more and more.

The emphasis also shifted from therapy to sport at the baths. The hot and cold sea-water baths were still patronized by some invalids, but as medical support for salt-water treatments began to decline, so the interest in swimming pools grew. Thus it was that the new baths opened at Torquay in 1857, Westward Ho! in 1866, Ilfracombe in 1880 and Teignmouth in 1883 provided not only hot and cold baths for invalids, but also swimming pools.[68]

Swimming clubs were formed at all the principal resorts. The Dawlish Swimming Association, for example, was established in 1864 and at once began organizing swimming matches in the sea.[69] Swimming competitions soon became one of the principal highlights of the summer season at many of the leading Devon resorts. Crowds of spectators assembled on the sea fronts and bands played to enliven the proceedings.

On the north Devon coast a heavy swell and strong tidal currents sometimes made swimming in the sea difficult, so two of the resorts began to stage aquatic sports at their baths. At Westward Ho! competitors would have had to face a buffeting from the Atlantic rollers, so from 1870 onwards swimming races were occasionally organized in the small pool at the Bath House.[70] In 1875 the Great Nassau Bath, measuring 133 feet by 33 feet, was opened at this resort[71] and swimming competitions were quite often held there.[72] At Ilfracombe the Hotel Baths, opened in 1880, had an even larger pool and swimming galas were frequently staged there.[73] These galas attracted many spectators, so in 1883 the Ilfracombe Hotel Company hired 'Professor' Parker, a self-styled 'Professor of the Natatory Arts', to organize a more ambitious programme of aquatic sports and entertainments. Up to a thousand people crowded in to see not only races, water polo matches and exhibitions of swimming and diving, but also comic turns including walking the greasy pole, tub races and swimming blindfold after live ducks.[74] R.D. Blackmore was present at one of these entertainments and watched in amazement while a 'male and female professor of the natatory art took afternoon tea at a table floating in the middle of the water'.[75]

Bathing exhibited the flesh and in so doing exposed some sensitive Victorian attitudes towards morality and propriety. There was a growing preoccupation with matters affecting public decency. Many Victorian visitors were concerned about dressing and undressing on the beaches, about the segregation of the sexes in the sea and particularly about nude bathing. The days when leering gallants ogled naked women bathers had long passed and it had become customary for ladies to bathe in voluminous costumes. Yet many English gentlemen still insisted on swimming in the buff, claiming that bathing drawers were cumbersome and a hindrance to their manly exercise. Francis Kilvert was a clergyman, but as late as 1873 he saw nothing wrong in bathing at Seaton without a costume:

A boy brought me to the machine door two towels as I thought, but when I came out of the water and began to use them, I found that one of the rags he had given me was a pair of very short red and white striped drawers to cover my nakedness. Unaccustomed to such things, I had in my ignorance bathed naked and set at nought the conventionalities of the place and scandalized the beach.[76]

Public decency became as important an issue as public health at many Devon resorts and sometimes the objective in forming a Local Board was as much to prevent bathers behaving improperly as it was to curb sanitary nuisances. In Chapter 9 it was shown that at Dawlish one of the principal reasons given in 1859 for seeking the powers of a Local Board was to put a stop to 'indecent bathing'.[77] Sidmouth was equally anxious to prohibit conduct which might drive away some of its wealthy patrons. It established a Local Board in 1863 after complaints about 'shameless men going stark naked in and out of the water close to the ladies' bathing places when a number of girls are waiting for the machines'.[78] When Seaton in 1877 applied to form a Local Board one of the principal reasons given was that 'in consequence of there being no local authority for the place, disgraceful and indecent scenes in regard to bathing ... are frequently occurring'.[79]

Once formed the new Local Boards were soon busy trying to stamp out nude bathing. The Teignmouth Local Board, for example, in 1866 passed a resolution stating: 'In future no person shall bathe ... whether from a machine or otherwise, after nine o'clock in the morning, without wearing bathing drawers'.[80] This measure was welcomed by some, but was greeted with outrage by others. One angry tourist insisted in a letter to the *Western Times* that visitors went to Teignmouth 'to have pure bathing unfettered by clammy, wet rags'.[81] Male nude bathing proved difficult to abolish, but by the late 1880s the forces of propriety had finally triumphed. In 1889 one visitor to Ilfracombe commented: 'Decency prevails to such an extent that every little boy of whatever class wears bathing drawers'.[82]

Mixed bathing was everywhere forbidden. Separate stretches of the beach were designated for ladies and gentlemen at resorts like Paignton and Exmouth. Many resorts went a stage further by reserving whole beaches for ladies and others for gentlemen. At Dawlish, for example, ladies bathed on the beach adjoining the Marine Parade, whilst the men were obliged to bathe at Coryton Cove, 'a very secluded locality about a quarter of a mile distant from the ladies' ground'.[83]

Many of the regulations enforcing segregated bathing seem ridiculous today. At Lynmouth, for example, a bye-law introduced in 1884 included the customary stipulation that no male bather over the age of ten years was permitted to approach within a hundred yards of the area set aside for female bathers, and that no female bather of any age was to approach nearer than a hundred yards to a male bather over the age of ten.[84] Such rules separated husband and wife, mother and son, sister and brother, all in the interests of public decency!

Social attitudes began to change at the end of the century and there were growing demands for the introduction of mixed bathing. Victorian taboos were gradually relaxing, and in any case one of the main reasons for segregated bathing was eliminated once men were prevented from swimming in the nude. There were also fears that some English holiday-makers were beginning to desert the English seaside in favour of French and Belgian watering places, where the sexes were allowed to swim together, and this increased the pressure on English resorts to provide the same facility. A letter published in the *Standard* in 1896 pointed out that 'on the Continent men and women bathe together and there is nothing to shock the sensibilities of the most prudish', and asked if in England there was a resort where they might do the same.[85] The newspaper was soon informed that Seaton was one of five English coastal resorts where mixed bathing was already allowed.[86]

Paignton was soon to join the small group of English resorts permitting mixed bathing. In the summer of 1896 a vigorous campaign was mounted to persuade the new Paignton Urban District Council to allow the sexes to bathe together. The Council received a number of letters from prospective visitors enquiring if mixed bathing was permitted and warning that if it was not they would holiday at Seaton or on the Continent instead of at Paignton.[87] One letter to the *Paignton Observer* asked:

> Why do we not adopt the continental idea of mixed bathing? And why should not Paignton, with its unrivalled sands, be a pioneer in this matter? . . . I feel confident that were the experiment tried that many, who like myself now take their wives and families to French watering places, would flock to Paignton.[88]

There was general concern at the threatened loss of trade and so in July the Council decided to 'wink at the bye-laws' for the remainder of the season.[89] In August the Council finally resolved to officially permit mixed bathing in 1897.[90] This decision received national publicity and Paignton benefited from an influx of visitors.[91]

Prudery was in retreat at Paignton, but it was still not completely vanquished. While the sexes were allowed to bathe together on the north side of the pier and were allowed to use tents for changing, the main beach was still reserved for segregated bathing. Only 'properly attired' men and boys were allowed to join the ladies in the mixed-bathing zone.[92] Even the keenest advocates of mixed bathing believed that the loin cloth then worn by many male bathers was a 'simply disgusting' form of attire in which to meet and bathe with ladies, and said that they would 'judge any dress indecent which did not completely cover the body from the neck to the knees'.[93] Thus it was that the all-concealing costumes already worn at the continental resorts became a required form of dress for gentlemen bathers at Paignton, as at other English resorts adopting the new practice of mixed bathing.

The whole edifice of Victorian propriety began to crumble on the Devon coast, for once Seaton and Paignton had removed the barriers to the sexes bathing together, they found that visitors flooded in, and other more conservative resorts were obliged to follow them, or run the risk of their patrons deserting them for more progressive watering places. In August 1897 Dawlish resolved to allow mixed bathing[94] while Torquay followed suit in October 1900.[95] At both resorts the decision reflected mounting concern at the loss of trade to Paignton where mixed bathing was proving so popular. These resorts were merely responding to changes in demand rather than attempting to alter public behaviour, so while they were in the vanguard of the movement to introduce mixed bathing, they were careful to reserve some sections of their beaches as segregated bathing areas to meet the needs of those who still regarded mixed bathing as immoral.

The shackles of Victorian prudery were somewhat slower to loosen on the north Devon coast. In 1905 the *North Devon Journal* instituted a campaign to allow mixed bathing, arguing that 'a large number of ladies would learn to swim if they could have the assistance of their father, husband or brother'.[96] Mixed bathing was finally allowed at Ilfracombe in 1906 and at Lynmouth in the following year.[97] Significantly at both resorts it was soon found that the number of ladies and gentlemen going for a swim greatly increased.[98]

In less than a decade mixed bathing had become acceptable and popular at resorts which had formerly banned it. This change in opinion and policy had come about partly as a result of a relaxation in moral attitudes, and partly as a consequence of the growing popularity of both family holidays and swimming, for it was absurd that members of a family had to be separated from each other while in the sea. Everywhere on the Devon coast the introduction of mixed bathing presaged the eventual demise of the bathing machine, for once the sexes were allowed to bathe together, there was no point in concealment before the water was reached. Bathing tents were less expensive to provide and more convenient to use for simply changing in.

There was a strong lobby at the Devon resorts campaigning against the introduction of rowdy, catchpenny entertainments. Middle-class visitors came seeking peace and self-improvement, and had a strong dislike of brash commercialism. Wealthy invalids and elderly residents were equally opposed to any innovations which might attract more excursionists and disrupt the quiet gentility of these sedate watering places. The established holiday industry depended on the patronage of this leisured company, and it was not prepared to seek the pence and problems of transitory trippers, if it risked losing the sovereigns and support of long-stay visitors and wealthy residents. So the Devon seaside resorts offered few man-made attractions, but instead relied heavily on their relatively unspoilt natural environment to attract discriminating holiday-makers.

'There is nothing to see there but respectability', complained one visitor after a visit to Lynton and Lynmouth in 1863,[99] yet this was precisely the quality that many visitors found so attractive. The Devon coastal watering places might be criticized for being dull, but many serious-minded holiday-makers felt secure there because they were protected from the vulgarity, noise and low social tone found at many more commercialized English seaside resorts.

Nothing more clearly demonstrated the Devon resorts' aversion to brash and uncultured commercial entertainment than their attitude towards beach entertainers. Stalls, sideshows and itinerant minstrels might clutter the beaches at many other English resorts, but on the Devon coast they were largely absent. An 1898 guidebook declared:

> Most of the more plebeian caterers for the amusement of holiday-makers have deserted the south Devon seaside resorts, because visitors have other and more healthy means of filling up their hours than listening to nigger songs or watching the antics of the puppets of a Punch and Judy show.[100]

The sedate Devon resorts were particularly proud of their freedom from 'nigger minstrels'. This offensive name was given in an age of blatant racialism to those groups of musical entertainers who blackened their faces with burnt cork and caricatured the songs and dance of negro slaves. Introduced to England from America in 1847, these minstrels had soon become a familiar sight on many English beaches. Twanging banjos, singing comic ballads and telling jokes, they played a major part in seaside culture.[101] At the Devon resorts, however, they were unwelcome. Westward Ho! in 1872 boasted that it was never 'annoyed by the vulgar, discordant songs of Ethiopian serenaders',[102] Lynton and Lynmouth in 1890 claimed to be 'far from the reach of the niggers and the thousand and one annoyances of an ordinary watering place',[103] while Torquay as late as 1898 was still announcing: 'There are no niggers on the sands or other garish pleasures, and holiday-makers who love the flesh-pots of Margate and Ramsgate had better keep away'.[104]

Only at the very end of the century did attitudes at last begin to change. In 1895 Exmouth, which had always boasted of its freedom from minstrel shows, allowed the 'Jackdaws' to perform for the summer season, while at Sidmouth the 'Black Hawk Minstrels' were given permission to entertain visitors.[105] Soon afterwards some pale-faced rivals began to try their fortune on the Devon beaches. Pierrots had been introduced into England from France in 1891. These entertainers, with faces as white as oxide of zinc could make them, were soon all the rage at many English seaside resorts.[106] More refined and better dressed than the black-faced minstrels, they were accepted at many of the Devon resorts[107] and by 1901 even select Lynton and Lynmouth had a professional troupe appearing daily for the summer season.[108]

Even at the end of the century the Devon seaside resorts were implacably opposed to any proposals for pleasure piers. At many rival resorts elsewhere on the English coast these symbols of vulgar commercialism had become the principal attraction, with their wide range of artificial amusements luring in huge crowds of fun-loving day-trippers.[109] Yet at the Devon seaside resorts not a single pleasure pier was built. In part this was because admission charges to pleasure piers were low and businessmen realized that at the relatively remote Devon seaside resorts it was unlikely that they would attract the large numbers of people needful to provide a reasonable return on the large capital investment. Of far more consequence was the fear that a pleasure pier would drive away affluent visitors who wanted to avoid both noisy, flashy amusements and the working-class excursionists they attracted.

Promenade piers were considered acceptable. Unlike the pleasure piers they offered few man-made amusements. They were simply intended to give visitors the novel experience of strolling above the heaving waves and of enjoying the thrill of being out at sea without the risks and discomforts of a boat trip. In reality they were little more than extensions of the seashore promenades, and as such they were thought to be ideal locations from which to inhale the health-giving sea breezes, to admire the marine views and to engage in social display.

Only four promenade piers were built at the Devon seaside resorts. The first was a 600-feet long structure opened at Teignmouth in 1867.[110] William Miller visited it in 1887 and found it was little frequented because the admission charge of 2d. was 'too high for the attractions it can offer'.[111] Entertainment on this pier was extremely limited; visitors could promenade, listen to the band or roller skate.[112] In 1873 a 500-foot promenade pier was completed at Westward Ho! but, as we have seen, it was soon destroyed by Atlantic storms.[113] Then in 1879 a 780-feet long pier was opened at Paignton. This pier did have a pavilion, a roller-skating room and a small billiard room, but in essence it was still a sedate promenade pier rather than a full-blown pleasure pier.[114] In 1885 an article in the *Paignton Observer* made it clear that only respectable entertainment was permitted: 'In place of the peripatetic minstrels, the shrimp teas and high jinks which form the staple amusement on many promenade piers, everything here is quiet and refined'.[115] Finally, in 1895 a stone promenade pier was opened in Torquay. It offered harbour views and band concerts, but once again rejected all vulgar amusements.

Steamer trips were one of the few commercial attractions available to holiday-makers at the Devon seaside resorts. Yet even this popular pastime was one which took advantage of Devon's natural assets rather than providing man-made indoor facilities, for these sea excursions were an ideal way for visitors to take the pure sea air and to admire the splendid coastal scenery. At many sleepy watering places the arrival of a steamer became the highlight in an otherwise uneventful day. Even those who had no intention of going on board found this maritime activity a novel focus of interest.

By the late nineteenth century pleasure steamers were picking up passengers at all the principal south Devon resorts. Where there was no pier or harbour to facilitate boarding, the pleasure steamers came in close to the beach and passengers had to scramble on board from mobile landing stages. A wide range of sea trips were on offer. From Torquay, for example, in 1890 the steamer *Prince* went on excursions to Sidmouth, Teignmouth, Seaton and Dawlish, while the *Lady of the Isles*, a new steamship, went to Torcross, Dartmouth, Start Point and Dawlish.[116] In 1891 a new company was formed to exploit the rapidly growing demand for steamer trips. The Devon Dock, Pier and Steamship Company first purchased Exmouth Docks and the piers at Teignmouth and Paignton, and then acquired a new pleasure steamer, *The Duchess of Devonshire*, to take trips from their dock and piers to places of interest all along the coast between Plymouth and Bournemouth. This steamer loaded and disembarked passengers from many of the harbours, piers and beaches along the south Devon coast. Such was its success that in 1894 the Company purchased a second vessel, *The Duke of Devonshire*, so that they could provide an even wider range of cruises.[117]

Even more marine excursions were available from the principal north Devon resorts. The well-appointed paddle-steamers which arrived there on day excursions from Bristol and South Wales often picked up passengers for a sea trip. In 1897 P. and A. Campbell were advertising a large number of excursions from Ilfracombe and Lynmouth to such attractive destinations as Clovelly, Woody Bay and Lundy Isle.[118]

By the end of the nineteenth century the commitment to improvement was at last beginning to weaken and visitors no longer felt obliged to devote so much of their holiday to recreations designed to exercise their mind and body. It was possible to rest and relax on the beach without feeling pangs of guilt. Bathing could be enjoyed instead of being regarded as an unpleasant but necessary activity for the recovery of good health. Prudery was beginning to lose its grip and already some resorts were allowing the sexes to swim together. The opposition to vulgar commercialism had lasted far longer than at most English seaside resorts. Yet by 1900 beach entertainers were performing at a growing number of Devon watering places and cinemas were to be opened at most of the Devon resorts in the years immediately preceding the First World War. Pleasure was at last replacing improvement as the principal objective when seeking recreation on the Devon coast.

Conclusion

This study has provided an example of a group of provincial seaside resorts which achieved national recognition despite their remote position. In their initial stage of development, the Devon coastal watering places catered mainly for a local clientele. Yet before long they they were proving their ability to attract visitors from distant parts of the country and no longer had to depend solely on local or even on regional sources of demand. Devon ended the nineteenth century with just one major seaside resort in Torquay, but with no less than eight middle-rank watering places, which likewise served a national clientele, and with a rapidly growing number of minor resorts proving that they too could attract visitors from distant parts of the country. These resorts owed their drawing power to the fact that the holidays they provided were markedly different from those available at most of their English competitors.

One key to the success of the Devon seaside resorts was that they developed reputations as specialized health resorts. Most English seaside resorts made some claims for the healthiness of their coastal location, but many of the Devon watering places had the important advantage of being recommended by eminent members of the medical fraternity. Invalids formed an unusually large proportion of their visiting public and they also played host to many elderly people. In addition, several south Devon seaside resorts at an early date developed a second season in winter, and this also helped to set them apart from the great majority of resorts.

Distance from the major centres of inland demand enabled the Devon seaside resorts to preserve a high social tone, and this was another factor which distinguished them from many of their rivals in other parts of the country. Even in the later nineteenth century, when rising real incomes were fuelling a growing demand for seaside holidays, their remoteness still insulated them from the massive working-class invasions experienced at so many other British seaside resorts. Their sedate, genteel ambience proved particularly attractive to those who disliked crowds and valued social status.

Another factor which set the Devon seaside resorts apart from many of their competitors was that they relied to an unusual extent on their natural assets to attract their clientele. It was their exceptionally mild sea air, splendid scenery and rich flora and fauna which made them attractive holiday destinations, despite their remote location. Elsewhere on the British coast, resorts like Weston-super-Mare and New Brighton could flourish with only the minimum of natural advantages, simply because they happened to be easy to reach from big cities and had some commercial attractions to lure in holiday-makers. In sharp contrast the Devon watering places in the second half of the nineteenth century were boasting of their freedom from tawdry commercialized entertainment. They set out to attract those holiday-makers who viewed the sparsity of artificial amusements as an advantage rather than a disadvantage.

Swings of the pendulum of fashion greatly affected the fortunes of individual watering places on the Devon coast. In the initial phase of development, in the years after 1750, the emphasis was on sea-bathing as a health-giving activity, and so Exmouth and Teignmouth, which had sandy beaches and were conveniently close to Exeter, were the first resorts to emerge. In the later part of the eighteenth century, attention began to swing towards the medical advantages of mild winters and pure sea air. Torquay, Sidmouth, Seaton and Budleigh Salterton all benefited, for while their beaches were not exceptional their climate was thought to be particularly suitable for invalids. At the same time the new cult of the picturesque also began to attract fashionable tourists, both to the south Devon coast and to Ilfracombe and Lynton and Lynmouth in north Devon.

The pendulum of fashion swung back in the later nineteenth century, as the importance attributed to climatic cures gradually diminished and interest increased in sea-bathing for pleasure, and in a variety of recreational activities associated with the sea and shore. The beach then took on a new importance as the focal point for a family holiday. Watering places with sandy beaches on the south Devon coast, such as Paignton, Dawlish, Teignmouth and Exmouth benefited from this shift of public interest, while, on the sandy Atlantic coast of north Devon, minor resorts began to emerge at Woolacombe, Croyde Bay and Saunton Sands. On the other hand, the shingle-beach resorts of Sidmouth, Seaton and Budleigh Salterton grew very little, because they were unable to attract many of the middle-class families who were forming a growing section of the holiday market.

Torquay was a major exception to the general trend, for it still flourished in the late nineteenth century despite the fact that its appeal centred principally on its climatic advantages and its beaches were not considered to be as good as some of its competitors. It was recognized as England's leading resort for the treatment of lung complaints, so it captured an increasing share of the contracting invalid market. It was also famous as the country's leading winter resort and this enabled it to attract many wealthy visitors and residents for a long winter season.

At the very end of the century another change of fashion began to affect the Devon seaside resorts, with a growing vogue for exotic foreign holidays causing some of their wealthiest patrons to desert them for the Alps, Norway, the Canaries, Egypt and other distant locations. This in turn gave added momentum to the trend towards shorter holidays, for whereas many of the rich visitors had spent whole summers or whole winters at the Devon resorts, most of the less-affluent holiday-makers who replaced them could only afford a week or at most a fortnight's stay.

Throughout the nineteenth century the Devon seaside resorts displayed a remarkable homogeneity, in sharp contrast to the diversity of coastal watering places developing in many other English coastal regions. Lowerson and Myerscough have shown that on the Sussex coast 'an array of towns developed, each offering its own brand of seaside attractions, vying in its different mix of natural and man-made facilities',[1] while Perkin has found equal variety among the resorts on the coast of north-west England, ranging from Blackpool, which developed into a predominantly working-class resort, to nearby Southport, a bastion of select respectability.[2] On the Devon coast the situation was quite different, for there was an unusual uniformity in the type of entertainment provided at each of the principal resorts, and there were only subtle gradations in the social standing of the watering places. Even at Ilfracombe, which became relatively easy to reach by Bristol Channel steamers and therefore suffered more than any other Devon resort from tripper invasions, the inhabitants tried hard to preserve its reputation as a highly respectable watering place where only refined and decorous entertainments were permitted. So, whilst in 1892 one travel writer found that Ilfracombe lacked 'the sad dignity of Torquay and the subdued gentility of Teignmouth', he pointed out that it could still 'turn up its nose at the high jinks' of Weston-super-Mare and many other boisterous coastal resorts.[3]

Why was it that the social ambience and pattern of entertainment remained so similar at each of the principal Devon seaside resorts? The answer would seem to be that in their formative years the Devon watering places were extremely difficult to reach from the principal centres of demand. On those English coasts which were more easily accessible from densely populated areas, differences in land ownership and in the policies of those residents with political power played the biggest part in determining how the resorts developed and whether they appealed more to the upper classes or to the urban masses. This brought about major differences in the social tone of watering places which were only a few miles apart. On the Devon coast the situation was strikingly different, for the difficulty of access outweighed all internal factors and played easily the most important part in shaping the character of the resorts. Early development at all the Devon seaside resorts was closely related to the high expectations of the privileged minority who alone could afford to travel there. Even in late Victorian times, the time and cost of travel still formed a barrier preventing mass influxes of the working class, though by then some of the well-born and well-off visitors had become residents and played their part in defending the select character of their resorts. The Devon watering places were not all exactly the same, but even at the very end of the nineteenth century they still exhibited a striking uniformity in their high social tone and in their blend of health and pleasure facilities.

There are some themes which could not be explored within the limits of this book, but which might form future lines of enquiry. This book has briefly considered the decline of the old maritime activities, but a more detailed examination of employment and its changing pattern at the resorts would be valuable. This might first look at the gradual loss of traditional occupations, and then move on to examine the new forms of employment created by tourism, the geographical origins of the work force, the seasonal nature of their jobs and the hardship suffered at most resorts during the period of winter unemployment. It would also be interesting to look more closely at the origins of business enterprise and capital, to see if it came mainly from within the resorts, or from elsewhere in Devon, or from outside the county.

Mention has been made of the formation of Local Boards, and of their work in safeguarding public health and public morality, but the evolution of local government at the Devon resorts is a topic which could form the basis of a separate research project. Such a study might profitably focus on the conflict between the tourist interest, which was frequently demanding improvements in sanitation, public utilities and amenities, and those pressure groups battling to prevent the ratepayers incurring additional expense.

It would also be rewarding to compare the tourist industry of Devon with that of Cornwall. Some of Cornwall's seaside resorts were favoured with even milder climates than the Devon watering places, while others could claim to have better beaches or more picturesque scenery. Yet the Cornish resorts were even further from the major centres of inland demand. It would be interesting to find out how far the period, pace and character of their development differed from that of the Devon seaside resorts.

A survey of twentieth-century growth and change at the Devon seaside resorts is also needed. This might study the impact made by further transport innovations, showing how the motor car and the charabanc began the process of opening up even the remotest coastal villages to the tourist. It should also consider how, as the holiday market became more democratized, so the holiday resorts became increasingly less alike, with some responding to the new opportunities by providing holiday camps, caravan sites and commercial entertainment to attract working-class visitors, while other more conservative resorts still tried to retain the quiet, genteel image they had cultivated in Victorian times.

It is hoped that this book has made some contribution to our knowledge and understanding of the development of tourism on the English coast. Previous studies of large, popular seaside resorts such as Blackpool and Margate have revealed some of the dynamics of holiday-making and resort growth in areas relatively close to the major centres of population. This book has broken new ground, for it has examined the rise of a county grouping of resorts in a remote part of the country, with many of them being comparatively small in size and all of them boasting a high social tone. It has shown that changes in medical and social fashion and in the local and national demand for holidays were of vital significance. But it has stressed that the most important factor shaping and controlling the pace and character of the development of the Devon seaside resorts was their distance from the chief inland centres of holiday demand. This in turn meant that any transport innovations which improved links with far-off parts of the country were of vital consequence. While remoteness was the principal barrier to their progress, it was also the principal defence of their high social tone. New transport services brought more trade, but they also brought change as they gradually opened up the Devon coast to a wider spectrum of society. Yet, even at the very end of the nineteenth century, the relatively remote location of the Devon resorts was still the major factor shaping their development. Changes were certainly taking place, but the world outside was being altered at a much faster rate, and visitors to the Devon watering places often went there seeking a refuge from the crowds and commercial amusements that were invading many more easily accessible English seaside resorts.

This then is a book about a very distinctive group of coastal resorts. The author hopes that it will inspire some studies of regional groups of watering places in other parts of the country and especially of clusters of resorts located in similarly isolated coastal areas. He also hopes that it will lead others to share his fascination with the remarkable rise of seaside resorts on the remote coast of Devon.

List of Principal Abbreviations

Abbreviations are listed here for works frequently cited in the notes. Other references are given in full on the first occasion they occur in the notes to a chapter and subsequent references for that chapter are abbreviated. Where no place of publication is given the work was published in London.

BG
> *Bideford Gazette*

Blewitt, *Panorama*
> O. Blewitt, *Panorama of Torquay* (2nd edn, 1832)

Clark, *Climate*
> J. Clark, *The Influence of Climate on the Prevention and Cure of Chronic Diseases* (1829)

DCNQ
> *Devon and Cornwall Notes and Queries*

Derry, ed., *Burney*
> J. Helmlow and W. Derry, eds, *The Journals and Letters of Fanny Burney (Madame D'Arblay)* (Oxford, 1982)

DRO
> Devon Record Office

EFP
> *Exeter Flying Post*

Ellis, ed., *Burney*
> A.R. Ellis, ed., *The Early Diary of Frances Burney, 1768–1778* (1907)

EPG
> *Exeter and Plymouth Gazette*

GM
> *The Gentleman's Magazine*

Granville, *Spas*
    A.B. Granville, *The Spas of England and Principal Sea-Bathing Places* (1841)

Greig, ed., *Farington*
    J. Greig, ed., *The Farington Diary: By Joseph Farington* (1925)

HLRO
    House of Lords Record Office

Hyett, *A Description*
    W. Hyett, *A Description of the Watering Places on the South-East Coast of Devon* (Exeter, 1803)

IC
    Ilfracombe Chronicle

IG
    Ilfracombe Gazette

LLR
    Lynton and Lynmouth Recorder

Maton, *Observations*
    W.G. Maton, *Observations Relative Chiefly to the Natural History, Picturesque Scenery and Antiquities of the Western Counties of England* (Salisbury, 1797)

May, 'Ilfracombe'
    F.B. May, 'The Development of Ilfracombe as a Resort in the Nineteenth Century' (unpublished MA thesis, University of Wales, 1978)

'Memoirs of Savage'
    Suffolk Record Office, Ipswich Branch, S9, 'Memoirs and Travels of John Savage' (1790)

Moncrieff, *Where?*
    A.R.H. Moncrieff, *Where Shall We Go?* (14th edn, 1899)

NDH
    North Devon Herald

NDJ
    North Devon Journal

Oliver, ed., *Curwen*
    A. Oliver, ed., *The Journal of Samuel Curwen, Loyalist* (Cambridge, Massachusetts, 1972)

Pimlott, *Holiday*
    J.A.R. Pimlott, *The Englishman's Holiday: A Social History* (Hassocks, 2nd edn, 1977)

PRO
Public Record Office

Sea-Bathing Places
A Guide to All the Watering and Sea-Bathing Places (1803)

Seaside Watering Places
Seaside Watering Places: Being a Guide to Strangers in Search of a Suitable Place in which to Spend their Holidays (new edn, 1896)

Sheldon, *Trackway*
G. Sheldon, *From Trackway to Turnpike: An Illustration from East Devon* (1928)

Sigsworth, ed., *Resorts*
E.M. Sigsworth, ed., *Ports and Resorts in the Regions* (Hull, 1980)

Swete, 'Picturesque'
DRO, 564/M, J. Swete, 'Picturesque Sketches of Devon', (1792–1801)

TD
Torquay Directory

TDA
Transactions of the Devon Association

Thomas, *Railways*
D.S.J. Thomas, *A Regional History of the Railways of Great Britain: Volume I, The West Country* (6th edn, 1988)

'Tour'
Bath Reference Library, 'Description of a Tour to the Isle of Wight and into the West of England in the Summer of 1810'

Travis, 'Holidaymaking'
J.F. Travis, 'The Rise of Holidaymaking on the Devon Coast, 1750 to 1900: With Particular Reference to Health and Entertainment' (unpublished PhD thesis, University of Exeter, 1989)

Vancouver, *General View*
C. Vancouver, *General View of the Agriculture of the County of Devon* (1808)

Walton, *Seaside Resort*
J.K. Walton, *The English Seaside Resort: A Social History, 1750–1914* (Leicester, 1983)

Walvin, *Seaside*
J. Walvin, *Beside the Seaside: A Social History of the Popular Seaside Holiday, 1750–1914* (1978)

Watering Places
   A Guide to the Watering Places on the Coast, between the Exe and the Dart (Teignmouth, 1817)

Whyman, 'Aspects'
   J. Whyman, 'Aspects of Holiday-making and Resort Development within the Isle of Thanet, with Particular Reference to Margate, *c*.1736 to *c*.1840' (PhD thesis, University of Kent, 1980, published New York, 1981)

Williams, *Picturesque*
   T.H. Williams, *Picturesque Excursions in Devonshire* (1804)

WL
   Western Luminary
WT
   Western Times

Notes

Introduction

1. Much of the research was for my thesis: Travis, 'Holidaymaking'.
2. W.G. Hoskins, *Devon* (1974), 117-20.
3. Pimlott, *Holiday*.
4. Walvin, *Seaside*.
5. Walton, *Seaside Resort*.
6. P. Russell, *A History of Torquay* (Torquay, 1960); J.A. Bulley, *Teignmouth in History* (Torquay, 1958); L. Lamplugh, *A History of Ilfracombe* (Chichester, 1984); R. Mayo, *The Story of Westward Ho!* (Yelland, 1973).
7. B. May, 'The Rise of Ilfracombe as a Seaside Resort', in S. Fisher, ed., *West Country Maritime and Social History: Some Essays* (Exeter, 1980), 137-59; F.B. May, 'Victorian and Edwardian Ilfracombe', in J.K. Walton and J. Walvin, eds, *Leisure in Britain, 1780–1939* (Manchester, 1983), 188-205; May, 'Ilfracombe'.
8. *Western Flying Post*, 29 June 1767. I am indebted to Chris Robinson for information about Plymouth.
9. S.H. Adamson, *Seaside Piers* (1977), 102.
10. F.M. Williams, *Plymouth as a Tourist and Health Resort* (Plymouth, 1898).
11. See esp. E.W. Gilbert, *Brighton: Old Ocean's Bauble* (Hassocks, 2nd edn, 1975); J.K. Walton, 'The Social Development of Blackpool, 1788–1914' (unpublished PhD thesis, University of Lancaster, 1974); Whyman, 'Aspects'.

Chapter One: South Devon Resorts, 1750–1788

1. J.J. Cartwright, ed., *The Travels through England of Dr Richard Pococke during 1750, 1751 and Later Years* (1888), I, 102. It is possible that Exmouth began to develop as a resort at a much earlier date. Polwhele's *History of Devonshire*, first published in 1793, stated that Exmouth had begun to attract visitors 'about a century ago', after a local judge 'in a very infirm state of health went thither to bathe and received great benefit': R. Polwhele, *The History of Devonshire* (1793), II, 215. I have not found any other reference to Exmouth having a resort function prior to 1750.
2. A. Brice, *The Grand Gazetteer* (Exeter, 1759), 1284.
3. Oliver, ed., *Curwen*, I, 104.

4. H. Downman, *Infancy: Or the Management of Children* (Exeter, 6th edn, 1803), 21, 116.

5. Walton, *Seaside Resort,* 11; Pimlott, *Holiday,* 52.

6. Walton, *Seaside Resort,* 11-5.

7. T. Short, *History of Mineral Waters* (1740) quoted in J.A. Patmore, 'The Spa Towns of Britain', in R.P. Beckinsale and J.M. Houston, eds, *Urbanisation and Its Problems* (Oxford, 1968), 47.

8. Pimlott, *Holiday,* 50-1, 54.

9. R. Russell, *A Disseration on the Use of Sea Water in the Diseases of the Glands* (1752), 6, 12.

10. Travis, 'Holidaymaking', 348-351.

11. 'Teignmouth', *The Royal Magazine,* VI, 128. A reference by J.A. Bulley led me to this article: J.A. Bulley, 'Teignmouth as a Seaside Resort before the Coming of the Railway', *TDA,* LXXXVIII (1958), 128.

12. *EFP,* 17 Sept. 1789.

13. Dr Lavington of Tavistock, 'The Case of a Lady Who Drank the Sea Water', *Royal Magazine: Philosophical Transactions: Abridged Version,* XII (1809), 6.

14. Whyman, 'Aspects', 145.

15. Brice, *Grand Gazetteer,* 551.

16. 'Teignmouth', *The Royal Magazine,* VI, 128.

17. Ellis, *Burney,* I, 254.

18. 'Ode Addressed to the Bathing Machines at Exmouth', *GM,* LII (1783), 607.

19. Brice, *Grand Gazetteer,* 551, 1284.

20. Downman, *Infancy,* 21, 116-8.

21. Swete, 'Picturesque', X, 159-60.

22. W.G. Hoskins, *Industry, Trade and People in Exeter, 1688-1800* (Exeter, 2nd edn, 1968), 28-58; W.G. Hoskins, *Two Thousand Years in Exeter* (Chichester, 1960), 80, 84-91.

23. See P. Borsay, 'The English Urban Renaissance: The Development of Provincial Urban Culture, *c.*1680–*c.*1760', *Social History,* I (1977), 581-603. Borsay identifies two distinct types of towns: those that created surplus wealth and those that attracted it.

24. 'An Essay on English Roads', *GM,* XXII (1752), 552-3.

25. Sheldon, *Trackway,* 71, 90.

26. P.H. Bagwell, *The Transport Revolution from 1770* (1974), 37-8.

27. W. Buckingham, *A Transport Key: An Account of the Proceedings of the Exeter Turnpike Trustees from 12 June 1753 to 1 November 1884* (Exeter, 1885), 7.

28. Sheldon, *Trackway,* 98-9, 134-5.

29. Buckingham, *Turnpike Key,* 38; Sheldon, *Trackway,* 99-100.

30. *EFP,* 6 May 1768.

31. *EFP,* 21 July 1769.

32. E.W. Gilbert, *Brighton: Old Ocean's Bauble* (Hassocks, 2nd edn, 1975), 116.

33. J. Whyman, 'Water Communications to Margate and Gravesend as Coastal

Resorts before 1840', *Southern History*, III (1981), 117: Travis, 'Holiday-making', 24.

34. *EFP*, 2 Mar. 1764, 5 June 1767, 13 Nov. 1778, 4 Jan. 1787.
35. *EFP*, 6 May 1768, 21 July 1769.
36. Gilbert, *Brighton*, 117.
37. Whyman, 'Water Communications', 117.
38. Whyman, 'Water Communications', 114.
39. Travis, 'Holidaymaking', 353-6.
40. Brice, *Grand Gazetteer*, 551.
41. M. Margarot, *Histoire ou Relation d'un Voyage* (1780), 17.
42. R. Newton, *Eighteenth Century Exeter* (Exeter, 1984), 69.
43. Sheldon, *Trackway*, 83, 100; *EFP*, 8 April 1768, 26 Dec. 1777.
44. Oliver, ed., *Curwen*, I, 205, 478, 561.
45. Ellis, *Burney*, I, 219-21, 224.
46. A. Hern, *The Seaside Holiday: The History of the English Seaside Resort* (1967), 15, 38, 155.
47. J.K. Walton and P.R. McGloin, 'Holiday Resorts and Their Visitors: Some Sources for the Local Historian', *Local Historian*, III (1979), 324-8.
48. *EFP*, 10-24 June, 15-22 July, 5 August 1774.
49. Oliver, ed., *Curwen*, I, 204-8.
50. Oliver, ed., *Curwen*, I, 461.
51. Oliver, ed., *Curwen*, I, 461.
52. Oliver, ed., *Curwen*, I, 455.
53. Oliver, ed., *Curwen*, I, 547.
54. Oliver, ed., *Curwen*, I, 544.
55. Oliver, ed., *Curwen*, I, 560.
56. Oliver, ed., *Curwen*, I, 547.
57. A.M. Northway, 'The Devon Fishing Industry, 1760-1860' (unpublished MA thesis, University of Exeter, 1969), 62; Hoskins, *Devon*, 217-8.
58. Oliver, ed., *Curwen*, I, 106.
59. Ellis, *Burney*, I, 220.
60. Oliver, ed., *Curwen*, I, 542.
61. W. Webb, *Memorials of Exmouth* (Exmouth, 1872), 23-4.
62. Brice, *Grand Gazetteer*, 1284.
63. *EFP*, 3 May 1776.
64. Oliver, ed., *Curwen*, I, 546-7.
65. *EFP*, 11 June 1773, 2 June 1780.
66. Oliver, ed., *Curwen*, I, 204-10, 448-80.
67. *EFP*, 25 May 1770.
68. *EFP*, 11 June 1773.
69. *EFP*, 10 Aug. 1781, 3 July 1783.
70. C.W. Chalklin, 'Capital Expenditure on Building for Cultural Purposes in Provincial England, 1730-1830', *Business History*, XXII (1980), 54-5; Walton, *Seaside Resort*, 158.

71. Pimlott, *Holiday*, 60; Walton, *Seaside Resort*, 158.
72. *EFP*, 31 Dec. 1773.
73. *EFP*, 10 Aug. 1781.
74. W. Everitt, *Memorials of Exmouth* (Exmouth, 2nd edn, 1885), 20.
75. Ellis, *Burney*, I, 248.
76. Ellis, *Burney*, I, 246-7.
77. Ellis, *Burney*, I, 245-6.
78. Ellis, *Burney*, I, 230.
79. *EFP*, 25 June 1779.
80. Ellis, *Burney*, I, 244.

Chapter Two: A North Devon Resort, 1770–1788

1. D. Defoe, *A Tour through the Whole Island of Great Britain* (6th edn, 1762), II, 9-10; A. Brice, *The Grand Gazetteer* (Exeter, 1759), 181-2; J. Watkins, *Essay towards a History of Bideford* (Exeter, 1792), 28, 58, 65-6, 71-5.
2. J.B. Gribble, *Memorials of Barnstaple* (Barnstaple, 1830), 542-3; Vancouver, *General View*, 385-6.
3. A.H. Slee, 'Some Dead Industries of North Devon', *TDA*, LXX (1938), 215; Brice, *Grand Gazetteer*, 1208; Vancouver, *General View*, 385.
4. Vancouver, *General View*, 440.
5. W.H. Rogers, 'The Barnstaple Turnpike Trust', *TDA*, LXXIV (1942), 145; Sheldon, *Trackway*, 133.
6. Rogers, 'Barnstaple Turnpike', 139-67.
7. *EFP*, 27 Nov. 1778, 4 Jan. 1787.
8. *EFP*, 27 Nov. 1778.
9. *EFP*, 2 Aug. 1771.
10. *EFP*, 17 July 1788.
11. Swete, 'Picturesque', I, 132-42.
12. Swete, 'Picturesque', I, 172.
13. 'Memoirs of Savage', 27 March–20 April 1790.

Chapter Three: South Devon Resorts, 1789–1815

1. W.G. Hoskins, *Industry, Trade and People in Exeter, 1688–1800* (Exeter, 2nd edn, 1968), 81-6.
2. A. Jenkins, *The History and Description of the City of Exeter and its Environs* (Exeter, 1806), 224, 227.
3. C.H. Lockett, *The Relations of French and English Society, 1763–1793* (1920), 19; 'The Wanderer's Diary in France', *GM*, LXI, Part 2 (1791), 1116.
4. J.G. Alger, *Napoleon's British Visitors and Captives, 1801–1815* (1904), 14.

5. C. Maxwell, *The English Traveller in France, 1698–1815* (1932), 22; Alger, *Napoleon's British Visitors*, 177-8, 212, 271, 303-4; R.S. Lambert, *The Fortunate Traveller* (1950), 80.
6. *The Gentleman's Guide in His Tour through France* (9th edn, 1787), 163-213; Maxwell, *The English Traveller*, 13-4.
7. Maxwell, *The English Traveller*, 16.
8. *EFP*, 16 June 1791.
9. R. Polwhele, *The History of Devonshire* (1793), III, 233.
10. *Sea-Bathing Places* (1803), 197.
11. Greig, ed., *Farington*, V, 264.
12. J. Ingenhousz, 'On the Degree of Salubrity of the Common Air at Sea, as Compared with that of the Seashore and that of Places far Removed from the Sea', *Royal Society: Philosophical Transactions*, LXX (1780), 354-77.
13. R. Fraser, *General View of the County of Devon, with Observations on the Means of its Improvement* (1794), 9.
14. *Sea-Bathing Places* (1803), 193-6.
15. E. Butcher, *An Excursion from Sidmouth to Chester in the Summer of 1803* (1805), 450.
16. C. Hussey, *The Picturesque: Studies in a Point of View* (1927), 110-24; W. Gilpin, *Observations on the River Wye* (Richmond, new edn, 1973), I-V.
17. Swete, 'Picturesque'; P. Hunt, ed., *Devon's Age of Elegance: Described by the Diaries of the Reverend John Swete, Lady Paterson and Miss Mary Cornish* (Exeter, 1984), 9-10, 156-7.
18. See, for example, Hyett, *A Description*, IV.
19. 'Dawlish, Teignmouth and Oxton-house, Devonshire', *GM*, LXIII (1793), Part 1, 593; 'Description of East Teignmouth and Its Environs', *GM*, LXIII (1793), Part 2, 785-6. The latter article was written by John Swete.
20. Maton, *Observations*, I, 101, 117-8.
21. Williams, *Picturesque*.
22. See, for example, J. Evans, *The Juvenile Tourist* (1810), 41, 54; J.A. De Luc, *Geological Travels* (1811), II, 300.
23. Jenkins, *History*, 223-9. *WL*, 10 Aug. 1813, 13 Sept. 1814.
24. Blewitt, *Panorama*, 36; Granville, *Spas*, III, 476.
25. E. Stone, *Chronicles of Fashion* (1845), II, 292-3.
26. M. Dunsford, *Miscellaneous Observations, in the Course of Two Tours, through Several Parts of the West of England* (Tiverton, 1800), 47.
27. Jenkins, *History*, 225-8; Sheldon, *Trackway*, 117.
28. Sheldon, *Trackway*, 117.
29. Swete, 'Picturesque', X, 160.
30. Greig, ed., *Farington*, V, 242-3.
31. Greig, ed., *Farington*, V, 242.
32. S. Ayling, *George III* (1972), 351.
33. 'Diary of their Majesties' Journey to Weymouth and Plymouth', *GM*, LIX, Part 2 (1789), 1204.

34. Granville, *Spas*, III, 475-6.
35. *EFP*, 24 April, 1-22 May 1806.
36. D.M.A. Espriella (R. Southey), *Letters from England* (1814), I, 348.
37. See, for example, *Sea-Bathing Places* (1810), 220.
38. *EFP*, 22 July 1783, 3 Nov. 1785. There was no further acceleration of coach times in this period. In 1815 the mail coach was scheduled to take 24½ hours to travel from London to Exeter: *EFP*, 4 May 1815.
39. *EFP*, 8 Oct. 1789.
40. *EFP*, 29 Sept. 1791.
41. See, for example, *EFP*, 25 Aug., 15 Sept. 1796.
42. National Library of Scotland, MS 2540, 'The Journal of the Hon. Frances Mackenzie', March-April 1811.
43. *DRO* 76/20, 'Memoirs of Henry Ellis', II, 21.
44. Greig, ed., *Farington*, V, 241-2, 255.
45. *EFP*, 6 Sept. 1792.
46. *EFP*, 28 Aug. 1796.
47. *EFP*, 9 June 1791.
48. G.D. and E.G.C. Griffiths, *History of Teignmouth* (Teignmouth, 1965), 76.
49. *EFP*, 20 Aug. 1795.
50. Swete, 'Picturesque', X, 45.
51. *EFP*, 23 Dec. 1790.
52. *EFP*, 18 Dec. 1794.
53. *EFP*, 25 Dec. 1794.
54. Maton, *Observations*, I, 84.
55. *EFP*, 29 Sept. 1791.
56. *WL*, 7 Sept. 1813.
57. Polwhele, *History*, III, 232.
58. E.W. Gilbert, *Brighton: Old Ocean's Bauble* (Hassocks, 2nd edn, 1975), 92; J. Whyman, 'Water Communications to Margate and Gravesend as Coastal Resorts before 1840', *Southern History*, III (1981), 117.
59. Swete, 'Picturesque', IX, 149.
60. Swete, 'Picturesque', X, 38.
61. J. Lackington, *Memoirs of the Forty-Five First Years of the Life of James Lackington* (1794), 313.
62. Swete, 'Picturesque', IX, 149.
63. S. Woolmer, *A Concise Account of the City of Exeter, its Neighbourhood and Adjacent Watering Places* (Exeter, 2nd edn, 1811), 92.
64. Swete, 'Picturesque', II, 112.
65. Maton, *Observations*, I, 117.
66. Hyett, *A Description*, 83.
67. Greig, ed., *Farington*, V, 263.
68. Walton, *Seaside Resort*, 45-6.
69. Tables 1 and 2 do not include figures for Seaton because in the 1801 and

1811 census statistics the returns for Beer and Seaton were added together instead of being shown separately.

70. Walton, *Seaside Resort*, 58.
71. *EFP*, 24 June 1790.
72. Griffiths, *History of Teignmouth*, 42.
73. Butcher, *An Excursion*, 452.
74. *EFP*, 31 Mar., 14 April 1791.
75. J.A. Bulley, 'Teignmouth as a Seaside Resort before the Coming of the Railway', *TDA*, LXXXVIII (1958), 149.
76. Swete, 'Picturesque', X, 12.
77. P. Russell, *A History of Torquay* (Torquay, 1960), 70.
78. D. Webb, *Observations and Remarks during Four Excursions Made to Various Parts of Great Britain in the Years 1810 and 1811* (1811), 69; Greig, ed., *Farington*, V, 257.
79. *EFP*, 9 June 1791.
80. *EFP*, 16 Jan. 1800; G. Griffiths, *The Book of Dawlish* (Buckingham, 1984), 45; *WL*, 9 Aug. 1814.
81. *EFP*, 16 Jan. 1800.
82. *EFP*, 23 July 1801.
83. J. Land, *A Treatise on the Hot, Cold, Tepid, Shower and Vapour Baths* (Exeter, c.1802), 1-2.
84. *EFP*, 8 Oct. 1789.
85. *EFP*, 15 Sept. 1796.
86. *Watering Places*, Part 1, 23.
87. *EFP*, 15 Sept. 1796.
88. *EFP*, 9 July 1801.
89. Woolmer, *Concise Account*, 88-9; *EFP*, 23 Dec. 1813, 15 Dec. 1814; *Watering Places*, Part 2, 17.
90. Butcher, *An Excursion*, 456-7.
91. H.M. Hamlyn, *Eighteenth Century Circulating Libraries in England* (1947), 198.
92. Swete, 'Picturesque', X, 12.
93. R.W. Chapman, ed., *Jane Austen's Letters to Her Sister Cassandra and Others* (1952), 98.
94. *Sea-Bathing Places* (1803), 193-6.
95. N.T. Carrington, *The Teignmouth, Dawlish and Torquay Guide* (Teignmouth, 1830), 28-9.
96. Chapman, ed., *Jane Austen's Letters*, 98.
97. *The Beauties of Sidmouth Displayed* (Sidmouth, 1810), 51-2. This book was published by Mr Wallis.
98. *The Beauties of Sidmouth*, 52.
99. *EFP*, 9 June 1791.
100. Butcher, *An Excursion*, 456.
101. G.A. Cooke, *A Topographical and Statistical Description of the County of Devon* (3rd edn, 1832), 99.

102. *EFP*, 20 Aug. 1795.
103. *EFP*, 14 July 1791; J. Britton and E.W. Brayley, *The Beauties of England and Wales: Devonshire*, 110.
104. *EFP*, 9 June 1791; Butcher, *An Excursion*, 456.
105. *EFP*, 26 Aug. 1802.
106. *Watering Places*, Part 2, 7.
107. *EFP*, 20 June 1816.
108. P. Borsay, 'The English Urban Renaissance: The Development of Provincial Urban Culture, *c*.1680–*c*.1760', *Social History*, I (1977), 582-3.
109. Suffolk Record Office, Bury St Edmunds Branch, E2/44/6, 'Tour in Devonshire by Rev. Sir Thomas Gery Cullum in 1789', 9 Aug. 1789.
110. *EFP*, 6 Sept. 1792.
111. Hyett, *A Description*, 12.
112. R. Bush, *The Book of Exmouth* (Buckingham, 1978), 44. Exmouth had had a promenade leading to the estuary as early as 1750; J.J. Cartwright, ed., *The Travels through England of Dr Richard Pococke during 1750, 1751 and Later Years* (1888), I, 102.
113. E. Butcher, *A New Guide Descriptive of the Beauties of Sidmouth* (Sidmouth, 1827), no pagination.
114. Dunsford, *Miscellaneous Observations*, 106.
115. 'Tour', 75.
116. Greig, ed., *Farington*, V, 245.
117. 'Dawlish, Teignmouth and Oxton-House', 593.
118. Dorset Record Office, NH140, 'Itinerary of Devonshire by Mrs Rackett, 1802', 5-6 Sept. 1802.
119. Cardiff Central Library, MS. 4.367, Robert Clutterbuck, 'Journal of a Tour through the Western Counties of England during the Summer of 1796', 322-4.
120. Berkshire Record Office, R 11A/401, 'Journal of Mrs Price', 24 June 1805.
121. *Western Morning News*, 17 May 1937.
122. *EFP*, 18 Aug. 1775.
123. *EFP*, 24 Sept. 1807, 22 Aug. 1811, 19 Sept. 1811.
124. *EFP*, 18 Aug. 1814.
125. *EFP*, 24 Sept. 1812.
126. J. Evans, *The Juvenile Tourist* (1810), 42.
127. *Watering Places*, Part 1, 47-8.
128. See, for example, T.H. Williams, *Picturesque Excursions in Devonshire; The Environs of Exeter* (Exeter, 1815), *passim*.
129. Hyett, *A Description*, 90. For an early description of this cavern see Maton, *Observations*, I, 119-21.
130. *Watering Places*, Part 1, 33-6, 75-82.
131. Swete, 'Picturesque', X, 12.
132. C. Granville, ed., *Lord Granville Leveson Gower: Private Correspondence, 1781–1821* (1817), I, 106-7.

133. Hyett, *A Description*, 83.

Chapter Four: North Devon Resorts, 1789–1815

1. R. Warner, *A Walk through Some of the Western Counties of England* (Bath, 1800), 123.
2. C. Dibdin, *Observations on a Tour through Almost the Whole of England and a Considerable Part of Scotland* (1801), I, 196.
3. Williams, *Picturesque*, 54-6.
4. Warner, *A Walk*, 123.
5. Vancouver, *General View*, 368.
6. J.R. Chanter, 'Devon Lanes', *TDA*, VI, Part 1 (1873), 191.
7. J.B. Gribble, *Memorials of Barnstaple* (Barnstaple, 1830), 597. In 1815 a new light coach started running between Barnstaple and London. It cut out the overnight stop and completed the journey in 32 hours; *EFP*, 23 March 1815.
8. *Sea-Bathing Places* (1803), 227.
9. Swete, 'Picturesque', XII, 116-7.
10. British Museum, Add MS. 33637, J. Skinner, 'Tour through Part of Somerset and Devon to Sidmouth, 1801', 8 May 1801.
11. G. Farr, *Ships and Harbours of Exmoor* (Dulverton, 1970), 20.
12. Lady Jackson, ed., *The Bath Archives: A Further Selection from the Letters of Sir George Jackson from 1809 to 1816* (1873), 131-4. I am indebted to Bernard Hallen for this reference.
13. The first royal visit was not until 1827, when the Duchess of Clarence stopped briefly at Ilfracombe before embarking on a steamer for Wales; *NDJ*, 27 July 1827.
14. D. Defoe, *A Tour through the Whole Island of Great Britain* (6th edn, 1762), I, 263.
15. Maton, *Observations*, II, 80-91.
16. See for example, J. Britton and E.W. Brayley, *The Beauties of England and Wales: Devonshire*, 271-5.
17. Swete, 'Picturesque', I, 159.
18. *Poetic Remembrances of Lynmouth* (Barnstaple, 1815), 26.
19. 'Tour', 99-101.
20. E. Moir, *The Discovery of Britain* (1964), 123-56.
21. J. Skinner, 'Tour through Devon', 8 May 1801.
22. J.W. Fortescue, *Records of the North Devon Staghounds* (Castle Hill, *c*.1883), 4-7; W. Marshall, *The Rural Economy of the West of England* (1796), I, 57, 165.
23. *EFP*, 2 June 1808.
24. *NDJ*, 14, 28 Aug. 1828, 30 July 1829.
25. 'Memoirs of Savage', 27 March 1790.

26. Jackson, *Bath Archives*, 135.
27. Derry, ed., *Burney*, X, 644-5.
28. *Tour through England Described in a Series of Letters from a Young Gentleman to his Sister* (1811), 71-2.
29. T.H. Cooper, *A Guide Containing a Short Historical Sketch of Lynton and Lynmouth* (1853), 8-9; Swete, 'Picturesque', I, 135.
30. Vancouver, *General View*, 440.
31. Warner, *A Walk*, 119.
32. *Sea-Bathing Places* (1803), 227.
33. *Sea-Bathing Places* (1803), 197.
34. W.C. Oulton, *The Traveller's Guide* (1805), II, 6.
35. *Sea-Bathing Places* (1803), 227. Humphrey Sibthorpe had died in 1797; *EFP*, 17 Aug. 1797.
36. *Sea-Bathing Places* (1815), 17.
37. A.G.K. Leonard, 'Poets Knew and Loved Lynmouth', *DCNQ*, XXVII (1956), 82-3.
38. K. Curry, ed., *New Letters of Robert Southey* (1965), I, 197.
39. E. Dowden, *The Life of Percy Bysshe Shelley* (1886), 279.
40. J.R. Chanter, 'A North Devon Record: Episode of the Poet Shelley', *The Western Antiquary*, V, (1886), 193-6.
41. Leonard, 'Poets', 84.
42. C.C. Southey, *Life and Correspondence of Robert Southey* (1849), II, 23.
43. Swete, 'Picturesque', I, 172.
44. Swete, 'Picturesque', I, 172.
45. Cooper, *A Guide*, 10-11.
46. *EFP*, 2 June 1808.
47. Mrs Jackson did find a shop at Ilfracombe which claimed to be a library, but she dismissed it as having 'far more quack medicines and articles of an all-sort description than books': Jackson, *Bath Archives*, 134.
48. Swete, 'Picturesque', I, 153.

Chapter Five: South Devon Resorts, 1816–1843

1. *EFP*, 27 July 1827.
2. *EPG*, 29 July 1815.
3. R.S. Lambert, *The Fortunate Traveller* (1950), 80.
4. G. Roberts, *The Social History of the People of the Southern Counties of England* (1856), 555.
5. Walton, *Seaside Resort*, 19, 57.
6. W. Harwood, *On the Curative Influence of the Southern Coast of England, Especially that of Hastings* (1828), 4; Clark, *Climate*, 25, 28-9; Granville, *Spas*, III, 598-600.
7. Blewitt, *Panorama*, 35-57.

8. *Watering Places*, Part 1, 16.

9. Clark, *Climate*, 49-50.

10. Clark, *Climate*, 51-4.

11. Granville, *Spas*, III, 483.

12. Granville, *Spas*, III, 474, 492.

13. Granville, *Spas*, III, 490-1.

14. Granville, *Spas*, III, 471.

15. Granville, *Spas*, III, 461.

16. Granville, *Spas*, III, 497.

17. Granville, *Spas*, III, 465-6.

18. *EPG*, 5, 12 October 1816; W.G. Hoskins, *Industry, Trade and People in Exeter, 1688–1800* (Exeter, 2nd edn, 1968), 84-6.

19. W.G. Hoskins, *Devon*, (1954), 98.

20. E.A.G. Clark, *The Ports of the Exe Estuary, 1660–1880* (Exeter, 1960), 130-3.

21. Walton, *Seaside Resort*, 19, 54, 59.

22. Walton, *Seaside Resort*, 21, 23; R.W. Ambler, 'Cleethorpes: The Development of an East Coast Resort', in Sigsworth, ed., *Resorts*, 180.

23. G.D. and E.G.C. Griffiths, *History of Teignmouth* (Teignmouth, 1965), 48.

24. Clark, *Ports*, 177-8; *WL*, 23 Oct. 1832.

25. Sheldon, *Trackway*, 124-6, 128-35.

26. *EFP*, 17 May 1828.

27. *EFP*, 22 Sept. 1831.

28. Sheldon, *Trackway*, 151-7.

29. Sheldon, *Trackway*, 131.

30. J.T. White, *The History of Torquay* (Torquay, 1878), 72; P. Russell, *A History of Torquay* (Torquay, 1960), 80-1.

31. Sheldon, *Trackway*, 158; J.R. Pike, *Torquay, Torbay: A Bibliographical Guide* (Torbay, 1973), 39.

32. Sheldon, *Trackway*, 168-9.

33. Walton, *Seaside Resort*, 58.

34. S. Woolmer, *A Concise Account of the City of Exeter, its Neighbourhood and Adjacent Watering Places* (Exeter, 3rd edn, 1821), 98.

35. Pike, *Torquay*, 5.

36. Woolmer, *Concise Account*, 98.

37. *EFP*, 18 Sept. 1828.

38. Granville, *Spas*, III, 486.

39. *Watering Places*, VII.

40. 'Old Letters from Teignmouth', *DCNQ*, XXXV (1983), 120-1.

41. *EFP*, 6 Nov. 1828.

42. Granville, *Spas*, III, 460-1.

43. Granville, *Spas*, III, 501-2.

44. Granville, *Spas*, III, 469.

45. Granville, *Spas*, III, 466.

46. Blewitt, *Panorama*, 102.

47. Westcountry Studies Library, Exeter, J. Milles, 'Devonshire Manuscript: Parochial Collections, 1753' (microfilm of original in Bodleian Library, Oxford), X, 211.

48. *The Alfred*, 11 Nov. 1828.

49. *EFP*, 30 Dec. 1819.

50. *EPG*, 25 Dec. 1819.

51. *DRO*, 76/20, 'Henry Ellis Memoirs', III, 171.

52. *EFP*, 20-27 Jan. 1820.

53. *EFP*, 7 Aug. 1828.

54. *EFP*, 8 Aug. 1833.

55. Walton, *Seaside Resort*, 18-9.

56. Granville, *Spas*, III, 486.

57. H.J. Trump, *Westcountry Harbour: The Port of Teignmouth, 1690–1975* (Teignmouth, 1976), 71-2.

58. *EFP*, 18 Sept. 1817.

59. D.M. Stirling, *The Beauties of the Shore: A Guide to the Watering Places on the South East Coast of Devon* (Exeter, 1838), 140.

60. W. Everitt, *Memorials of Exmouth* (Exmouth, 2nd edn, 1885), 48.

61. H. Cunningham, *Leisure in the Industrial Revolution, c.1780–c.1880* (1980), 76.

62. *EPG*, 2 Sept. 1826.

63. *EFP*, 29 Oct. 1835, 13 Oct. 1836.

64. *EFP*, 6 July 1826.

65. *EPG*, 26 Aug. 1826.

66. *The Stranger's Guide: The Handbook of Exmouth* (Exmouth, c.1840), 14.

67. J. Mockett, *Mockett's Journal* (Canterbury, 1836), 252.

68. *Watering Places*, Part 1, 17, 20, 28.

69. *The Alfred*, 11 Nov. 1828.

70. *EFP*, 4 April 1816; E. Butcher, *A New Guide Descriptive of the Beauties of Sidmouth* (Sidmouth, 4th edn, c.1828), no pagination.

71. *EFP*, 26 Oct. 1820.

72. *EFP*, 9 July 1835.

73. *EPG*, 14 Aug. 1824.

74. Mockett, *Journal*, 232-3.

75. E. Welsh, ed., 'Lady Sylvester's Tour', *DCNQ*, XXXI (1968-70), 23.

Chapter Six: North Devon Resorts, 1816–1843

1. Derry, ed., *Burney*, X, 534-5.

2. *EFP*, 29 June 1826; J.B. Gribble, *Memorials of Barnstaple* (Barnstaple, 1830), 597.

3. *NDJ*, 20 July 1827.

4. *NDJ*, 4 Nov. 1830.

5. Sheldon, *Trackway*, 133.
6. *NDJ*, 20 July 1827.
7. Gribble, *Memorials*, 592.
8. Clark, *Climate* (2nd edn, 1830), 58-9.
9. *EFP*, 8 March 1832.
10. *NDJ*, 19 May 1842.
11. T.H. Cooper, *A Guide Containing a Short Historical Sketch of Lynton and Lynmouth* (1853), 20.
12. Mrs Selwyn, *Journal of Excursions through the Most Interesting Parts of England, Wales and Scotland* (1824), 25 Aug. 1823.
13. *Sea-Bathing Places* (1825), 399-400.
14. DRO, 2579 A/PV1, 'Lynton Vestry Minutes'.
15. *NDJ*, 27 April, 4 May 1827.
16. *NDJ*, 21 April 1831.
17. *NDJ*, 16 May 1832.
18. J. Dugdale, *The New British Traveller: Or a Modern Panorama of England and Wales* (1819), II, 147.
19. *Ilfracombe as It Is* (Ilfracombe, 1839), VI-VII.
20. Gribble, *Memorials*, 596.
21. *North Devon Advertiser*, 29 June 1838.
22. Dugdale, *British Traveller*, II, 147.
23. G. Farr, *West Country Passenger Steamers* (Prescot, 2nd edn, 1967), 6-7.
24. May, 'Ilfracombe', 244.
25. *EFP*, 11 May 1826.
26. T.H. Cornish, *Sketch of the Rise and Progress of the Principal Towns of the North of Devon* (Bristol, 1828), 28-9.
27. *NDJ*, 1 Sept. 1831.
28. *NDJ*, 12 Aug. 1830.
29. *NDJ*, 11 Sept. 1834, 29 Jan. 1835.
30. *NDJ*, 23 Feb., 26 July 1832.
31. *NDJ*, 11 Aug. 1836. May's thesis led me to this news item: May, 'Ilfracombe', 247.
32. *NDJ*, 18 Aug. 1836.
33. Farr, *Passenger Steamers*, 79-80; May, 'Ilfracombe', 247.
34. *NDJ*, 12 May 1842.
35. E.T. MacDermot, *The History of the Great Western Railway* (1972), I, 66.
36. *NDJ*, 22 July–12 Aug. 1841.
37. *NDJ*, 30 June 1842.
38. *NDJ*, 4-11 May 1843.
39. *EPG*, 13 May 1843.
40. *NDJ*, 4-11 May 1843.
41. *NDJ*, 20 July 1843.
42. *NDJ*, 8-15 June 1843.
43. *NDJ*, 17 Aug. 1843.

44. Derry, ed., *Burney*, X, 591.
45. *NDJ*, 9 Aug. 1832.
46. *NDJ*, 29 July 1869.
47. S. Dixon, *A Journal of Eighteen Days Excursion on the Eastern and Southern Side of Dartmoor and on the Western Vicinity of Exmoor* (Plymouth, 1830), 47.
48. 'The Sketcher', *Blackwood's Edinburgh Magazine*, XXXV (1834), 178.
49. Cornish, *Sketch*, 24.
50. *North Devon Advertiser*, 13 July 1838.
51. *NDJ*, 11 May–4 Oct. 1827.
52. British Parliamentary Papers, *Population: Enumeration Abstract* (1843), 62.
53. Details obtained from the census enumerator's books: PRO, HO 107/245.
54. *NDJ*, 4, 18 Aug. 1842.
55. It was claimed that Blackpool had 2,000 visitors in mid-August 1835, while Margate was said to have 20,000 at the peak of the summer season in 1840: Walton, *Seaside Resort*, 18-9.
56. *NDJ*, 11 May–4 Oct. 1827.
57. May, 'Ilfracombe', 306-7; Cooper, *A Guide*, 11.
58. R. Warner, *A Walk through Some of the Western Counties of England* (Bath, 1800), 113-4, 120.
59. T.H. Williams, *Picturesque Excursions in Devonshire and Cornwall* (1804), 43-4.
60. *NDJ*, 22 Aug. 1833.
61. J. Murray, *A Handbook for Travellers in Devon and Cornwall* (1851), 107.
62. Dugdale, *British Traveller*, 147.
63. D. Lyson, *Magna Britannia: Devonshire* (1822), 289.
64. J. Banfield, *A Guide to Ilfracombe and the Neighbouring Towns* (Ilfracombe, 1830), 9.
65. Banfield, *A Guide* (1830), 10; May, 'Ilfracombe', 377.
66. *Ilfracombe as It Is*, 20.
67. Dixon, *A Journal*, 47.
68. *North Devon Advertiser*, 13 July 1838.
69. Derry, ed., *Burney*, X, 634-5.
70. *NDJ*, 20 Aug., 17 Sept. 1824.
71. *Times Past in Ilfracombe and Combe Martin* (Ilfracombe, 1981), 14-5.
72. Derry, ed., *Burney*, XI, 176.
73. *Robson's London and Western Counties Directory: Devonshire* (1838), 157.
74. Banfield, *A Guide* (1830), 8.
75. Banfield, *A Guide* (1840), 10.
76. Derry, ed., *Burney*, X, 644.
77. Banfield, *A Guide* (1830), 10.
78. *NDJ*, 7 Sept. 1843.
79. Cooper, *A Guide*, 22.
80. *North Devon Advertiser*, 13 July 1838.
81. *NDJ*, 31 July 1828.
82. *NDJ*, 7 Aug. 1828.

83. *NDJ*, 7 Aug. 1828.
84. *NDJ*, 31 July 1828.
85. *NDJ*, 6 Aug. 1829.
86. *NDJ*, 21 Aug. 1846.
87. *North Devon Advertiser*, 13 July 1838.
88. Cornish, *Sketch*, 30.

Chapter Seven: South Devon Resorts, 1844–1900

1. *WL*, 7 May 1844; *EPG*, 4 May 1844; *WT*, 4 May 1844.
2. Walton, *Seaside Resort*, 24-5, 36-8.
3. Pimlott, *Holiday*, 142-3; H. Cunningham, *Leisure in the Industrial Revolution, c.1780–c.1880* (1980), 141-51.
4. Pimlott, *Holiday*, 144-9; Walvin, *Seaside*, 58-63.
5. *WT*, 4 May 1844.
6. E.T. MacDermot, *History of the Great Western Railway* (2nd edn, 1972), I, 92, 340; II, 68-75.
7. HLRO, Minutes of Evidence, H.C., 1844, vol. 37, 'South Devon Railway Bill', 30 April; DRO, 58/9, Box 160, 'Torquay and Newton Abbot Railway'.
8. MacDermot, *G.W.R.*, I, 337, 348; II, 135.
9. MacDermot, *G.W.R.*, I, 103.
10. It was intended that the railway would soon be operated by the 'atmospheric system', with trains being drawn along by a partial vacuum rather than being pulled by locomotives. 'Atmospheric trains' began carrying passengers in September 1847 but there were many problems and the system was abandoned in September 1848: Thomas, *Railways*, 78-81.
11. *EFP*, 4 June 1846.
12. Thomas, *Railways*, 66.
13. *WT*, 23 Dec. 1848; *EPG*, 23 Dec. 1848; MacDermott, *G.W.R.*, II, 112.
14. *EFP*, 8 Feb. 1849.
15. DRO, 58/9, Box 160, 'Torquay and Newton Abbot Railway'.
16. J.R. Pike, *Paignton, Torbay: A Bibliographical Guide* (Torbay, 1974), 16.
17. Thomas, *Railways*, 23-4, 51-7; MacDermot, *G.W.R.*, I, 142-5.
18. Thomas, *Railways*, 63-8; R.A. Williams, *The London and South Western Railway* (Newton Abbot, 1968), 214, 217.
19. Thomas, *Railways*, 237-9.
20. C.S. Ward and M.J. Baddaley, *South Devon and Cornwall* (1884), 15.
21. MacDermot, *G.W.R.*, II, 196-207; Thomas, *Railways*, 252-5.
22. *Torquay Times*, 27 May 1892.
23. PRO, RAIL 631/1, 'South Devon Railway', 6 June 1848.
24. Thomas, *Railways*, 115.
25. *WT*, 5 Sept. 1857, 28 Aug. 1858.
26. *Exmouth Chronicle*, 31 May 1890.

27. H.J. Dyos and D.H. Aldcroft, *British Transport: An Economic Survey from the Seventeenth Century to the Twentieth* (Harmondsworth, 1974), 159.
28. *Seaside Watering Places*, 22.
29. *TD*, 16 May 1894.
30. Walton, *Seaside Resort*, 62-4.
31. W.G. Hoskins, *Devon* (1954), 67, 130.
32. Hoskins, *Devon*, 67, 120, 175.
33. Blackpool is a good example. The centre of the resort became an ill-planned mass of small properties: H.J. Perkin, 'The Social Tone of Victorian Seaside Resorts in the North West', *Northern History*, XI (1976), 186-7.
34. P. Russell, *A History of Torquay* (Torquay, 1960), 81-2, 86-7, 105.
35. A.C. Ellis, *An Historical Survey of Torquay* (Torquay, 1930), 285; Russell, *Torquay*, 87, 101.
36. Ellis, *Torquay*, 281-7; Russell, *Torquay*, 89-90.
37. Russell, *Torquay*, 92, 95-7.
38. Russell, *Torquay*, 171-2.
39. W.H. Mallock, *Memoirs of Life and Literature* (1920), 10; Russell, *Torquay*, 126-30.
40. Russell, *Torquay*, 130-1.
41. PRO, MH 13/141, 'Correspondence between Paignton Local Board and the General Board of Health', 1 Feb. 1866; Pike, *Paignton*, 4.
42. F. R. Penwill, *Paignton in Six Reigns* (Paignton, 1953), 12, 18; Pike, *Paignton*, 21.
43. C.H. Patterson, *The History of Paignton* (Paignton, 1952), 132; Pike, *Paignton*, 19.
44. Penwill, *Paignton*, 32.
45. Quoted in Penwill, *Paignton*, 28.
46. Quote in Patterson, *Paignton*, 132-3.
47. T.W. Rammell, *Report to the Board of Health on the Sanitary Condition of Exmouth* (1850), 7.
48. E.R. Delderfield, *Exmouth Milestones* (Exmouth, 1948), 53, 122-3.
49. Delderfield, *Exmouth*, 178-9.
50. C.G. Harper, *The South Devon Coast* (1907), 66.
51. PRO, RAIL 1066/177, 'Devon and Dorset Railway Bill', 17 June 1853.
52. Decennial Census.
53. Walton, *Seaside Resort*, 69.
54. *Seaside Watering Places*, 233.
55. Moncrieff, *Where?*, 192.
56. *Seaside Watering Places*, 233.
57. Thomas, *Railways*, 85; Hoskins, *Devon*, 163.
58. Moncrieff, *Where?*, 92.
59. J. Clark, *The Sanative Influence of Climate* (1841), 141.
60. Thomas, *Railways*, 99-100.
61. Moncrieff, *Where?*, 67.

62. *Seaside Watering Places*, 238.
63. *Seaside Watering Places*, 240.
64. *Seaside Watering Places*, 240.
65. *TD*, 9 Jan., 7 Aug. 1850.
66. *TD*, 1 Jan., 6 Aug. 1890.
67. *Teignmouth Gazette*, 7 Jan., 5 Aug. 1850.
68. *Teignmouth Gazette*, 1 Jan., 6 Aug. 1880.
69. Walton, *Seaside Resort*, 71-2.
70. *IC*, 4 Aug. 1900.
71. *EFP*, 17 Jan. 1872.
72. Quoted in *EFP*, 17 Jan. 1872.
73. Granville, *Spas*, III, 494.
74. *EFP*, 18 Sept. 1817.
75. *EFP*, 6 Aug. 1857.
76. *WT*, 13 Aug. 1859.
77. *WT*, 13 Aug. 1859.
78. *TD*, 24 June 1885.
79. *TD*, 25 July 1900.
80. *TD*, 24 June 1885.
81. *Black's Guide to Torquay* (1901), 68.
82. Moncrieff, *Where?*, 188.
83. Moncrieff, *Where?*, 78.
84. *A New Pictorial and Descriptive Guide to Dawlish* (1899), 2.
85. Quoted in Patterson, *Paignton*, 135-6.
86. *WT*, 4 Aug. 1891, 2 Aug. 1892.
87. *Exmouth Journal*, 7 Aug. 1897.
88. F.M. Stafford, 'Holidaymaking in Victorian Margate, 1870-1900' (unpublished MA thesis, University of Kent, 1979), 103.
89. Walton, *Seaside Resort*, 71.
90. M. Huggins, 'Social Tone and Resort Development in North-East England', *Northern History*, XX (1984), 195-6.
91. *WT*, 27 Aug. 1859.
92. *WT*, 21 Aug. 1858; *EPG* 28 Aug. 1858; PRO, RAIL 631/5, 'South Devon Railway', 17 Aug. 1858.
93. *WT*, 4 Sept. 1858.
94. *WT*, 30 July 1859.
95. *WT*, 27 Aug. 1859.
96. W. Plomer, ed., *Kilvert's Diary: Selections from the Diary of the Rev. Francis Kilvert* (new edn, 1960), I, 387.
97. W. Miller, *Our English Shores* (Edinburgh, 1888), 25.
98. Miller, *English Shores*, 7.
99. *Teignmouth Times*, 10 Aug. 1888.
100. Walton, *Seaside Resort*, 187-215.

Chapter Eight: North Devon Resorts, 1844–1900

1. *NDJ*, 22 May 1851.
2. C.M. MacInnes and W.F. Whittard, eds, *Bristol and its Adjoining Counties* (Bristol, 1955), 214-5, 231-4.
3. *NDJ*, 18 Sept. 1851.
4. *NDJ*, 18 Sept. 1851.
5. *EFP*, 25 April, 24 Oct. 1844.
6. Thomas, *Railways*, 101-3.
7. *NDJ*, 13 July 1854.
8. *NDJ*, 5 Jan. 1854.
9. Quoted in *Western Morning News*, 15 May 1852.
10. *NDJ*, 17 Aug. 1854.
11. *NDJ*, 24 Aug. 1854.
12. *NDJ*, 12 Oct., 9 Nov. 1854.
13. *WT*, 3 Nov. 1855.
14. *BG*, 2 June 1863.
15. *BG*, 9 Aug. 1870.
16. R. Mayo, *The Story of Westward Ho!: From Fashionable Watering Place to Self-Service Resort* (Yelland, 1973), 35-9.
17. *NDJ*, 14 Aug. 1862.
18. C.G. Maggs, *The Barnstaple and Ilfracombe Railway* (Headington, 2nd edn, 1988), 9-10.
19. *NDJ*, 30 April, 7 May, 11 June, 6 Aug. 1863.
20. HLRO, Minutes of Evidence, H.L., 1864, vol. 23, 'North Devon and Somerset Railway' and 'The London and South Western Railway: North Devon Extension'.
21. F.F. Box, 'The Barnstaple and Ilfracombe Railway', *Railway Magazine*, XLVI (1919-20), 24-9, 80-4.
22. *IC*, 22 July 1874; *NDJ*, 23 July 1874.
23. *EFP*, 5, 12 Nov. 1873.
24. *NDJ*, 26 March, 21 May, 4 June 1874.
25. *NDJ*, 4, 20 June 1874; Box, 'Ilfracombe Railway', 80-3.
26. *IC* 1 Aug., 5-19 Sept. 1874.
27. *NDJ*, 17 May, 7 June, 6 Sept. 1855.
28. *NDJ*, 7 Oct. 1858.
29. *EFP*, 21 May 1873.
30. *BG*, 11 Aug. 1870.
31. *BG*, 29 July 1873.
32. Mayo, *Westward Ho!*, 19, 20, 31.
33. J. Travis, 'Lynton in the Nineteenth Century: An Isolated and Exclusive Resort', in Sigsworth, *Resorts*, 152-67.
34. *NDJ*, 4 Feb. 1897.

35. B.J.H. Brown, 'Bristol's Second Outport: Portishead in the Nineteenth Century', *Transport History,* IV (1971), 80-93.
36. *NDJ,* 12-26 Aug. 1869.
37. *NDJ,* 28 July 1870.
38. *Stewart's Arrival List,* 22 Aug. 1873.
39. In 1882 a First Class rail ticket from Paddington to Ilfracombe was £2, whereas to travel First Class from Paddington to Portishead and then by steamer to Ilfracombe cost £1 9s. 6d.: *IC,* 17 June 1882.
40. The Devon and Somerset Railway had been converted to standard gauge in 1881, removing one obstacle to the through running of trains. On 1 June 1887 a link line was opened at Barnstaple connecting the GWR system to the LSWR system and this made it possible for GWR carriages to be shunted along to join LSWR trains to Ilfracombe: *IC,* 2 June 1887; *NDJ,* 2 June 1887. In 1889 the GWR were given permission to run through trains to Ilfracombe: Box, 'Ilfracombe Railway', 24-9, 80-4.
41. *IC,* 22 Oct. 1887.
42. *LLR,* 25 Oct. 1887.
43. *NDJ,* 4 July 1843.
44. *NDJ,* 20 April 1854.
45. G. Farr, *West Country Passenger Steamers* (Prescot, 2nd edn, 1967), 222-37.
46. *NDJ,* 7 Aug. 1890.
47. *LLR,* 19 June 1894.
48. *NDJ,* 22 Nov. 1894.
49. *NDJ,* 6 Dec. 1894.
50. *NDJ,* 28 March 1895.
51. *NDH,* 12 May 1898.
52. *The Route Book of Devon: A Guide for the Stranger and Tourist* (Exeter, 1850), 56.
53. May, 'Ilfracombe', 65-71.
54. May, 'Ilfracombe', 72-5.
55. *IC,* 9 Oct. 1869.
56. May, 'Ilfracombe', 76-92; F.B. May, 'Victorian and Edwardian Ilfracombe', in J.K. Walton and J. Walvin, eds, *Leisure in Britain, 1780–1939* (Manchester, 1983), 81-3.
57. *LLR,* 25 Nov. 1885, 6 July 1886, 18 Jan., 23 Aug., 4 Oct. 1887, 10 Jan. 1888.
58. *LLR,* 18 Nov. 1890, 24 March 1891.
59. *LLR,* 24 Feb., 1 Dec. 1891; *NDJ,* 12 March, 21 May, 27 Aug., 30 Oct., 19 Nov., 31 Dec. 1891.
60. *LLR,* 12 May 1891.
61. *LLR,* 10, 17 March 1892.
62. *NDJ,* 14 April, 13 Oct. 1892; *LLR,* 2 Aug. 1892.
63. *NDH,* 20 Oct. 1898; *NDJ,* 5 Oct. 1899, 12 April, 5 July 1900.

64. *BG*, 2 June 1863.
65. *NDJ*, 11 Feb. 1864; *BG*, 11 Feb. 1864.
66. *BG*, 9 Aug. 1864; *EFP*, 1 March 1865.
67. *EFP*, 22 Aug. 1866; Mayo, *Westward Ho!*, 12.
68. *EFP*, 17 May 1871.
69. The vicar drew attention to this in a pamphlet: I.H. Gossett, *To the Ratepayers of Northam Parish* (Northam, 1869).
70. *NDJ*, 15 July 1875.
71. Mayo, *Westward Ho!*, 28, 30-3, 40-1.
72. W. Walters, *Guide to Ilfracombe and North Devon* (Ilfracombe, 1888), 150.
73. *Seaside Watering Places*, 293-4.
74. *Seaside Watering Places*, 292-3.
75. PRO, MT 10 589/H6613, 'Change of Ownership in the Manor of Martinhoe'.
76. *LLR*, 13 March 1894; *NDJ*, 19 Sept. 1895.
77. *NDJ*, 19 Sept. 1895.
78. *NDJ*, 17 May 1894.
79. *NDJ*, 19 Sept. 1895, 3 Sept. 1896.
80. *NDJ*, 5 July 1900.
81. *NDH*, 8 Nov. 1900.
82. *NDJ*, 24 Jan. 1901.
83. *NDJ*, 18 Oct. 1900.
84. *NDJ*, 25 Aug. 1842.
85. *Seaside Watering Places*, 281-3.
86. M.J. Baddaley and I.S. Ward, eds, *North Devon and Cornwall* (1884), 44.
87. *Black's Guide to Devonshire* (13th edn, 1889), 179.
88. *IC*, 15 Feb. 1873.
89. J.J. Hissey, *On the Box Seat* (1886), 338-9.
90. L.J. Jennings, 'In the Wilds of North Devon', *Murray's Magazine*, IV (1888), 81.
91. Jennings, 'In the Wilds', 80.
92. *Bright's Intelligencer*, 3 Aug. 1860; *IC*, 4 Aug. 1900.
93. *Bright's Intelligencer*, 3 Aug. 1860; 5 Aug. 1890. The onerous task of preparing visitor lists had been abandoned at Lynton and Lynmouth by 1900.
94. *Stewart's Arrival List*, 5 Aug. 1873; 7 Aug. 1874.
95. *NDH*, 4 Aug. 1898; *LLR*, 25 April 1899.
96. *IG*, 2 Sept. 1896.
97. *NDH*, 24 Sept. 1896.
98. *IG*, 21 Nov. 1896.
99. *IC*, 24 Jan., 7 Feb. 1891; *NDJ*, 11 Jan. 1894.
100. *IC*, 17 Dec. 1892.
101. *IC*, 24 Jan. 1891.
102. *IC*, 14 March 1891.
103. Walton, *Seaside Resort*, 63.

104. Travis, 'Holidaymaking', 309-11, 13-4.
105. Travis, 'Holidaymaking', 310-14.
106. *LLR*, 18 Feb. 1890.
107. *LLR*, 15 March 1881.
108. Moncrieff, *Where?*, 219.
109. *IC*, 30 Oct. 1869.
110. Quoted in *NDJ*, 7 Sept. 1871.
111. The *Bristol Mercury* in 1893 suggested that the boarding house system was better established at Ilfracombe than anywhere else in the country: Quoted in *Ilfracombe Observer*, 13 Jan. 1893.
112. Walters, *Guide to Ilfracombe*, 23.
113. *IG*, 15 April, 27 May 1890.
114. For a description of this boarding house see *Times Past in Ilfracombe and Combe Martin* (Ilfracombe, 1981), 22-5.
115. *IG*, 30 Dec. 1893.
116. *NDJ*, 4 July 1843.
117. *NDJ*, 21 Aug. 1845.
118. *NDJ*, 28 May 1846.
119. *NDJ*, 20 July 1848. Quoted in May, 'Ilfracombe', 328.
120. *NDJ*, 28 June 1849.
121. *NDJ*, 25 Aug. 1853, 3 July 1854.
122. M. Palmer, 'A Diarist in Devon', *TDA*, LXXVI (1944), 200.
123. *NDJ*, 25 Aug. 1864.
124. *IC*, 30 May 1874. May's thesis led me to this news item: May, 'Ilfracombe', 329.
125. *NDJ*, 9 Aug. 1877.
126. *NDJ*, 9 Aug. 1860.
127. *NDJ*, 25 Aug. 1864.
128. *NDJ*, 30 July, 20 Aug. 1896.
129. Walton, *Seaside Resort*, 213-4.
130. *IC*, 12 Aug. 1893.
131. *Weston Mercury*, 31 May, 8 Aug. 1890.
132. Walton, *Seaside Resort*, 208-10.
133. Moncrieff, *Where?*, 103.
134. *IG*, 22 June 1899.
135. *IC*, 21 Oct. 1899.
136. *IC*, 28 Oct. 1899.
137. *NDH*, 20 Sept. 1900.
138. *IG*, 4 June 1898; *NDJ*, 4 Aug. 1898.
139. *NDJ*, 12 May 1898.
140. *NDJ*, 11 Aug. 1898.

Chapter Nine: Health at the Devon Resorts, 1844–1900

1. 'Death at the Seaside', *The Lancet*, II (1859), 170-1.
2. T. Shapter, *The Climate of South Devon and its Influence Upon Health* (1842), 144, 148, 150, 154-5, 159.
3. T.H. Cooper, *A Guide Containing a Short Historical Sketch of Lynton and Lynmouth* (1853), 12-3.
4. *EFP*, 17 May 1871.
5. E.J. Slade-King, *An Enquiry into the Causes which Render Ilfracombe the Healthiest Devonshire Watering Place* (2nd edn, 1875).
6. *Ilfracombe: The Healthiest of All English Watering Places* (Ilfracombe, 1867), 7.
7. N. Longmate, *King Cholera: The Biography of a Disease* (1966), 17-9.
8. Memories were stirred by the publication of a book recalling the horrors of the 1832 epidemic in Exeter: T. Shapter, *The History of the Cholera in Exeter in 1832* (1849).
9. C. Creighton, *A History of Epidemics in Britain* (1965), II, 822. Exmouth had suffered an outbreak in 1832: *EFP*, 30 Aug., 6 Sept. 1832.
10. *TD,* 5 Sept. 1849.
11. *EPG*, 15 Sept. 1849.
12. PRO, MH 13/184, 'General Board of Health Correspondence with Tormoham Local Board', 27 Sept. 1849. At Torquay the Local Board was responsible for the parish of Tormohun, but it was known as the Tormoham Local Board.
13. *NDJ*, 13 Sept. 1849.
14. *NDJ*, 20 Sept. 1849.
15. PRO, MH 1399, 'General Board of Health Correspondence with Ilfracombe Local Board', 19 Oct. 1849.
16. H.J. Smith, 'Local Reports to the General Board of Health', *History*, LVI (1971), 46-9.
17. *The Stranger's Guide: The Handbook of Exmouth* (Exmouth, *c.*1840), 15.
18. T.W. Rammell, *Report to the Board of Health on the Sanitary Condition of Exmouth* (1850), 4, 11, 24-7.
19. T.W. Rammell, *Report to the Board of Health on the Sanitary Condition of Torquay* (1850), 23-4.
20. T.W. Rammell, *Report to the Board of Health on the Sanitary Condition of Ilfracombe* (1850), 14, 16.
21. W. Thornhill, *The Growth and Reform of English Local Government* (1971), 6.
22. PRO, MH 13/61, 'Local Government Act Office Correspondence with Dawlish Local Board', 24 Aug. 1849; *EPG*, 27 Aug. 1859.
23. Travis, 'Holidaymaking', 401-9.
24. The work of the Lynton and Lynmouth Local Board is made a case study in Travis, 'Holidaymaking', 418-35.

25. *EFP*, 24 Feb. 1855; J.T. White, *The History of Torquay* (Torquay, 1878), 204-6.
26. *TD*, 12 May, 14 July 1858; *EFP*, 10 June 1858.
27. DRO, R 2458A (C2/3) C, 'Ilfracombe Local Board Minute Book IV', 24 Feb., 3 April 1860; *NDJ*, 5 April 1860.
28. DRO, R 2360A (5/5) C3, 'Teignmouth Local Board Minute Book', 5 Nov. 1870, 1 April 1871; *WT*, 8 Nov. 1870.
29. PRO, MH 13/181, 'Local Government Act Office Correspondence with Teignmouth Local Board', 23 Aug. 1870; *WT*, 16 Sept. 1870.
30. *Dawlish Times*, 5 Feb., 2 Sept., 7 Oct. 1880.
31. E.R. Delderfield, *Exmouth Milestones* (Exmouth, 1948), 52, 55; *EPG*, 18 Oct., 1 Nov., 29 Nov. 1867.
32. *NDJ*, 23 Aug. 1866, 7 Nov. 1867.
33. J.R. Pike, *Paignton: A Bibliographical Guide* (Torbay, 1952), 19.
34. R. Mayo, *The Story of Westward Ho!* (Yelland, 1973), 31.
35. W. White, *History, Gazetteer and Directory of Devonshire* (Sheffield, 3rd edn, 1890), 872-3.
36. DRO, R7/6/C/1, 'Seaton Local Board Minute Book I', 5 Oct. 1888.
37. At Exmouth in 1902: *Exmouth Chronicle*, 4 Jan., 10 May 1902; at Paignton in 1888: *Devon County Standard*, 9 June 1888; at Seaton in 1888: DRO, R 7/6/C/1, 'Seaton Local Board Minute Book I', 5 Oct., 2 Nov., 7 Dec. 1888.
38. *NDJ*, 4 Jan. 1877; *NDH*, 8 Feb. 1877.
39. *LLR*, 1 Feb. 1887.
40. *LLR*, 9 Sept. 1890.
41. *NDJ*, 14 Aug. 1890.
42. HLRO, Minutes of Evidence, H.L., 1891, Vol. 8, 'Lynton Water Bill'.
43. *LLR*, 20 Dec. 1892, *NDJ*, 29 Dec. 1892.
44. Walton, *Seaside Resort*, 128-9.
45. Only Westward Ho! disposed of its sewage on land, and there only because piping to the sea was made difficult by the Pebble Ridge. When the new resort was sewered in 1870 the untreated sewage was allowed to flow onto an adjacent common known as Northam Burrows: *NDJ*, 20 Jan., 24 Feb. 1870. This turned the Burrows into a 'pestilential drain' and polluted the wells: *NDJ*, 15 July 1875.
46. White, *History* (1st edn, 1850), 446.
47. Rammell, *Torquay*, 23.
48. *Devon Weekly Times*, 30 Aug. 1878; *WT*, 27 Aug. 1878; *EFP*, 30 Aug. 1878.
49. *Dawlish Times*, 9 April, 20 Sept. 1885; DRO, R 2369A (5/3) C4, 'Dawlish Local Board Minute Book', 20 July, 2 Dec. 1886, 10 March-3 Nov. 1887.
50. Ilfracombe in 1881: May, 'Ilfracombe', 185; Exmouth in 1882: *EFP*, 15 Feb. 1882; Paignton in 1885: *Paignton Gazette*, 11 July 1885; Lynton and Lynmouth in 1895: PRO, MH 12/2156, 'Correspondence with the Lynton Urban District Council', 26 Feb. 1895; Sidmouth in 1896: *Sidmouth Observer*, 25 March 1896; Teignmouth in 1898: *Teignmouth Gazette*, 12 Jan. 1898.

51. *Illustrated Guide to Ilfracombe and North Devon* (Ilfracombe, 1885), 1-3.
52. Slade-King, *Ilfracombe*, 26-37.
53. PRO, MH 12/2141, 'Correspondence with Ilfracombe Local Board', 9 Oct. 1878.
54. W. Walters, *Ilfracombe: A Health Resort* (Ilfracombe, 1878), 4-5.
55. May, 'Ilfracombe', 183-5.
56. *Illustrated Guide to Ilfracombe*, 1-3.
57. A. Hern, *The Seaside Holiday: The History of the English Seaside Resort* (1967), 115-6.
58. D. Read, *England 1868–1914: The Age of Urban Democracy* (1979), 214.
59. S. Thomson, *Torquay Past and Present* (Torquay, 1877), 18.
60. G.F. Munsford, *Seaton, Beer and Neighbourhood* (Yeovil, 1890), 7.
61. Read, *England*, 214.
62. *The Visitor's Guide to Exmouth* (Exeter, 1893), 8.
63. N. MacVean and L. Williams, *The English Riviera: A Guide to Sidmouth* (Sidmouth, 1894), 68.
64. *Lynton and Lynmouth: The English Switzerland* (Lynton, 1890), no pagination.
65. Thomson, *Torquay*, 85.

Chapter Ten: Recreations at the Devon Resorts, 1844–1900

1. 'At the Seaside', *Cornhill Magazine*, XXII (1875), 415.
2. P. Bailey, *Leisure and Class: Rational Recreation and the Contest for Control* (1978), 35-79.
3. C. Kingsley, *Glaucus: Or the Wonders of the Shore* (Cambridge, 4th edn, 1859), 61.
4. For a full description of Gosse's life see E.W. Gosse, *The Naturalist on the Seashore: The Life of Philip Henry Gosse* (1896).
5. P.H. Gosse, *A Naturalist's Rambles on the Devonshire Coast* (1853), V.
6. P.H. Gosse, *Seaside Sketches in the Neighbourhood of Ilfracombe* (new edn, 1861).
7. P.H. Gosse, *Land and Sea* (new edn, 1879), 107-26, 229-303.
8. 'Ilfracombe', *London Society*, XII (1867), 28.
9. Gosse, *Land and Sea*, 251.
10. Gosse, *Land and Sea*, 251.
11. C. Chanter, *Ferny Combes: A Ramble after Ferns in the Glens and Valleys of Devonshire* (3rd edn, 1857), preface.
12. R. Stewart, *Handbook of the Torquay Flora: Comprising the Flowering Plants and Ferns Growing in and around Torquay* (Torquay, 1860); P.O. Hutchinson, *The Ferns of Sidmouth* (Sidmouth, 1862); Z.I. Edmunds, *The Ferns of the Axe and its Tributaries* (1862).
13. F.G. Heath, *The Fern Paradise: A Plea for the Culture of Ferns* (1875), 14-5.
14. F.G. Heath, *The Fern World* (1877), 123, 125-51, 166-91.

15. P.H. Gosse, *The Aquarium: An Unveiling of the Wonders of the Deep Sea* (1854), 22; Gosse, *A Naturalist's Rambles*, 26.

16. Heath, *The Fern World*, 110-1.

17. Morris and Co., eds, *Commercial Directory and Gazetteer of Devonshire* (Nottingham, 1870), 93.

18. Morris and Co., eds, *Commercial Directory*, 326, 328; W. White, *History, Gazetteer and Directory of Devonshire* (Sheffield, 2nd edn, 1878), 22.

19. *IC*, 8 Feb, 1879.

20. *IG*, 9 Aug. 1890.

21. 'A Sketch from Ilfracombe', *Blackwood's Edinburgh Magazine*, CXLIII (1887), 39.

22. S. Chitty, *The Beast and the Monk: A Life of Charles Kingsley* (1974), 168-71.

23. J.R. Chanter, 'R.D. Blackmore and *Lorna Doone*', *TDA*, XXXV (1903), 244-5.

24. *NDH*, 7 Nov. 1901.

25. S. Baring-Gould, *Devon* (7th edn, 1924), 235.

26. *EFP*, 18 Dec. 1794, 25 Aug. 1796.

27. E. Royle, *Modern Britain: A Social History, 1750–1985* (1987), 254-6.

28. J. Walvin, *Leisure and Society, 1830–1950* (1978), 104.

29. *EFP*, 10 Oct. 1850, 4 Nov. 1852, 20 Jan., 21 May 1853.

30. A.C. Ellis, *An Historical Survey of Torquay* (Torquay, 1930), 291.

31. The business community at Lynton and Lynmouth, for example, in 1890 collected subscriptions with which to hire a German band from Bath, but the band still had to be allowed to supplement its income by asking for donations: *NDH*, 22 May-19 June 1890.

32. *NDJ*, 21 Sept. 1843.

33. *NDJ*, 4-18 June 1863.

34. L. Lamplugh, *A History of Ilfracombe* (Chichester, 1984), 75.

35. *NDJ*, 21 May, 4-18 June 1863.

36. *NDJ*, 9 July 1863.

37. *NDJ*, 18 June 1863.

38. *NDJ*, 18-25 June 1863.

39. *NDJ*, 4-11 June 1863.

40. *NDJ*, 18 June 1863.

41. *NDJ*, 20 July 1876.

42. Westcountry Studies Library, Exeter, C. Drewett, 'An Autumn Holiday in Devon, 1891–7', 1892, no pagination.

43. *IC*, 17-24 Aug. 1889, 16 Aug. 1892; *TD*, 16 July 1890; May, 'Ilfracombe', 416.

44. *NDH*, 5 March 1903; May, 'Ilfracombe', 414.

45. W. Miller, *Our English Shores* (Edinburgh, 1888), 10-1.

46. R. Holt, *Sport and the British: A Modern History* (Oxford, 1989), 74-134; H. Cunningham, *Leisure in the Industrial Revolution* (1980), 110-37.

47. *EFP*, 7 Aug. 1856.

48. *EFP*, 23 Sept. 1852, 14 July 1853.

49. *EFP*, 14 Oct. 1852, 30 Aug. 1855, 26 June, 17 July, 4 Sept. 1856, 3 July, 21 Aug. 1861, 17 Aug. 1864.

50. *EFP*, 2 Aug. 1871.

51. *EFP*, 17 Aug. 1881.

52. *EFP*, 16 Aug. 1882, 22 Aug. 1883, 13 Aug. 1884; *Exmouth Journal*, 11 Aug. 1888.

53. *EFP*, 22-29 Aug., 19 Sept. 1883, 22 July, 26 Aug. 1885; *Pictorial and Historical Guide to Ilfracombe* (1887), 25.

54. *The Royal North Devon Golf Club: A Century Anthology, 1864–1964* (Westward Ho!, 1964), 27.

55. B. Darwin, *The Royal North Devon Golf Club* (1955), 13-5.

56. *Rules for the Government of the Royal North Devon and West of England Golf Club* (Westward Ho!, 1875), 3.

57. Darwin, *North Devon Golf Club*, 27. 94.

58. *EFP*, 23 May, 19 Sept. 1866; *BG*, 24 May 1870; *WT*, 5 Dec. 1871.

59. A.R.H. Moncrieff quoted in Walton, *Seaside Resort*, 185.

60. *EFP*, 24 June 1868.

61. *NDJ*, 15 Oct. 1868.

62. *NDJ*, 1 July 1869.

63. R. Mayo, *The Story of Westward Ho!* (Yelland, 1973), 22.

64. *EFP*, 4 Sept. 1878, 16 June, 22 Sept. 1880; *TD*, 6 Aug. 1879.

65. D. Rubinstein, 'Cycling Eighty Years Ago', *History Today*, XXVIII (1978), 544-7; D. Rubinstein, 'Cycling in the 1890s', *Victorian Studies*, XXI (1977), 47-51.

66. M. Spearman, 'Wish You Were Here', *Devon Life*, XXXIV (April 1970), 36. I am indebted to Bernard Hallen for this reference.

67. *EFP*, 14 Aug. 1867.

68. *EFP*, 6 Aug. 1857; Mayo, *Westward Ho!*, 12; *NDJ*, 5 Aug. 1880; *EFP*, 20 June, 7 Nov. 1883.

69. *Cornelius's Guide to Dawlish* (Dawlish, c.1880), 18; *EFP*, 14 Aug. 1867.

70. *EFP*, 31 Aug. 1870, 31 July 1872.

71. *NDJ*, 8-15 July 1875.

72. *EFP*, 25 Aug. 1875; *IC*, 3 Sept 1892.

73. *NDJ*, 2 Sept. 1880, 21 July, 4 Aug., 18 Aug. 1881.

74. *EFP*, 8 Aug. 1883; *IC*, 27 July 1889, 11 July 1891, 11 June, 6 Aug., 10 Sept. 1892.

75. Quoted in Lamplugh, *Ilfracombe*, 83.

76. W. Plomer, ed., *Kilvert's Diary: Selections from the Diary of the Rev. Francis Kilvert* (new edn, 1960), II, 358.

77. PRO, MH 13/61, 'Local Government Act Office Correspondence with Dawlish Local Board', 1859.

78. *Sidmouth Directory*, 1 Aug. 1863.

79. PRO, MH 12/2111, 'Correspondence with Seaton', 12 Jan. 1877.

80. DRO, R 2360A (5/5) C3, 'Teignmouth Local Board Minute Book', 3 July 1866; *WT*, 6 July 1866.
81. *WT*, 10 July 1866.
82. Quoted in May, 'Ilfracombe', 381.
83. *EFP*, 19 May 1875.
84. PRO, MH 12/2145, 'Draft Bye Laws for Lynton', 1883; R.J. Ferrar, 'Bathing Machines in Lynmouth', *Lyn Valley News* (Sept. 1984), 2.
85. *The Standard*, 13 June 1896.
86. *The Standard*, 15-16 June 1896. Pimlott suggests that in 1901 Bexhill in Sussex became one of the first English resorts to allow mixed bathing, but this is not the case: Pimlott, *Holiday*, 182.
87. *Paignton Observer*, 25 June, 9, 23 July 1896.
88. *Paignton Observer*, 11 June 1896.
89. *Paignton Observer*, 23 July 1896.
90. *Paignton Observer*, 13 Aug. 1896.
91. *Paignton Observer*, 20 Aug. 1896.
92. *Paignton Observer*, 23 July, 13 Aug. 1896.
93. *Paignton Observer*, 30 July 1896.
94. *Teignmouth Times*, 13 Aug. 1897.
95. *Torquay Times*, 14 Sept. 5 Oct. 1900.
96. *NDJ*, 10-17 Aug. 1905.
97. *NDJ*, 6 Sept. 1906, 22 Aug. 1907.
98. *NDH*, 22 Aug. 1907.
99. 'Off the Rails', *Temple Bar*, VII (1863), 287.
100. *A New Pictorial and Descriptive Guide to Torquay* (1898), 1-2. May's thesis led me to this guide: May, 'Ilfracombe', 368-9.
101. C. Rose, *Beside the Seaside* (1960), 59, 63.
102. *EFP*, 24 Jan. 1872.
103. *LLR*, 18 Feb. 1890.
104. *New Guide to Torquay*, X.
105. E.R. Delderfield, *Exmouth Yesterdays* (Exmouth, 1952), 60; A. Sutton, *A History of Sidmouth* (Sidmouth, 2nd edn, 1953), 100.
106. Rose, *Beside the Seaside*, 17, 63.
107. At Teignmouth in 1897: *Teignmouth Times*, 16 July 1897. Two groups at Ilfracombe by 1897: Drewett, 'Autumn Holiday', 1897, no pagination.
108. *NDH*, 29 Aug. 1901.
109. S.H. Adamson, *Seaside Piers* (1977), 9-46, 100-4.
110. Adamson, *Piers*, 19, 101, 112.
111. Miller, *Our English Shores*, 6.
112. *Teignmouth Times*, 29 July, 12 Aug., 16 Sept. 1876.
113. *BG*, 29 July 1873; Mayo, *Westward Ho*, 31.
114. J.R. Pike, *Paignton, Torbay: A Bibliographical Guide* (Torbay, 1952), 33.
115. Quoted in C.H. Patterson, *The History of Paignton* (Paignton, 1952), 135-6.
116. *TD*, 6 Aug. 1890.

117. E.R. Delderfield, *Exmouth Milestones* (Exmouth, 1948), 88-9.
118. Drewett, 'Autumn Holiday', 1897, no pagination.

Conclusion

1. J. Lowerson and J. Myerscough, *Time to Spare in Victorian England* (Hassocks, 1977), 38.
2. H.J. Perkin, 'The Social Tone of Victorian Seaside Resorts in the North-West', *Northern History*, XI (1976), 180-94.
3. A.R.H. Moncrieff, *Where Shall We Go?* (12th edn, 1892), 115.

Bibliography

Primary Sources

Manuscripts

Public Record Office
General Board of Health and Local Government Act Office correspondence with
    Local Boards:
Dawlish (1859–1871), MH 13/61
Exmouth (1848–1871), MH 13/72
Ilfracombe (1848–1871), MH 13/99
Lynton (1866–1871), MH 13/121
Northam (1868–1871), MH 13/135
Paignton (1863–1871), MH 13/141
Sidmouth (1863–1871), MH 13/168
Teignmouth (1858–1871), MH 13/181
Tormoham (1849–1871), MH 13/184

Local Government Board correspondence with Local Boards and Urban District
    Councils:
Ilfracombe, MH 12/2161-5
Lynton, MH 12/2141-56
Seaton, MH 12/2111

Railway records:
Bristol and Exeter Railway, directors' minute books, RAIL 75
South Devon Railway, directors' minute books, RAIL 631
Devon and Dorset Railway Bill (1853), RAIL 1066/177

Board of Trade Harbour Department correspondence:
Manor of Martinhoe (1885), MT 10/589/H6613

House of Lords Record Office
Minutes of Evidence taken before Select Committees:
Ilfracombe Railway Bill, H.L., 1864, vol. 23

London and South Western Railway: North Devon Extensions Bill, H.L., 1864, vol. 23

Lynton Water Bill, H.L., 1891, vol. 8

North Devon and Somerset Railway Bill, H.L., 1864, vol. 23

South Devon Railway Bill, H.C., 1844, vol. 37

British Museum

J. Skinner, Tour through Part of Somerset and Devon to Sidmouth, 1801, Add MS. 33637

Devon Record Office

Minute books of Local Boards and Vestries:

Dawlish Local Board, R 2369A(5/3)C

Exmouth Local Board of Health, R 7/4/C

Ilfracombe Local Board of Health, R 2458A(C2/3)C

Lynton Vestry Minutes, 2579A/P VI

Seaton Local Board, R 7/6/C

Sidmouth Urban District Council, R 7/7/C/17

Teignmouth Local Board, R 2360 A(5/5)C

Miscellaneous records:

John Swete, Picturesque Sketches of Devon (1792–1801), 564/M

Henry Ellis, Memoirs (1790–1857), 76/20

Torquay and Newton Abbot Railway, 58/9, Box 160

Westcountry Studies Library, Exeter

C. Drewett, An Autumn Holiday in Devon (1891–7)

J. Milles, Devonshire Manuscript: Parochial Collections (1753). (microfilm of original in Bodleian Library, Oxford)

Bath Reference Library

Description of a Tour to the Isle of Wight and into the West of England in the Summer of 1810

Berkshire Record Office

Journal of Mrs Price (1805), R 11A/401

Cardiff Central Library

Robert Clutterbuck, Journal of a Tour through the Western Counties of England during the Summer of 1796, MS. 4. 367

Dorset Record Office
Itinerary of Devonshire by Mrs Rackett (1802), NH 140

National Library of Scotland
The Journal of the Hon. Frances Mackenzie (1811), MS. 2540

Suffolk Record Office, Ipswich Branch
Memoirs and Travels of John Savage (1790), S 92

Suffolk Record Office, Bury St Edmunds Branch
Tour in Devonshire by Rev. Sir Thomas Gery Cullum in 1789, E 2/44/6

Directories

Kelly's Post Office Directory of Devonshire (edns for 1856, 1866, 1883, 1897)
Morris and Co., *Commercial Directory and Gazetteer of Devonshire* (Nottingham, 1870)
Robson's London and Western Counties Directory: Devonshire (1838)
W. White, *History, Gazetteer and Directory of Devonshire* (Sheffield; edns for 1850, 1878, 1890)

Newspapers

The Alfred, 1815–1832
Bideford Gazette, 1856–1870; 1873–1900
Bright's Intelligencer and Arrival Lists for Ilfracombe and Lynton, 1860–1861
Dawlish Times, 1868–1898; 1898–1900
Devon Weekly Times, 1861–1900
Exeter and Plymouth Gazette, 1813–1901
Exeter Flying Post, 1768–1900
Exmouth Journal, 1869–1900
Ilfracombe Chronicle, 1869; 1872–1900
Ilfracombe Gazette, 1875–1893
Ilfracombe Gazette and Observer, 1894–1900
Ilfracombe Observer, 1884–1893
Lynton and Lynmouth Recorder, 1880–1903
North Devon Advertiser, 1855–1895
North Devon Herald, 1870–1910
North Devon Journal, 1824–1914
Paignton Gazette, 1877–1887
Paignton Observer, 1895–1900
Sidmouth Directory, 1850; 1862–1864

Sidmouth Journal, 1858; 1870–1888
The Standard, 1896
Stewart's Arrival List for Ilfracombe and Lynton, 1873–1874
Teignmouth Gazette, 1849–1873; 1875–1896; 1898–1900
Teignmouth Times, 1856–1873; 1875–1895; 1897; 1899–1900
Torquay Directory, 1846–1847; 1849–1900
Torquay Times, 1869–1872; 1873–1895; 1897–1900
Western Luminary, 1813–1857
Western Flying Post, 1767
Western Times, 1829–1900
Weston Mercury, 1890

Books

M.J. Baddaley and I.S. Ward, eds, *North Devon and Cornwall* (1884)
J. Banfield, *A Guide to Ilfracombe and the Neighbouring Towns* (Ilfracombe, 1830 and 1840 edns)
The Beauties of Sidmouth Displayed (Sidmouth, 1810)
Black's Guide to Devonshire (13th edn, 1889)
Black's Guide to Torquay (1901)
O. Blewitt, *Panorama of Torquay* (2nd edn, 1832)
A. Brice, *The Grand Gazetteer* (Exeter, 1759)
J. Britton and E.W. Brayley, *The Beauties of England and Wales: Devonshire* (1803)
W. Buckingham, *A Transport Key: An Account of the Proceedings of the Exeter Turnpike Trustees from 12 June 1753 to 1 November 1884* (Exeter, 1885)
E. Butcher, *A New Guide Descriptive of the Beauties of Sidmouth* (Sidmouth, 1827)
E. Butcher, *An Excursion from Sidmouth to Chester in the Summer of 1803* (1805)
N.T. Carrington, *The Teignmouth, Dawlish and Torquay Guide* (Teignmouth, 1830)
J.J. Cartwright, ed., *The Travels through England of Dr Richard Pococke during 1750, 1751 and Later Years* (1888)
C. Chanter, *Ferny Combes: A Ramble after Ferns in the Glens and Valleys of Devonshire* (3rd edn, 1857)
J. Clark, *The Influence of Climate on the Prevention and Cure of Chronic Diseases* (1829)
J. Clark, *The Sanative Influence of Climate* (1841)
G.A. Cooke, *A Topographical and Statistical Description of the County of Devon* (3rd edn, 1832)
T.H. Cooper, *A Guide Containing a Short Historical Sketch of Lynton and Lynmouth* (1853)
Cornelius's Guide to Dawlish (Dawlish, c.1880)
T.H. Cornish, *Sketch of the Rise and Progress of the Principal Towns of the North of Devon* (Bristol, 1828)
J.A. De Luc, *Geological Travels* (1811)
D. Defoe, *A Tour through the Whole Island of Great Britain* (6th edn, 1762)

C. Dibdin, *Observations on a Tour through Almost the Whole of England and a Considerable Part of Scotland* (1801)

S. Dixon, *A Journal of Eighteen Days Excursion on the Eastern and Southern Side of Dartmoor and on the Western Vicinity of Exmoor* (Plymouth, 1830)

E. Dowden, *The Life of Percy Bysshe Shelley* (1886)

H. Downman, *Infancy: Or the Management of Children* (Exeter, 6th edn, 1803)

J. Dugdale, *The New British Traveller: Or a Modern Panorama of England and Wales* (1819)

M. Dunsford, *Miscellaneous Observations, in the Course of Two Tours, through Several Parts of the West of England* (Tiverton, 1800)

Z.I. Edmunds, *The Ferns of the Axe and its Tributaries* (1862)

D.M.A. Espriella (R. Southey), *Letters from England* (1814)

J. Evans, *The Juvenile Tourist* (3rd edn., 1810)

W. Everitt, *Memorials of Exmouth* (Exmouth, 2nd edn, 1885)

J.W. Fortescue, *Records of the North Devon Staghounds* (Castle Hill, *c*.1883)

R. Fraser, *General View of the County of Devon, with Observations on the Means of its Improvement* (1794)

The Gentleman's Guide in His Tour through France (9th edn, 1787)

W. Gilpin, *Observations on the River Wye* (Richmond, new edn, 1973)

E.W. Gosse, *The Naturalist on the Seashore: The Life of Philip Henry Gosse* (1896)

P.H. Gosse, *The Aquarium: An Unveiling of the Wonders of the Deep Sea* (1854)

P.H. Gosse, *A Naturalist's Rambles on the Devonshire Coast* (1853)

P.H. Gosse, *Land and Sea* (new edn, 1879)

P.H. Gosse, *Seaside Sketches in the Neighbourhood of Ilfracombe* (new edn, 1861)

I.H. Gossett, *To the Ratepayers of Northam Parish* (Northam, 1869)

A.B. Granville, *The Spas of England and Principal Sea-Bathing Places* (1841)

C. Granville, ed., *Lord Granville Leveson Gower: Private Correspondence, 1781–1821* (1817)

J.B. Gribble, *Memorials of Barnstaple* (Barnstaple, 1830)

A Guide to All the Watering and Sea-Bathing Places (1803)

A Guide to the Watering Places on the Coast, between the Exe and the Dart (Teignmouth, 1817)

C.G. Harper, *The South Devon Coast* (1907)

W. Harwood, *On the Curative Influence of the Southern Coast of England, Especially that of Hastings* (1828)

F.G. Heath, *The Fern Paradise: A Plea for the Culture of Ferns* (1875)

F.G. Heath, *The Fern World* (1877)

J.J. Hissey, *On the Box Seat* (1886)

P.O. Hutchinson, *The Ferns of Sidmouth* (Sidmouth, 1862)

W. Hyett, *A Description of the Watering Places on the South-East Coast of Devon* (Exeter, 1803)

Ilfracombe as It Is (Ilfracombe, 1839)

Ilfracombe: The Healthiest of All English Watering Places (Ilfracombe, 1867)

Illustrated Guide to Ilfracombe and North Devon (Ilfracombe, 1885)

Lady Jackson, ed., *The Bath Archives: A Further Selection from the Letters of Sir George Jackson from 1809 to 1816* (1873)

Alexander Jenkins, *The History and Description of the City of Exeter and its Environs* (Exeter, 1806)

C. Kingsley, *Glaucus: Or the Wonders of the Shore* (Cambridge, 4th edn, 1859)

J. Lackington, *Memoirs of the Forty-Five First Years of the Life of James Lackington* (1794)

J. Land, *A Treatise on the Hot, Cold, Tepid, Shower and Vapour Baths* (Exeter, c.1802)

Lynton and Lynmouth: The English Switzerland (Lynton, 1890)

D. Lyson, *Magna Britannia: Devonshire* (1822)

N. MacVean and L. Williams, *The English Riviera: A Guide to Sidmouth* (Sidmouth, 1894)

W.H. Mallock, *Memoirs of Life and Literature* (1920)

M. Margarot, *Histoire ou Relation d'un Voyage* (1780)

W. Marshall, *The Rural Economy of the West of England* (1796)

W.G. Maton, *Observations Relative Chiefly to the Natural History, Picturesque Scenery and Antiquities of the Western Counties of England* (Salisbury, 1797)

W. Miller, *Our English Shores* (Edinburgh, 1888)

J. Mockett, *Mockett's Journal* (Canterbury, 1836)

A.R.H. Moncrieff, *Where Shall We Go?* (14th edn, 1899)

G.F. Munsford, *Seaton, Beer and Neighbourhood* (Yeovil, 1890)

J. Murray, *A Handbook for Travellers in Devon and Cornwall* (1851)

A New Pictorial and Descriptive Guide to Dawlish (1899)

A New Pictorial and Descriptive Guide to Torquay (1898)

W.C. Oulton, *The Traveller's Guide* (1805)

Pictorial and Historical Guide to Ilfracombe (1887)

Poetic Remembrances of Lynmouth (Barnstaple, 1815)

R. Polwhele, *The History of Devonshire* (1793)

T.W. Rammell, *Report to the Board of Health on the Sanitary Condition of Exmouth* (1850)

T.W. Rammell, *Report to the Board of Health on the Sanitary Condition of Ilfracombe* (1850)

T.W. Rammell, *Report to the Board of Health on the Sanitary Condition of Torquay* (1850)

G. Roberts, *The Social History of the People of the Southern Counties of England* (1856)

The Route Book of Devon: A Guide for the Stranger and Tourist (Exeter, 1850)

Rules for the Government of the Royal North Devon and West of England Golf Club (Westward Ho!, 1875)

R. Russell, *A Disseration on the Use of Sea Water in the Diseases of the Glands* (1752)

Seaside Watering Places: Being a Guide to Strangers in Search of a Suitable Place in which to Spend their Holidays (new edn, 1896)

Mrs Selwyn, *Journal of Excursions through the Most Interesting Parts of England, Wales and Scotland* (1824)

T. Shapter, *The Climate of South Devon and its Influence Upon Health* (1842)

T. Shapter, *The History of the Cholera in Exeter in 1832* (1849)

E.J. Slade-King, *An Enquiry into the Causes which Render Ilfracombe the Healthiest Devonshire Watering Place* (2nd edn, 1875)

C.C. Southey, *Life and Correspondence of Robert Southey* (1849)

R. Stewart, *Handbook of the Torquay Flora: Comprising the Flowering Plants and Ferns Growing in and around Torquay* (Torquay, 1860)

D.M. Stirling, *The Beauties of the Shore: A Guide to the Watering Places on the South East Coast of Devon* (Exeter, 1838)

E. Stone, *Chronicles of Fashion* (1845)

The Stranger's Guide: The Handbook of Exmouth (Exmouth, c.1840)

S. Thomson, *Torquay Past and Present* (Torquay, 1877)

Tour through England Described in a Series of Letters from a Young Gentleman to his Sister (1811)

C. Vancouver, *General View of the Agriculture of the County of Devon* (1808)

The Visitor's Guide to Exmouth (Exeter, 1893)

W. Walters, *Guide to Ilfracombe and North Devon* (Ilfracombe, 1888)

W. Walters, *Ilfracombe: A Health Resort* (Ilfracombe, 1878)

C.S. Ward and M.J. Baddaley, *South Devon and Cornwall* (1884)

R. Warner, *A Walk through Some of the Western Counties of England* (Bath, 1800)

J. Watkins, *Essay towards a History of Bideford* (Exeter, 1792)

D. Webb, *Observations and Remarks during Four Excursions Made to Various Parts of Great Britain in the Years 1810 and 1811* (1811)

W. Webb, *Memorials of Exmouth* (Exmouth, 1872)

J.T. White, *The History of Torquay* (Torquay, 1878)

F.M. Williams, *Plymouth as a Tourist and Health Resort* (Plymouth, 1898)

T.H. Williams, *Picturesque Excursions in Devonshire and Cornwall* (1804)

T.H. Williams, *Picturesque Excursions in Devonshire; The Environs of Exeter* (Exeter, 1815)

S. Woolmer, *A Concise Account of the City of Exeter, its Neighbourhood and Adjacent Watering Places* (Exeter; 2nd edn, 1811; also 3rd edn, 1821)

Articles and Essays

'At the Seaside', *Cornhill Magazine*, XXII (1875)

J.R. Chanter, 'Devon Lanes', *TDA*, VI, Part 1 (1873)

J.R. Chanter, 'A North Devon Record: Episode of the Poet Shelley', *The Western Antiquary*, V (1886)

J.R. Chanter, 'R.D. Blackmore and *Lorna Doone*', *TDA*, XXXV (1903)

'Dawlish, Teignmouth and Oxton-house, Devonshire', *GM*, LXIII, Part 1 (1793)

'Death at the Seaside', *The Lancet*, II (1859)

'Description of East Teignmouth and Its Environs', *GM*, LXIII, Part 2 (1793)

'Diary of their Majesties' Journey to Weymouth and Plymouth', *GM*, LIX, Part 2 (1789)

'An Essay on English Roads', *GM*, XXII (1752)

'Ilfracombe', *London Society*, XII (1867)

J. Ingenhousz, 'On the Degree of Salubrity of the Common Air at Sea, as Compared with that of the Seashore and that of Places far Removed from the Sea', *Royal Society: Philosophical Transactions*, LXX (1780)

L.J. Jennings, 'In the Wilds of North Devon', *Murray's Magazine*, IV (1888)

Dr Lavington of Tavistock, 'The Case of a Lady Who Drank the Sea Water', *Royal Magazine: Philosophical Transactions: Abridged Version*, XII (1809)

'Ode Addressed to the Bathing Machines at Exmouth', *GM*, LII (1783)

'Off the Rails', *Temple Bar*, VII (1863)

'A Sketch from Ilfracombe', *Blackwood's Edinburgh Magazine*, CXLIII (1887)

'The Sketcher', *Blackwood's Edinburgh Magazine*, XXXV (1834)

'Teignmouth', *The Royal Magazine*, VI (1762)

Secondary Sources

Books

S.H. Adamson, *Seaside Piers* (1977)

J.G. Alger, *Napoleon's British Visitors and Captives, 1801–1815* (1904)

S. Ayling, *George III* (1972)

P.H. Bagwell, *The Transport Revolution from 1770* (1974)

P. Bailey, *Leisure and Class in Victorian England: Rational Recreation and the Contest for Control, 1830–1885* (1978)

J.A. Bulley, *Teignmouth in History* (Torquay, 1958)

R. Bush, *The Book of Exmouth* (Buckingham, 1978)

R.W. Chapman, ed., *Jane Austen's Letters to Her Sister Cassandra and Others* (1952)

S. Chitty, *The Beast and the Monk: A Life of Charles Kingsley* (1974)

E.A.G. Clark, *The Ports of the Exe Estuary, 1660-1860* (Exeter, 1960)

C. Creighton, *A History of Epidemics in Britain* (1965)

H. Cunningham, *Leisure in the Industrial Revolution, c.1780–c.1880* (1980)

K. Curry, ed., *New Letters of Robert Southey* (1965)

E.R. Delderfield, *Exmouth Milestones* (Exmouth, 1948)

E.R. Delderfield, *Exmouth Yesterdays* (Exmouth, 1952)

E. Dowden, *The Life of Percy Bysshe Shelley* (1886)

H.J. Dyos and D.H. Aldcroft, *British Transport: An Economic Survey from the Seventeenth Century to the Twentieth* (Harmondsworth, 1974)

A.C. Ellis, *An Historical Survey of Torquay* (Torquay, 1930)

A.R. Ellis, ed., *The Early Diary of Fanny Burney, 1776–1778* (1907)

G. Farr, *Ships and Harbours of Exmoor* (Dulverton, 1970)

G. Farr, *West Country Passenger Steamers* (Prescot, 2nd edn, 1967)

E.W. Gilbert, *Brighton: Old Ocean's Bauble* (Hassocks: Harvester Press, 1975)

J. Greig, ed., *The Farington Diary: By Joseph Farington* (1925)

G.D. and E.G.C. Griffiths, *History of Teignmouth* (Teignmouth, 1965)

G. Griffiths, *The Book of Dawlish* (Buckingham, 1984)

H.M. Hamlyn, *Eighteenth Century Circulating Libraries in England* (1947)

J. Helmlow and W. Derry, eds, *The Journals and Letters of Fanny Burney* (*Madame D'Arblay*) (Oxford, 1982)

A. Hern, *The Seaside Holiday: The History of the English Seaside Resort* (1967)

R. Holt, *Sport and the British: A Modern History* (Oxford, 1989)

W.G. Hoskins, *Devon* (1954)

W.G. Hoskins, *Industry, Trade and People in Exeter, 1688–1800* (Exeter, 2nd edn, 1968)

W.G. Hoskins, *Two Thousand Years in Exeter* (Chichester, 1960)

P. Hunt, ed., *Devon's Age of Elegance: Described by the Diaries of the Reverend John Swete, Lady Paterson and Miss Mary Cornish* (Exeter, 1984)

C. Hussey, *The Picturesque: Studies in a Point of View* (1927)

R.S. Lambert, *The Fortunate Traveller* (1950)

L. Lamplugh, *A History of Ilfracombe* (Chichester, 1984)

C.H. Lockett, *The Relations of French and English Society, 1763–1793* (1920)

N. Longmate, *King Cholera: The Biography of a Disease* (1966)

J. Lowerson and J. Myerscough, *Time to Spare in Victorian England* (Hassocks, 1977)

E.T. MacDermot, *History of the Great Western Railway* (2nd edn, 1972)

C.M. MacInnes and W.F. Whittard, eds, *Bristol and its Adjoining Counties* (Bristol, 1955)

C.G. Maggs, *The Barnstaple and Ilfracombe Railway* (Headington, 2nd edn, 1988)

C. Maxwell, *The English Traveller in France, 1698–1815* (1932)

R. Mayo, *The Story of Westward Ho!* (Yelland, 1973)

E. Moir, *The Discovery of Britain* (1964)

R. Newton, *Eighteeenth Century Exeter* (Exeter, 1984)

A. Oliver, ed., *The Journal of Samuel Curwen, Loyalist* (Cambridge, Massachusetts, 1972)

C.H. Patterson, *The History of Paignton* (Paignton, 1952)

F.R. Penwill, *Paignton in Six Reigns* (Paignton, 1953)

J.R. Pike, *Paignton: A Bibliographical Guide* (Torbay, 1974)

J.R. Pike, *Torquay: A Bibliographical Guide* (Torbay, 1973)

J.A.R. Pimlott, *The Englishman's Holiday: A Social History* (Hassocks, 2nd edn, 1977)

W. Plomer, ed., *Kilvert's Diary: Selections from the Diary of the Rev. Francis Kilvert* (new edn, 1960)

D. Read, *England 1868–1914: The Age of Urban Democracy* (1979)

C. Rose, *Beside the Seaside* (1960)

The Royal North Devon Golf Club: A Century Anthology, 1864–1964 (Westward Ho!, 1964)

E. Royle, *Modern Britain: A Social History, 1750–1985* (1987)

P. Russell, *A History of Torquay* (Torquay, 1960)

G. Sheldon, *From Trackway to Turnpike: An Illustration from East Devon* (1928)

E.M. Sigsworth, ed., *Ports and Resorts in the Regions* (Hull, 1980)

J.V. Somers Cocks, *Devon Topographical Prints, 1660-1870: A Catalogue and Guide* (Exeter, 1977)

A. Sutton, *A History of Sidmouth* (Sidmouth, 2nd edn, 1953)

D.S.J. Thomas, *A Regional History of the Railways of Great Britain I, The West Country* (1960)

W. Thornhill, *The Growth and Reform of English Local Government* (1971)

Times Past in Ilfracombe and Combe Martin (Ilfracombe, 1981)

H.J. Trump, *Westcountry Harbour: The Port of Teignmouth, 1690–1975* (Teignmouth, 1976)

J.K. Walton, *The English Seaside Resort: A Social History* (Leicester, 1983)

J.K. Walton and J. Walvin, eds, *Leisure in Britain, 1780–1939* (Manchester, 1983)

J. Walvin, *Beside the Seaside: A Social History of the Popular Seaside Holiday, 1750–1914* (1978)

J. Walvin, *Leisure and Society, 1830–1950* (1978)

R.A. Williams, *The London and South Western Railway* (Newton Abbot, 1968)

Articles and Essays

P. Borsay, 'The English Urban Renaissance: The Development of Provincial Urban Culture, *c.*1680–*c.*1760', *Social History*, I (1977)

F.F. Box, 'The Barnstaple and Ilfracombe Railway', *Railway Magazine*, XLVI (1919-1920)

B.J.H. Brown, 'Bristol's Second Outport: Portishead in the Nineteenth Century', *Transport History*, IV (1971)

J.A. Bulley, 'Teignmouth as A Seaside Resort before the Coming of the Railway', *TDA*, LXXXVIII (1958)

C.W. Chalklin, 'Capital Expenditure on Building for Cultural Purposes in Provincial England, 1730-1830', *Business History* XXII (1980)

R.J. Ferrar, 'Bathing Machines in Lynmouth', *Lyn Valley News* (1984)

M. Huggins, 'Social Tone and Resort Development in North-East England', *Northern History*, XX (1984)

A.G.K. Leonard, 'Poets Knew and Loved Lynmouth', *DCN*, XXVII (1956)

B. May, 'The Rise of Ilfracombe as a Seaside Resort in the Nineteenth and Early Twentieth Centuries', in H.E.S. Fisher, ed., *West Country Maritime and Social History: Some Essays* (Exeter, 1980)

F.B. May, 'Victorian and Edwardian Ilfracombe', in J. K. Walton and J. Walvin, eds., *Leisure in Britain, 1780–1939* (Manchester, 1983)

'Old Letters from Teignmouth', *DCNQ*, XXXV (1983)

M. Palmer, 'A Diarist in Devon', *TDA*, LXXV (1943); LXXVI (1944)

J.A. Patmore, 'The Spa Towns of Britain', in R.P. Beckinsale and J.M. Houston, eds, *Urbanisation and Its Problems* (Oxford, 1968)

H.J. Perkin, 'The Social Tone of Victorian Seaside Resorts in the North West', *Northern History*, XI (1976)

W.H. Rogers, 'The Barnstaple Turnpike Trust', *TDA*, LXXIV (1942)

D. Rubinstein, 'Cycling Eighty Years Ago', *History Today*, XXVIII (1978)

D. Rubinstein, 'Cycling in the 1890s', *Victorian Studies*, XXI (1977)

A.H. Slee, 'Some Dead Industries of North Devon', *TDA*, LXX (1938)

H.J. Smith, 'Local Reports to the General Board of Health', *History*, LVI (1971)

M. Spearman, 'Wish You Were Here', *Devon Life*, XXXIV (April 1970)

J. Travis, 'Devon Seaside Tourism and its Relationship with the Coastal Environment, 1750–1900', in Stephen Fisher, ed., *Man and the Maritime Environment* (Exeter, 1993)

J. Travis, 'Lynton in the Nineteenth Century: An Isolated and Exclusive Resort', in E.M. Sigsworth, ed., *Ports and Resorts in the Regions* (Hull, 1980)

J.K. Walton and P.A. McGloin, 'Holiday Resorts and Their Visitors: Some Sources for the Local Historian', *Local Historian*, XIII (1979)

E. Welsh, ed., 'Lady Sylvester's Tour', *DCNQ*, XXXI (1968–1970)

J. Whyman, 'Water Communications to Margate and Gravesend as Coastal Resorts before 1840', *Southern History*, III (1981)

Theses

F.B. May, 'The Development of Ilfracombe as a Resort in the Nineteenth Century' (unpublished MA thesis, University of Wales, 1978)

R. Newton, 'Victorian Exeter, 1837–1914' (unpublished PhD thesis, University of Exeter, 1966)

A.M. Northway, 'The Devon Fishing Industry, 1760–1860' (unpublished MA thesis, University of Exeter, 1969)

F.M. Stafford, 'Holiday-making in Victorian Margate, 1870–1900' (unpublished MA thesis, University of Kent, 1979)

J.F. Travis, 'The Rise of Holidaymaking on the Devon Coast, 1750 to 1900: with Particular Reference to Health and Entertainment' (unpublished PhD thesis, University of Exeter, 1989)

J.K. Walton, 'The Social Development of Blackpool, 1788–1914' (unpublished PhD thesis, University of Lancaster, 1974)

J. Whyman, 'Aspects of Holiday-making and Resort Development within the Isle of Thanet, with Particular Reference to Margate, c.1736–c.1840' (PhD thesis, University of Kent, 1980, published New York, 1981)

Index